Bloom's Modern Critical Views

Bloom's Modern Critical Views

Bloom's Modern Critical Views

CHARLES DICKENS
Updated Edition

Edited and with an introduction by
Harold Bloom
Sterling Professor of the Humanities
Yale University

CHELSEA HOUSE
P U B L I S H E R S
An imprint of Infobase Publishing

Bloom's Modern Critical Views: Charles Dickens, Updated Edition

©2006 Infobase Publishing

Introduction © 2006 by Harold Bloom

Chelsea House
An imprint of Infobase Publishing
132 West 31st Street
New York NY 10001

Library of Congress Cataloging-in-Publication Data
Charles Dickens / Harold Bloom, editor. — Updated ed.
  p. cm. — (Bloom's modern critical views)
 Includes bibliographical references and index.
 ISBN 0-7910-8568-6 (hardcover)
 1. Dickens, Charles, 1812-1870—Criticism and interpretation.
I. Bloom, Harold. II. Series.
 PR4588.C358 2006
 823'.8—dc22   2006011660

Chelsea House books are available at special discounts when purchased in bulk quantities for businesses, associations, institutions, or sales promotions. Please call our Special Sales Department in New York at (212) 967-8800 or (800) 322-8755.

You can find Chelsea House on the World Wide Web at http://www.chelseahouse.com

Contributing Editor: Mei Chin
Cover design by Keith Trego
Cover photo © Hulton-Deutsch Collection/CORBIS

Printed in the United States of America
Bang EJB 10 9 8 7 6 5 4 3 2 1

This book is printed on acid-free paper.

All links and web addresses were checked and verified to be correct at the time of publication. Because of the dynamic nature of the web, some addresses and links may have changed since publication and may no longer be valid.

Contents

Editor's Note

My Introduction centers upon Dickens's staging of the will in *David Copperfield*, *Bleak House*, *Hard Times*, and *A Tale of Two Cities*.

G.K. Chesterton, to me still the best of Dickens's critics, emphasizes the novelist's extraordinary contemporary popularity, which continues until this day.

For George Orwell, Dickens was an implicit radical and a humane liberal, of a kind now virtually extinct.

Great Expectations is praised as Dickens's best story by George Bernard Shaw, while Lionel Trilling praises *Little Dorrit* as a triumph of fantasy.

Dickens's heroines and heroes are regarded by Angus Wilson with an exuberant ambivalence, after which William Oddie exalts Mr. Micawber as a humorous creation so powerful as to wrest *David Copperfield* away from its autobiographical hero.

Violence in Dickens is seen by John Carey as aesthetically effective only where it is extreme, while *Bleak House*, Dickens's authentic masterpiece, is analyzed by D.A. Miller as an intricate representation of "discipline in different voices," with a particular emphasis upon Dickens's juxtaposed visions of the police and the family.

George Levine usefully contrasts Charles Darwin and Charles Dickens, after which *Our Mutual Friend* is read by Pam Morris as a virtual national apocalypse.

Garrett Stewart finds Dickens's relation to language to be one that "frays the very assurances it seems to bind," while John Cosnett details the remarkably acute Dickensian observations of neurological morbidities.

My Afterthought attempts a brief general overview of Dickens's perpetual relevance.

HAROLD BLOOM

Introduction

I

Courage would be the critical virtue most required if anyone were to attempt an essay that might be called "The Limitations of Shakespeare." Tolstoy, in his most outrageous critical performance, more or less tried just that, with dismal results, and even Ben Jonson might not have done much better, had he sought to extend his ambivalent *obiter dicta* on his great friend and rival. Nearly as much courage, or foolhardiness, is involved in discoursing on the limitations of Dickens, but the young Henry James had a critical gusto that could carry him through every literary challenge. Reviewing *Our Mutual Friend* in 1865, James exuberantly proclaimed that "*Bleak House* was forced; *Little Dorrit* was labored; the present work is dug out as with a spade and pickaxe." At about this time, reviewing *Drum-Taps*, James memorably dismissed Whitman as an essentially prosaic mind seeking to lift itself, by muscular exertion, into poetry. To reject some of the major works of the strongest English novelist and the greatest American poet, at about the same moment, is to set standards for critical audacity that no one since has been able to match, even as no novelist since has equalled Dickens, nor any poet, Walt Whitman.

James was at his rare worst in summing up Dickens's supposedly principal inadequacy:

Such scenes as this are useful in fixing the limits of Mr. Dickens's insight. Insight is, perhaps, too strong a word; for we are convinced that it is one of the chief conditions of his genius not to see beneath the surface of things. If we might hazard a definition of his literary character, we should, accordingly, call him the greatest of superficial novelists. We are aware that this definition confines him to an inferior rank in the department of letters which he adorns; but we accept this consequence of our proposition. It were, in our opinion, an offence against humanity to place Mr. Dickens among the greatest novelists. For, to repeat what we have already intimated, he has created nothing but figure. He has added nothing to our understanding of human character. He is master of but two alternatives: he reconciles us to what is commonplace, and he reconciles us to what is odd. The value of the former service is questionable; and the manner in which Mr. Dickens performs it sometimes conveys a certain impression of charlatanism. The value of the latter service is incontestable, and here Mr. Dickens is an honest, an admirable artist.

This can be taken literally, and then transvalued: to see truly the surface of things, to reconcile us at once to the commonplace and the odd—these are not minor gifts. In 1860, John Ruskin, the great seer of the surface of things, the charismatic illuminator of the commonplace and the odd together, had reached a rather different conclusion from that of the young Henry James, five years before James's brash rejection:

The essential value and truth of Dickens's writings have been unwisely lost sight of by many thoughtful persons merely because he presents his truth with some colour of caricature. Unwisely, because Dickens's caricature, though often gross, is never mistaken. Allowing for his manner of telling them, the things he tells us are always true. I wish that he could think it right to limit his brilliant exaggeration to works written only for public amusement; and when he takes up a subject of high national importance, such as that which he handled in *Hard Times*, that he would use severer and more accurate analysis. The usefulness of that work (to my mind, in several respects, the greatest he has written) is with many persons seriously diminished because Mr. Bounderby is a dramatic monster, instead of a characteristic example of a worldly master; and Stephen Blackpool a dramatic perfection, instead of a characteristic example of an honest workman. But let us not lose the use of Dickens's wit and insight, because he chooses to speak in a circle of stage fire. He is entirely right in his main drift and purpose in every book he has written; and all of them, but especially *Hard Times*, should be studied with close and earnest care by persons interested in social questions. They will find much that is partial, and, because partial, apparently unjust; but if they examine all the evidence on the other side, which Dickens seems to overlook, it will appear, after all their trouble, that his view was the finally right one, grossly and sharply told.

To say of Dickens that he chose "to speak in a circle of stage fire" is exactly right, since Dickens is the greatest actor among novelists, the finest master of dramatic projection. A superb stage performer, he never stops performing in his novels, which is not the least of his many Shakespearean characteristics. Martin Price usefully defines some of these as "his effortless invention, his brilliant play of language, the scope and density of his imagined world." I like also Price's general comparison of Dickens to the strongest satirist in the language, Swift, a comparison that Price shrewdly turns into a confrontation:

But the confrontation helps us to define differences as well: Dickens is more explicit, more overtly compassionate, insisting always upon the perversions of feeling as well as of thought. His outrage is of the same consistency as his generous celebration, the satirical wit of the same copious extravagance as the comic elaborations. Dickens' world is alive with things that snatch, lurch, teeter, thrust, leer; it is the animate world of Netherlandish genre painting or of Hogarth's prints, where all space is a field of force, where objects vie or intrigue with each other, where every human event spills over into the things that surround it. This may become the typically crowded scene of satire, where persons are reduced to things and things to matter in motion; or it may pulsate with fierce energy and noisy feeling. It is different from Swift; it is the distinctive Dickensian plenitude, which we find again in his verbal play, in his great array of vivid characters, in his massed scenes of feasts or public declamations. It creates rituals as compelling as the resuscitation of Rogue Riderhood, where strangers participate

solemnly in the recovery of a spark of life, oblivious for the
moment of the unlovely human form it will soon inhabit.

That animate, Hogarthian world, "where all space is a field of force,"
indeed is a plenitude and it strikes me that Price's vivid description suggests
Rabelais rather than Swift as a true analogue. Dickens, like Shakespeare in
one of many aspects and like Rabelais, is as much carnival as stage fire, a kind
of endless festival. The reader of Dickens stands in the midst of a festival,
which is too varied, too multiform, to be taken in even by innumerable
readings. Something always escapes our ken; Ben Jonson's sense of being
"rammed with life" is exemplified more even by Dickens than by Rabelais, in
that near-Shakespearean plenitude that is Dickens's peculiar glory.

Is it possible to define that plenitude narrowly enough so as to
conceptualize it for critical use, though by "conceptualize" one meant only a
critical metaphor? Shakespearean representation is no touchstone for
Dickens or for anyone else, since above all modes of representation it turns
upon an inward changing brought about by characters listening to
themselves speak. Dickens cannot do that. His villains are gorgeous, but
there are no Iagos or Edmunds among them. The severer, more relevant test,
which Dickens must fail, though hardly to his detriment, is Falstaff, who
generates not only his own meaning, but meaning in so many others besides,
both on and off the page. Probably the severest test is Shylock, most
Dickensian of Shakespeare's characters, since we cannot say of Dickens's
Shylock, Fagin, that there is much Shakespearean about him at all. Fagin is
a wonderful grotesque, but the winds of will are not stirred in him, while they
burn on hellishly forever in Shylock.

Carlyle's injunction, to work in the will, seems to have little enough
place in the cosmos of the Dickens characters. I do not say this to indicate a
limitation, or even a limit, nor do I believe that the will to live or the will to
power is ever relaxed in or by Dickens. But nothing is got for nothing, except
perhaps in or by Shakespeare, and Dickens purchases his kind of plenitude at
the expense of one aspect of the will. T.S. Eliot remarked that "Dickens's
characters are real because there is no one like them." I would modify that to
"They are real because they are not like one another, though sometimes they
are a touch more like some of us than like each other." Perhaps the will, in
whatever aspect, can differ only in degree rather than in kind among us. The
aesthetic secret of Dickens appears to be that his villains, heroes, heroines,
victims, eccentrics, ornamental beings do differ from one another *in the kinds
of will that they possess*. Since that is hardly possible for us, as humans, it does
bring about an absence in reality in and for Dickens. That is a high price to
pay, but it is a good deal less than everything and Dickens got more than he

paid for. We also receive a great deal more than we ever are asked to surrender when we read Dickens. That may indeed be his most Shakespearean quality, and may provide the critical trope I quest for in him. James and Proust hurt you more than Dickens does, and the hurt is the meaning, or much of it. What hurts in Dickens never has much to do with meaning, because there cannot be a poetics of pain where the will has ceased to be common or sadly uniform. Dickens really does offer a poetics of pleasure, which is surely worth our secondary uneasiness at his refusal to offer us any accurately mimetic representations of the human will. He writes always the book of the drives, which is why supposedly Freudian readings of him always fail so tediously. The conceptual metaphor he suggests in his representations of character and personality is neither Shakespearean mirror nor Romantic lamp, neither Rabelaisian carnival nor Fieldingesque open country. "Stage fire" seems to me perfect, for "stage" removes something of the reality of the will, yet only as modifier. The substantive remains "fire." Dickens is the poet of the fire of the drives, the true celebrant of Freud's myth of frontier concepts, of that domain lying on the border between psyche and body, falling into matter, yet partaking of the reality of both.

II

If the strong writer be defined as one who confronts his own contingency, his own dependent relation on a precursor, then we can discover only a few writers after Homer and the Yahwist who are strong without that sense of contingency. These are the Great Originals, and they are not many; Shakespeare and Freud are among them and so is Dickens. Dickens, like Shakespeare and Freud, had no true precursors, or perhaps it might be more accurate to say he swallowed up Tobias Smollett rather as Shakespeare devoured Christopher Marlowe. Originality, or an authentic freedom from contingency, is Dickens's salient characteristic as an author. Since Dickens's influence has been so immense, even upon writers so unlikely as Dostoevski and Kafka, we find it a little difficult now to see at first how overwhelmingly original he is.

Dickens now constitutes a facticity or contingency that no subsequent novelist can transcend or evade without the risk of self-maiming. Consider the difference between two masters of modern fiction, Henry James and James Joyce. Is not Dickens the difference? *Ulysses* comes to terms with Dickens, and earns the exuberance it manifests. Poldy is larger, I think, than any single figure in Dickens, but he has recognizably Dickensian qualities. Lambert Strether in *The Ambassadors* has none, and is the poorer for it. Part of the excitement of *The Princess Casamassima* for us must be that, for once,

James achieves a Dickensian sense of the outward life, a sense that is lacking even in *The Portrait of a Lady*, and that we miss acutely (at least I do) amidst even the most inward splendors of *The Wings of the Dove* and *The Golden Bowl*.

The Personal History of David Copperfield, indeed the most personal and autobiographical of all Dickens's novels, has been so influential upon all subsequent portraits of the artist as a young man that we have to make a conscious effort to recover our appreciation of the book's fierce originality. It is the first therapeutic novel, in part written to heal the author's self, or at least to solace permanent anxieties incurred in childhood and youth. Freud's esteem for *David Copperfield* seems inevitable, even if it has led to a number of unfortunate readings within that unlikely compound oddly called "Freudian literary criticism."

Dickens's biographer Edgar Johnson has traced the evolution of *David Copperfield* from an abandoned fragment of autobiography, with its powerful but perhaps self-deceived declaration: "I do not write resentfully or angrily: for I know how all these things have worked together to make me what I am." Instead of representing his own parents as being David Copperfield's, Dickens displaced them into the Micawbers, a change that purchased astonishing pathos and charm at the expense of avoiding a personal pain that might have produced greater meaningfulness. But *David Copperfield* was, as Dickens said, his "favourite child," fulfilling his deep need to become his own father. Of no other book would he have said: "I seem to be sending some part of myself into the Shadowy World."

Kierkegaard advised us that "he who is willing to do the work gives birth to his own father," while Nietzsche even more ironically observed that "if one hasn't had a good father, then it is necessary to invent one." *David Copperfield* is more in the spirit of Kierkegaard's adage, as Dickens more or less makes himself David's father. David, an illustrious novelist, allows himself to narrate his story in the first person. A juxtaposition of the start and conclusion of the narrative may be instructive:

> Whether I shall turn out to be the hero of my own life, or whether that station will be held by anybody else, these pages must show. To begin my life with the beginning of my life, I record that I was born (as I have been informed and believe) on a Friday, at twelve o'clock at night. It was remarked that the clock began to strike, and I began to cry, simultaneously.
>
> In consideration of the day and hour of my birth, it was declared by the nurse, and by some sage women in the neighbourhood who had taken a lively interest in me several

months before there was any possibility of our becoming personally acquainted, first, that I was destined to be unlucky in life; and secondly, that I was privileged to see ghosts and spirits; both these gifts inevitably attaching, as they believed, to all unlucky infants of either gender, born towards the small hours on a Friday night.

I need say nothing here, on the first head, because nothing can show better than my history whether that prediction was verified or falsified by the result. On the second branch of the question, I will only remark, that unless I ran through that part of my inheritance while I was still a baby, I have not come into it yet. But I do not at all complain of having been kept out of this property; and if anybody else should be in the present enjoyment of it, he is heartily welcome to keep it.

And now, as I close my task, subduing my desire to linger yet, these faces fade away. But one face, shining on me like a Heavenly light by which I see all other objects, is above them and beyond them all. And that remains.

I turn my head, and see it, in its beautiful serenity, beside me.

My lamp burns low, and I have written far into the night; but the dear presence, without which I were nothing, bears me company.

O Agnes, O my soul, so may thy face be by me when I close my life indeed; so may I, when realities are melting from me, like the shadows which I now dismiss, still find thee near me, pointing upward!

No adroit reader could prefer the last four paragraphs of *David Copperfield* to the first three. The high humor of the beginning is fortunately more typical of the book than the sugary conclusion. Yet the juxtaposition does convey the single rhetorical flaw in Dickens that matters, by which I do not mean the wild pathos that marks the death of Steerforth, or the even more celebrated career of the endlessly unfortunate little Em'ly. If Dickens's image of voice or mode of representation is "stage fire," then his metaphors always will demand the possibility of being staged. Micawber, Uriah Heep, Steerforth in his life (not at the end) are all of them triumphs of stage fire, as are Peggotty, Murdstone, Betsey Trotwood, and even Dora Spenlow. But Agnes is a disaster, and that dreadful "pointing upward!" is not to be borne. You cannot stage Agnes, which would not matter except that she does represent the idealizing and self-mystifying side of David and so she raises the question, Can you, as a reader, stage David? How much stage fire got into him? Or, to be hopelessly reductive, has he a will, as Uriah Heep and Steerforth in their very different ways are wills incarnate?

If there is an aesthetic puzzle in the novel, it is why David has and conveys so overwhelming a sense of disordered suffering and early sorrow in his Murdstone phase, as it were, and before. Certainly the intensity of the pathos involved is out of all proportion to the fictive experience that comes through to the reader. Dickens both invested himself in and withdrew from David, so that something is always missing in the self-representation. Yet the will—to live, to interpret, to repeat, to write—survives and burgeons perpetually. Dickens's preternatural energy gets into David, and is at some considerable variance with the diffidence of David's apparent refusal to explore his own inwardness. What does mark Dickens's representation of David with stage fire is neither the excess of the early sufferings nor the tiresome idealization of the love for Agnes. It is rather the vocation of novelist, the drive to tell a story, particularly one's own story, that apparels David with the fire of what Freud called the drives.

Dickens's greatness in *David Copperfield* has little to do with the much more extraordinary strength that was to manifest itself in *Bleak House*, which can compete with *Clarissa, Emma, Middlemarch, The Portrait of a Lady, Women in Love*, and *Ulysses* for the eminence of being the inescapable novel in the language. *David Copperfield* is of another order, but it is the origin of that order, the novelist's account of how she or he burned through experience in order to achieve the Second Birth, into the will to narrate, the storyteller's destiny.

III

Bleak House may not be "the finest literary work the nineteenth century produced in England," as Geoffrey Tillotson called it in 1946. A century that gave us *The Prelude* and Wordsworth's major crisis lyrics, Blake's *Milton* and *Jerusalem*, Byron's *Don Juan*, the principal poems of Shelley, Keats, Tennyson, and Browning, and novels such as *Pride and Prejudice, Emma, Middlemarch*, and Dickens's own *Hard Times* and *Our Mutual Friend*, is an era of such literary plenitude that a single choice is necessarily highly problematic. Yet there is now something close to critical agreement that *Bleak House* is Dickens's most complex and memorable single achievement. W. J. Harvey usefully sketches just how formidably the novel is patterned:

> *Bleak House* is for Dickens a unique and elaborate experiment in narration and plot composition. It is divided into two

intermingled and roughly concurrent stories; Esther Summerson's first-person narrative and an omniscient narrative told consistently in the historic present. The latter takes up thirty-four chapters; Esther has one less. Her story, however, occupies a good deal more than half the novel. The reader who checks the distribution of these two narratives against the original part issues will hardly discern any significant pattern or correlation. Most parts contain a mixture of the two stories; one part is narrated entirely by Esther and five parts entirely by the omniscient author. Such a check does, however, support the view that Dickens did not, as is sometimes supposed, use serial publication in the interest of crude suspense. A sensational novelist, for example, might well have ended a part issue with chapter 31; Dickens subdues the drama by adding another chapter to the number. The obvious exception to this only proves the rule; in the final double number the suspense of Bucket's search for Lady Dedlock is heightened by cutting back to the omniscient narrative and the stricken Sir Leicester. In general, however, Dickens's control of the double narrative is far richer and subtler than this.

I would add to Harvey the critical observation that Dickens's own narrative will in "his" thirty-four chapters is a will again different in kind from the will to tell her story of the admirable Esther Summerson. Dickens's (or the omniscient, historical present narrator's) metaphor of representation is one of "stage fire": wild, free, unconditioned, incessant with the force of Freud's domain of those grandly indefinite frontier concepts, the drives. Esther's mode of representation is certainly not flat or insipid; for all of her monumental repressions, Esther finally seems to me the most mysteriously complex and profound personage in *Bleak House*. Her narrative is not so much plain style as it is indeed repressed in the precise Freudian sense of "repression," whose governing metaphor, in Esther's prose as in Freud's, is flight from, rather than a pushing down or pushing under. Esther frequently forgets, purposefully though "unconsciously," what she cannot bear to remember, and much of her narrative is her strong defense against the force of the past. Esther may not *appear* to change as she goes from little girl to adult, but that is because the rhythm of her psyche, unlike Dickens's own, is one of unfolding rather than development. She is Dickens's Muse, what Whitman would have called his "Fancy," as in the great death-lyric "Good-bye, my Fancy!" or what Stevens would have called Dickens's "Interior Paramour."

Contrast a passage of Esther's story with one of Dickens's own narrative, from the end of chapter 56, "Pursuit," and toward the close of the next chapter, "Esther's Narrative":

Mr. Jarndyce, the only person up in the house, is just going to bed; rises from his book, on hearing the rapid ringing at the bell; and comes down to the door in his dressing-gown.

"Don't be alarmed sir." In a moment his visitor is confidential with him in the hall, has shut the door, and stands with his hand upon the lock. "I've had the pleasure of seeing you before. Inspector Bucket. Look at that handkerchief, sir, Miss Esther Summerson's. Found it myself put away in a drawer of Lady Dedlock's, quarter of an hour ago. Not a moment to lose. Matter of life or death. You know. Lady Dedlock?"

"Yes."

"There has been a discovery there, to-day. Family affairs have come out. Sir Leicester Dedlock, Baronet, has had a fit— apoplexy or paralysis—and couldn't be brought to, and precious time has been lost. Lady Dedlock disappeared this afternoon, and left a letter for him that looks bad. Run your eye over it. Here it is!"

Mr. Jarndyce having read it, asks him what he thinks? "I don't know. It looks like suicide. Anyways, there's more and more danger, every minute, of its drawing to that. I'd give a hundred pound an hour to have got the start of the present time. Now, Mr. Jarndyce, I am employed by Sir Leicester Dedlock, Baronet, to follow her and find her—to save her, and take her his forgiveness. I have money and full power, but I want something else. I want Miss Summerson."

Mr. Jarndyce, in a troubled voice, repeats "Miss Summerson?"

"Now, Mr. Jarndyce"; Mr. Bucket has read his face with the greatest attention all along: "I speak to you as a gentleman of a humane heart, and under such pressing circumstances as don't often happen. If ever delay was dangerous, it's dangerous now; and if ever you couldn't afterwards forgive yourself for causing it, this is the time. Eight or ten hours, worth, as I tell you, a hundred pound apiece at least, have been lost since Lady Dedlock disappeared. I am charged to find her. I am Inspector Bucket. Besides all the rest that's heavy on her, she has upon her, as she believes, suspicion of murder. If I follow her alone, she, being in ignorance of what Sir Leicester Dedlock, Baronet, has communicated to me, may be driven to desperation. But if I follow her in company with a young lady, answering to the description of a young lady that she has a tenderness for—I ask no question, and I say no more than that—she will give me credit for being friendly. Let me come up with her, and be able to have the hold upon her of putting that young lady for'ard, and I'll save her and prevail with her if she is alive. Let me come up with her alone—a harder matter—and I'll do my best; but I don't answer for what the best may be. Time flies; it's getting on for one o'clock. When one strikes, there's another hour gone; and it's worth a thousand pound now, instead of a hundred."

This is all true, and the pressing nature of the case cannot be questioned. Mr. Jarndyce begs him to remain there, while he speaks to Miss Summerson. Mr. Bucket says he will; but acting on his usual principle, does no such thing—following up-stairs instead, and keeping his man in sight. So he remains, dodging and lurking about in the gloom of the staircase while they confer. In a very little time, Mr. Jarndyce comes down, and tells him that Miss Summerson will join him directly, and place herself under his protection, to accompany him where he pleases. Mr. Bucket, satisfied, expresses high approval; and awaits her coming, at the door.

There, he mounts a high tower in his mind, and looks out far and wide. Many solitary figures he perceives, creeping through the streets; many solitary figures out on heaths, and roads, and lying under haystacks. But the figure that he seeks is not among them. Other solitaries he perceives, in nooks of bridges, looking over; and in shadowed places down by the river's level; and a dark, dark, shapeless object drifting with the tide, more solitary than all, clings with a drowning hold on his attention.

Where is she? Living or dead, where is she? If, as he folds the handkerchief and carefully puts it up, it were able, with an enchanted power, to bring before him the place where she found it, and the night landscape near the cottage where it covered the little child, would he descry her there? On the waste, where the brick-kilns are burning with a pale blue flare; where the straw-roofs of the wretched huts in which the bricks are made, are being scattered by the wind; where the clay and water are hard frozen, and the mill in which the gaunt blind horse goes round all day, looks like an instrument of human torture; traversing this deserted blighted spot, there is a lonely figure with the sad world to itself, pelted by the snow and driven by the wind, and cast out, it would seem, from all companionship. It is the figure of a woman, too; but it is miserably dressed, and no such clothes ever came through the hall, and out at the great door, of the Dedlock mansion.

The transparent windows with the fire and light, looking so bright and warm from the cold darkness out of doors, were soon gone, and again we were crushing and churning the loose snow. We went on with toil enough; but the dismal roads were not much worse than they had been, and the stage was only nine miles. My companion smoking on the box—I had thought at the last inn of begging him to do so, when I saw him standing at a great fire in a comfortable cloud of tobacco—was as vigilant as ever; and as quickly down and up again, when we came to any human abode or any human creature. He had lighted his little dark lantern, which seemed to be a favourite with him, for we had lamps to the carriage; and every now and then he turned it upon me, to see that I was doing well. There was a folding-window to the carriage-head, but I never closed it, for it seemed like shutting out hope.

We came to the end of the stage, and still the lost trace was not recovered. I looked at him anxiously when we stopped to change; but I knew by his yet graver face, as he stood watching the ostlers, that he had heard nothing. Almost in an instant afterwards, as I leaned back in my seat, he looked in, with his lighted lantern in his hand, an excited and quite different man.

"What is it?" said I, starting. "Is she here?"

"No, no. Don't deceive yourself, my dear. Nobody's here. But I've got it!"

The crystallised snow was in his eyelashes, in his hair, lying in ridges on his dress. He had to shake it from his face, and get his breath before he spoke to me.

"Now, Miss Summerson," said he, beating his finger on the apron, "don't you be disappointed at what I'm a going to do. You know me. I'm Inspector Bucket, and you can trust me. We've come a long way; never mind. Four horses out there for the next stage up! Quick!"

There was a commotion in the yard, and a man came running out of the stables to know "if he meant up or down?" "Up, I tell you! Up! Ain't it English? Up!"

"Up?" said I, astonished. "To London! Are we going back?"

"Miss Summerson," he answered, "back. Straight back as a die. You know me. Don't be afraid. I'll follow the other, by G——."

"The other?" I repeated. "Who?"

"You called her Jenny, didn't you? I'll follow her. Bring those two pair out here, for a crown a man. Wake up, some of you!"

"You will not desert this lady we are in search of; you will not abandon her on such a night, and in such a state of mind as I know her to be in!" said I, in an agony, and grasping his hand.

"You are right, my dear, I won't. But I'll follow the other. Look alive here with them horses. Send a man for'ard in the saddle to the next stage, and let him send another for'ard again, and order four on, up, right through. My darling, don't you be afraid!"

These orders, and the way in which he ran about the yard, urging them, caused a general excitement that was scarcely less bewildering to me than the sudden change. But in the height of the confusion, a mounted man galloped away to order the relays, and our horses were put to with great speed.

"My dear," said Mr. Bucket, jumping up to his seat, and looking in again—"you'll excuse me if I'm too familiar—don't you fret and worry yourself no more than you can help. I say nothing else at present; but you know me, my dear; now, don't you?"

I endeavoured to say that I knew he was far more capable than I of deciding what we ought to do; but was he sure that this was right? Could I not go forward by myself in search of—I grasped his hand again in my distress, and whispered it to him—of my own mother.

"My dear," he answered, "I know, I know, and would I put you wrong, do you think? Inspector Bucket. Now you know me, don't you?"

What could I say but yes!

"Then you keep up as good a heart as you can, and you rely upon me for standing by you, no less than by Sir Leicester Dedlock, Baronet. Now, are you right there?"

"All right, sir!"

"Off she goes, then. And get on, my lads!"

We were again upon the melancholy road by which we had come; tearing up the miry sleet and thawing snow, as if they were torn up by a waterwheel.

Both passages are extraordinary, by any standards, and certainly "Pursuit" has far more stage fire than "Esther's Narrative," but this timelier repressive shield, in part, is broken through, and a fire leaps forth out of her. If we start with "Pursuit," however, we are likelier to see what it is that returns from the repressed in Esther, returns under the sign of negation (as Freud prophesied), so that what comes back is primarily cognitive, while the affective aspect of the repression persists. We can remember the opening of *David Copperfield*, where Dickens in his *persona* as David disavows the gift of second sight attributed to him by the wise women and gossips. Inspector Bucket, at the conclusion of the "Pursuit" chapter, is granted a great vision, a preternatural second sight of Esther's lost mother, Lady Dedlock. What Bucket *sees* is stage fire at its most intense, the novelist's will to tell become an absolute vision of the will. Mounting a high tower in his mind, Bucket (who thus becomes Dickens's authorial will) looks out, far and wide, and sees the truth: "a dark, dark, shapeless object drifting with the tide, more solitary than all," which "clings with a drowning hold on his attention." That "drowning hold" leads to the further vision: "where the clay and water are hard frozen, and the mill in which the gaunt blind horse goes round all day." I suspect that Dickens here has a debt to Browning's great romance, "Childe Roland to the Dark Tower Came," where another apparent instrument of human torture in a deserted, blighted spot, is seen by a companionless figure as being in association with a starving blind horse, cast out from the Devil's stud, who provokes in Browning's narrator the terrible outcry that he never saw a beast he hated so, because: "He must be wicked to deserve such pain."

The ensuing chapter of "Esther's Narrative" brilliantly evokes the cognitive return of Esther's acknowledgment of her mother, under the sign of a negation of past affect. Here the narrative vision proceeds, not in the sublime mode of Bucket's extraordinary second sight, but in the grave, meditative lyricism that takes us first to a tentative return from unconscious flight through an image of pursuit of the fleeing, doomed mother: "The transparent windows with the fire and light, looking so bright and warm from the cold darkness out of doors, were soon gone, and again we were crushing and churning the loose snow." That "crushing and churning" images the breaking of the repressive shield, and Dickens shrewdly ends the chapter with Esther's counterpart to Bucket's concluding vision of a Browningesque demonic water mill, torturing consciousness into a return from flight. Esther whispers to Bucket that she desires to go forward by herself in search of her own mother, and the dark pursuit goes on in the sinister metaphor of the sleet and thawing snow, shield of repression, being torn up by a waterwheel that recirculates the meaning of memory's return, even as it buries part of the pains of abandonment by the mother once more: "We were again upon the melancholy road by which we had come; tearing up the miry sleet and thawing snow, as if they were torn up by a waterwheel."

It is a terrifying triumph of Dickens's art that, when "Esther's Narrative" resumes, in chapter 59, we know inevitably that we are headed straight for an apocalyptic image of what Shakespeare, in *King Lear*, calls "the promised end" or "image of that horror," here not the corpse of the daughter, but of the mother. Esther goes, as she must, to be the first to touch and to see, and with no affect whatsoever, unveils the truth:

> I passed on to the gate, and stooped down. I lifted the heavy head, put the long dank hair aside, and turned the face. And it was my mother, cold and dead.

IV

Hard Times is, for Dickens, a strikingly condensed novel, being about one-third of the length of *David Copperfield* and *Bleak House*, the two masterpieces that directly preceded it. Astonishing and aesthetically satisfying as it is, I believe it to be somewhat overpraised by modern criticism, or perhaps praised for some less than fully relevant reasons. Ruskin and Bernard Shaw after him admired the book as a testament to Dickens's conversion away from a commercialized and industrialized England and back towards a supposed juster and more humane society. But to like *Hard Times* because of its anti-Utilitarian ideology is to confuse the book with Carlyle and William Morris, as well as with Ruskin and Shaw. The most balanced judgment of the novel is that of Monroe Engel, who observes that "the greatest virtues of *Hard Times* are Dickens's characteristic virtues, but less richly present in the book than in many others." Gradgrind is poor stuff, and is not even an effective parody of Jeremy Bentham. The strength of the novel is indeed elsewhere, as we might expect in the theatrical Dickens.

And yet *Hard Times* is lacking in stage fire; compared to *Bleak House*, it possesses only a tiny component of the Sublime. Again, as an instance of the plain style, the mode of Esther Summerson's narrative, it is curiously weak, and has moreover such drab characterizations as Sissy Jupe and Stephen Blackpool. Indeed, the book's rhetoric is the most colorless in all of Dickens's work. Though, as Engel insisted, many of Dickens's authorial virtues are present, the book lacks the preternatural exuberance that makes Dickens unique among all novelists. Has it any qualities of its own to recommend our devotion?

I would suggest that the start of any critical wisdom about *Hard Times* is to dismiss every Marxist or other moral interpretation of the book. Yes, Dickens's heart was accurate, even if his notion of Benthamite social philosophy was not, and a great novelist's overt defense of imagination cannot fail to move us. Consider however the outrageous first chapter of *Hard Times*, "The One Thing Needful":

> "Now, what I want is, Facts. Teach these boys and girls nothing but Facts. Facts alone are wanted in life. Plant nothing else, and root out everything else. You can only form the minds of reasoning animals upon Facts; nothing else will ever be of any service to them. This is the principle on which I bring up my own children, and this is the principle on which I bring up these children. Stick to Facts, sir!"
>
> The scene was a plain, bare, monotonous vault of a schoolroom, and the speaker's square forefinger emphasized his observations by underscoring every sentence with a line on the schoolmaster's sleeve. The emphasis was helped by the speaker's square wall of a forehead, which had his eyebrows for its base, while his eyes found commodious cellarage in two dark caves, overshadowed by the wall. The emphasis was helped by the speaker's mouth, which was wide, thin, and hard set. The emphasis was helped by the speaker's voice, which was inflexible, dry, and dictatorial. The emphasis was helped by the speaker's hair, which bristled on the skirts of his bald head, a plantation of firs to keep the wind from its shining surface, all covered with knobs, like the crust of a plum pie, as if the head had scarcely warehouse-room for the hard facts stored inside. The speaker's obstinate carriage, square coat, square legs, square shoulders— nay, his very neckcloth, trained to take him by the throat with an unaccommodating grasp, like a stubborn fact, as it was—all helped the emphasis.
>
> "In this life, we want nothing but Facts, sir; nothing but Facts!"
>
> The speaker, and the schoolmaster, and the third grown person present, all backed a little, and swept with their eyes the inclined plane of little vessels then and there arranged in order, ready to have imperial gallons of facts poured into them until they were full to the brim.

Gradgrind is doubtless Dickens's ultimate revenge upon his own school sufferings; Gradgrind might be called Murdstone run wild, except that Murdstone stays within the circle of caricature, whereas Gradgrind's will is mad, is a drive towards death. And that is where, I now think, the peculiar aesthetic strength of *Hard Times* is to be located. The novel survives as phantasmagoria or nightmare, and hardly as a societal or conceptual bad dream. What goes wrong in it is what Freud called "family romances," which become family horrors. Critics always have noted how really dreadful family relations are in *Hard Times*, as they so frequently are elsewhere in Dickens. A particular power is manifest if we analyze a passage near the conclusion of the penultimate chapter of the first book of the novel, chapter 15, "Father and Daughter":

"Louisa," returned her father, "it appears to me that nothing can be plainer. Confining yourself rigidly to Fact, the question of Fact you state to yourself is: Does Mr. Bounderby ask me to marry him? Yes, he does. The sole remaining question then is: Shall I marry him? I think nothing can be plainer than that?"

"Shall I marry him?" repeated Louisa, with great deliberation. "Precisely. And it is satisfactory to me, as your father, my clear Louisa, to know that you do not come to the consideration of that question with the previous habits of mind, and habits of life, that belong to many young women."

"No, father," she returned, "I do not."

"I now leave you to judge for yourself," said Mr. Gradgrind. "I have stated the case, as such cases are usually stated among practical minds; I have stated it, as the case of your mother and myself was stated in its time. The rest, my dear Louisa, is for you to decide."

From the beginning, she had sat looking at him fixedly. As he now leaned back in his chair, and bent his deep-set eyes upon her in his turn, perhaps he might have seen one wavering moment in her, when she was impelled to throw herself upon his breast, and give him the pent-up confidences of her heart. But, to see it, he must have overleaped at a bound the artificial barriers he had for many years been erecting, between himself and all those subtle essences of humanity which will elude the utmost cunning of algebra until the last trumpet ever to be sounded shall blow even algebra to wreck. The barriers were too many and too high for such a leap. With his unbending, utilitarian, matter-of-fact face, he hardened her again; and the moment shot away into the plumbless depths of the past, to mingle with all the lost opportunities that are drowned there.

Removing her eyes from him, she sat so long looking silently towards the town, that he said, at length: "Are you consulting the chimneys of the Coketown works, Louisa?"

"There seems to be nothing there but languid and monotonous smoke. Yet when the night comes, Fire bursts out, father!" she answered, turning quickly.

"Of course I know that, Louisa. I do not see the application of the remark." To do him justice he did not, at all.

She passed it away with a slight motion of her hand, and concentrating her attention upon him again, said, "Father, I have often thought that life is very short."—This was so distinctly one of his subjects that he interposed.

"It is short, no doubt, my dear. Still, the average duration of human life is proved to have increased of late years. The calculations of various life assurance and annuity offices, among other figures which cannot go wrong, have established the fact."

"I speak of my own life, father."

"O indeed? Still," said Mr. Gradgrind, "I need not point out to you, Louisa, that it is governed by the laws which govern lives in the aggregate."

"While it lasts, I would wish to do the little I can, and the little I am fit for. What does it matter?"

Mr. Gradgrind seemed rather at a loss to understand the last four words; replying, "How, matter? What matter, my dear?"

"Mr. Bounderby," she went on in a steady, straight way, without regarding this, "asks me to marry him. The question I have to ask myself is, shall I marry him? That is so, father, is it not? You have told me so, father. Have you not?"

"Certainly, my dear."

"Let it be so. Since Mr. Bounderby likes to take me thus, I am satisfied to accept his proposal. Tell him, father, as soon as you please, that this was my answer. Repeat it, word for word, if you can, because I should wish him to know what I said."

"It is quite right, my dear," retorted her father approvingly, "to be exact. I will observe your very proper request. Have you any wish in reference to the period of your marriage, my child?"

"None, father. What does it matter?"

Mr. Gradgrind had drawn his chair a little nearer to her, and taken her hand. But, her repetition of these words seemed to strike with some little discord on his ear. He paused to look at her, and, still holding her hand, said:

"Louisa, I have not considered it essential to ask you one question, because the possibility implied in it appeared to me to be too remote. But perhaps I ought to do so. You have never entertained in secret any other proposal?"

"Father," she returned, almost scornfully, "what other proposal can have been made to me? Whom have I seen? Where have I been? What are my heart's experiences?"

"My dear Louisa," returned Mr. Gradgrind, reassured and satisfied. "You correct me justly. I merely wished to discharge my duty."

"What do *I* know, father," said Louisa in her quiet manner, "of tastes and fancies; of aspirations and affections; of all that part of my nature in which such light things might have been nourished? What escape have I had from problems that could be demonstrated, and realities that could be grasped?" As she said it, she unconsciously closed her hand, as if upon a solid object, and slowly opened it as though she were releasing dust or ash.

Caricature here has leaped into Ruskin's "stage fire." Gradgrind, quite mad, nevertheless achieves the wit of asking Louisa whether she is consulting the oracular vapors of the Coketown chimneys. Her magnificent, "Yet when the night comes, Fire bursts out, father!" is more than a prophecy of the return of the repressed. It prophesies also the exuberance of Dickens himself, which comes flooding forth in the obvious yet grand metaphor a page later, when poor Louisa closes her hand, as if upon a graspable reality, and slowly opens it to disclose that her heart, like that of Tennyson's protagonist in *Maud*, is a handful of dust.

That is the true, dark power of *Hard Times*. Transcending Dickens's social vision, or his polemic for imagination, is his naked return to the domain of the drives, Eros and Death. The novel ends with an address to the reader that necessarily is far more equivocal than Dickens can have intended:

Dear Reader! It rests with you and me, whether, in our two fields of action, similar things shall be or not. Let them be! We shall sit with lighter bosoms on the hearth, to see the ashes of our fires turn grey and cold.

Presumably, our imaginative escape from Gradgrindism into poetry will lighten our bosoms, even as we watch the reality principle overtake us. But the power of Dickens's rhetoric is in those gray and cold ashes, handfuls of dust that gather everywhere in the pages of *Hard Times*. Gradgrind, or the world without imagination, fails as a satire upon Utilitarianism, but triumphs frighteningly as a representation of the drive beyond the pleasure principle.

V

Except perhaps for *Pickwick Papers*, *A Tale of Two Cities* always has been the most popular of Dickens's books, if we set aside also the annual phenomenon of *A Christmas Carol* and the other Christmas books. No critic however would rank it with such other later novels as *Great Expectations* and *Our Mutual Friend* or the unfinished *Edwin Drood,* or with the many earlier and middle period masterpieces. The harshest single judgment remains that of the now forgotten but formidably pungent reviewer Sir James Fitzjames Stephen, who left Dickens nothing:

> The moral tone of the *Tale of Two Cities* is not more wholesome than that of its predecessors, nor does it display any nearer approach to a solid knowledge of the subject-matter to which it refers. Mr. Dickens observes in his preface—"It has been one of my hopes to add something to the popular and picturesque means of understanding that terrible time, though no one can hope to add anything to the philosophy of Mr. Carlyle's wonderful book." The allusion to Mr. Carlyle confirms the presumption which the book itself raises, that Mr. Dickens happened to have read the *History of the French Revolution*, and, being on the look-out for a subject, determined off-hand to write a novel about it. Whether he has any other knowledge of the subject than a single reading of Mr. Carlyle's work would supply does not appear, but certainly what he has written shows no more. It is exactly the sort of story which a man would write who had taken down Mr. Carlyle's theory without any sort of inquiry or examination, but with a comfortable conviction that "nothing could be added to its philosophy." The people, says Mr. Dickens, in effect, had been degraded by long and gross misgovernment, and acted like wild beasts in consequence. There is, no doubt, a great deal of truth in this view of the matter, but it is such very elementary truth that, unless a man had something new to say about it, it is hardly worth mentioning; and Mr. Dickens supports it by specific assertions which, if not absolutely false, are at any rate so selected as to convey an entirely false impression. It is a shameful thing for a popular writer to exaggerate the faults of the French aristocracy in a book which

will naturally find its way to readers who know very little of the subject except what he chooses to tell them; but it is impossible not to feel that the melodramatic story which Mr. Dickens tells about the wicked Marquis who violates one of his serfs and murders another, is a grossly unfair representation of the state of society in France in the middle of the eighteenth century. That the French *noblesse* had much to answer for in a thousand ways, is a lamentable truth; but it is by no means true that they could rob, murder, and ravish with impunity. When Count Horn thought proper to try the experiment under the Regency, he was broken on the wheel, notwithstanding his nobility; and the sort of atrocities which Mr. Dickens depicts as characteristic of the eighteenth century were neither safe nor common in the fourteenth.

The most palpable hit here is certainly Dickens's extraordinary reliance upon Carlyle's bizarre but effective *French Revolution*, which is not the history it purports to be but rather has the design, rhetoric, and vision of an apocalyptic fantasy. No one now would read either Carlyle or Dickens in order to learn anything about the French Revolution, and sadly enough no one now reads Carlyle anyway. Yet Stephen's dismay remains legitimate; countless thousands continue to receive the only impressions they ever will have of the French Revolution through the reading of *A Tale of Two Cities*. The book remains a great tale, a vivid instance of Dickens's preternatural gifts as a pure storyteller, though except for its depiction of the superbly ghastly Madame Defarge and her Jacobin associates it lacks the memorable grotesques and driven enthusiasts that we expect from Dickens.

The most palpable flaw in the novel is the weakness as representations of Lucie and Darnay, and the relative failure of the more crucial Carton, who simply lacks the aesthetic dignity that Dickens so desperately needed to give him. If Carton and Darnay, between them, really were meant to depict the spiritual form of Charles Dickens, then their mutual lack of gusto renders them even more inadequate. When Madame Defarge dies, slain by her own bullet, we are very moved, particularly by relief that such an unrelenting version of the death drive will cease to menace us. When Carton, looking "sublime and prophetic," goes to execution, Dickens attempts to move us: we receive the famous and unacceptable, "It is a far, far better thing that I do, than I have ever done; it is a far, far better rest that I go to than I have ever known." Dickens owes us a far, far better rhetoric than that, and generally he delivers it.

The life of *A Tale of Two Cities* is elsewhere, centered upon the negative sublimity of Madame Defarge and her knitting, which is one of Dickens's finest inventions, and is clearly a metaphor for the storytelling of the novel itself. Dickens hardly would have said: "I am Madame Defarge," but she, like the author, remorselessly controls the narrative, until she loses her struggle with the epitome of a loving Englishwoman, Miss Pross. The book's penultimate chapter, in which we are rid of Madame Defarge, is shrewdly called "The Knitting Done."

Even Dickens rarely surpasses the nightmare intensity of Madame Defarge, her absolute command of stage fire, and his finest accomplishment in the book is to increase her already stark aura as the narrative knits onwards. Here is a superb early epiphany of the lady, putting heart into her formidable husband, who seems weak only in comparison to his wife, less a force of nature than of history:

> The night was hot, and the shop, close shut and surrounded by so foul a neighbourhood, was ill-smelling. Monsieur Defarge's olfactory sense was by no means delicate, but the stock of wine smelt much stronger than it ever tasted, and so did the stock of rum and brandy and aniseed. He whiffed the compound of scents away, as he put down his smoked-out pipe.
>
> "You are fatigued," said madame, raising her glance as she knotted the money. "There are only the usual odours."
>
> "I am a little tired," her husband acknowledged.
>
> "You are a little depressed, too," said madame, whose quick eyes had never been so intent on the accounts, but they had had a ray or two for him. "Oh, the men, the men!"
>
> "But my dear!" began Defarge.
>
> "But my dear!" repeated madame, nodding firmly; "but my dear! You are faint of heart to-night, my dear!"
>
> "Well, then," said Defarge, as if a thought were wrung out of his breast, "it *is* a long time."
>
> "It is a long time," repeated his wife; "and when is it not a long time? Vengeance and retribution require a long time; it is the rule."
>
> "It does not take a long time to strike a man with Lightning," said Defarge.
>
> "How long," demanded madame, composely, "does it take to make and store the lightning? Tell me."
>
> Defarge raised his head thoughtfully, as if there were something in that too.

"It does not take a long time," said madame, "for an earthquake to swallow a town. Eh well! Tell me how long it takes to prepare the earthquake?"

"A long time, I suppose," said Defarge.

"But when it is ready, it takes place, and grinds to pieces everything before it. In the meantime, it is always preparing, though it is not seen or heard. That is your consolation. Keep it."

She tied a knot with flashing eyes, as if it throttled a foe.

"I tell thee," said madame, extending her right hand, for emphasis, "that although it is a long time on the road, it is on the road and coming. I tell thee it never retreats, and never stops. I tell thee it is always advancing. Look around and consider the lives of all the world that we know, consider the faces of all the world that we know, consider the rage and discontent to which the Jacquerie addresses itself with more and more of certainty every hour. Can such things last? Bah! I mock you."

"My brave wife," returned Defarge, standing before her with his head a little bent, and his hands clasped at his back, like a docile and attentive pupil before his catechist, "I do not question all this. But it has lasted a long time, and it is possible—you know well, my wife, it is possible—that it may not come, during our lives."

"Eh well! How then?" demanded madame, tying another knot, as if there were another enemy strangled.

"Well!" said Defarge, with a half-complaining and half-apologetic shrug. "We shall not see the triumph."

"We shall have helped it," returned madame, with her extended hand in strong action. "Nothing that we do, is done in vain. I believe, with all my soul, that we shall see the triumph. But even if not, even if I knew certainly not, show me the neck of an aristocrat and tyrant, and still I would—"

Then madame, with her teeth set, tied a very terrible knot indeed.

"Hold!" cried Defarge, reddening a little as if he felt charged with cowardice; "I too, my dear, will stop at nothing."

"Yes! But it is your weakness that you sometimes need to see your victim and your opportunity, to sustain you. Sustain yourself without that. When the time comes, let loose a tiger and a devil; but wait for the time with the tiger and the devil chained—not shown—yet always ready."

To be always preparing, unseen and unheard, is Madame Defarge's one consolation. Dickens has made her childless, somewhat in the mysterious mode of Lady Macbeth, since somehow we believe that Madame Defarge too must have nursed an infant. Her dialogue with Defarge has overtones of Lady Macbeth heartening Macbeth, keying up his resolution to treason and a kind of parricide. What Dickens has learned from Shakespeare is the art of counterpointing degrees of terror, of excess, so as to suggest a dread that otherwise would reside beyond representation. Macbeth, early doubting, seems weak in contrast to his wife's force, but we will see him at his bloody work, until he becomes an astonishing manifestation of tyranny. Similarly, Defarge seems little in juxtaposition to his implacable wife, but we will see him as a demon of courage, skill, and apocalyptic drive, leading the triumphant assault upon the Bastille.

In his final vision of Madame Defarge, Dickens brilliantly reveals his masochistic passion for her:

> Madame Defarge slightly waved her hand, to imply that she heard, and might be relied upon to arrive in good time, and so went through the mud, and round the corner of the prison wall. The Vengeance and the Juryman, looking after her as she walked away, were highly appreciative of her fine figure, and her superb moral endowments.
>
> There were many women at that time, upon whom the time laid a dreadfully disfiguring hand; but, there was not one among them more to be dreaded than this ruthless woman, now taking her way along the streets. Of a strong and fearless character, of shrewd sense and readiness, of great determination, of that kind of beauty which not only seems to impart to its possessor firmness and animosity, but to strike into others an instinctive recognition of those qualities; the troubled time would have heaved her up, under any circumstances. But, imbued from her childhood with a brooding sense of wrong, and an inveterate hatred of a class, opportunity had developed her into a tigress. She was absolutely without pity. If she had ever had the virtue in her, it had quite gone out of her.
>
> It was nothing to her, that an innocent man was to die for the sins of his forefathers; she saw, not him, but them. It was nothing to her, that his wife was to be made a widow and his daughter an orphan; that was insufficient punishment, because they were her natural enemies and her prey, and as such had no right to live. To appeal to her, was made hopeless by her having no sense of pity, even for herself. If she had been laid low in the streets, in any of the many encounters in which she had been engaged, she would

not have pitied herself; nor, if she had been ordered to the axe to-morrow, would she have gone to it with any softer feeling than a fierce desire to change places with the man who sent her there.

Such a heart Madame Defarge carried under her rough robe. Carelessly worn, it was a becoming robe enough, in a certain weird way, and her dark hair looked rich under her coarse red cap. Lying hidden in her bosom, was a loaded pistol. Lying hidden at her waist, was a sharpened dagger. Thus accoutred, and walking with the confident tread of such a character, and with the supple freedom of a woman who had habitually walked in her girlhood, bare-foot and bare-legged, on the brown sea-sand, Madame Defarge took her way along the streets.

We can discount Dickens's failed ironies here ("her superb moral endowments") and his obvious and rather tiresome moral judgments upon his own creation. What comes through overwhelmingly is Dickens's desire for this sadistic woman, which is the secret of our desire for her also, and so for her nightmare power over us. "Her fine figure," "that kind of beauty ... firmness and animosity," "a tigress ... absolutely without pity," "a becoming robe enough, in a certain weird way," "her dark hair looked rich," "confident tread ... supple freedom ... bare-foot and bare-legged"—these are the stigmata of a dominatrix. Loaded pistol in her bosom, sharpened dagger at her waist, Madame Defarge is the ultimate phallic woman, a monument to fetishism, to what Freud would have called the splitting of Dickens's ego in the defensive process.

That splitting attains a triumph in the grand wrestling match, where Miss Pross, a Jacob wrestling with the Angel of Death, holds off Madame Defarge in what is supposed to be an instance of Love stronger than Death, but which is all the more effective for its sexual overtones:

Madame Defarge made at the door. Miss Pross, on the instinct of the moment, seized her round the waist in both her arms, and held her tight. It was in vain for Madame Defarge to struggle and to strike; Miss Pross, with the vigorous tenacity of love, always so much stronger than hate, clasped her tight, and even lifted her from the floor in the struggle that they had. The two hands of Madame Defarge buffeted and tore her face; but, Miss Pross, with her head down, held her round the waist, and clung to her with more than the hold of a drowning woman.

Soon, Madame Defarge's hands ceased to strike, and felt at her encircled waist. "It is under my arm," said Miss Pross, in

smothered tones, "you shall not draw it. I am stronger than you,
I bless Heaven for it. I'll hold you till one or other of us faints or
dies!"

Madame Defarge's hands were at her bosom. Miss Pross
looked up, saw what it was, struck at it, struck out a flash and a
crash, and stood alone—blinded with smoke.

The embrace of Miss Pross clearly has a repressed lesbian passion for
Madame Defarge in it, so that more than a transcendent love for Lucie here
endows the force of the good with its immovable tenacity. But for the pistol
blast, Madame Defarge would have been held until one or the other lady
fainted or died. Miss Pross had never struck a blow in her life, but then her
father Jacob had been no warrior either. Dickens, master of stage fire,
destroyed Madame Defarge in the grand manner, the only fate worthy of so
vivid and so passionately desired a creation.

G.K. CHESTERTON

The Great Popularity

There is one aspect of Charles Dickens which must be of interest even to that subterranean race which does not admire his books. Even if we are not interested in Dickens as a great event in English literature, we must still be interested in him as a great event in English history. If he had not his place with Fielding and Thackeray, he would still have his place with Wat Tyler and Wilkes; for the man led a mob. He did what no English statesman, perhaps, has really done; he called out the people. He was popular in a sense of which we moderns have not even a notion. In that sense there is no popularity now. There are no popular authors today. We call such authors as Mr. Guy Boothby or Mr. William Le Queux popular authors. But this is popularity altogether in a weaker sense; not only in quantity, but in quality. The old popularity was positive; the new is negative. There is a great deal of difference between the eager man who wants to read a book, and the tired man who wants a book to read. A man reading a Le Queux mystery wants to get to the end of it. A man reading the Dickens novel wished that it might never end. Men read a Dickens story six times because they knew it so well. If a man can read a Le Queux story six times it is only because he can forget it six times. In short, the Dickens novel was popular, not because it was an

From *Charles Dickens, The Last of the Great Men.* © 1942 The Readers Club.

unreal world, but because it was a real world; a world in which the soul could live. The modern "shocker" at its very best is an interlude in life. But in the days when Dickens's work was coming out in serial, people talked as if real life were itself the interlude between one issue of "Pickwick" and another.

In reaching the period of the publication of "Pickwick," we reach this sudden apotheosis of Dickens. Henceforward he filled the literary world in a way hard to imagine. Fragments of that huge fashion remain in our daily language; in the talk of every trade or public question are embedded the wrecks of that enormous religion. Men give out the airs of Dickens without even opening his books; just as Catholics can live in a tradition of Christianity without having looked at the New Testament. The man in the street has more memories of Dickens, whom he has not read, than of Marie Corelli, whom he has. There is nothing in any way parallel to this omnipresence and vitality in the great comic characters of Boz. There are no modern Bumbles and Pecksniffs, no modern Gamps and Micawbers. Mr. Rudyard Kipling (to take an author of a higher type than those before mentioned) is called, and called justly, a popular author; that is to say, he is widely read, greatly enjoyed, and highly remunerated; he has achieved the paradox of at once making poetry and making money. But let any one who wishes to see the difference try the experiment of assuming the Kipling characters to be common property like the Dickens characters. Let any one go into an average parlour and allude to Strickland as he would allude to Mr. Bumble, the Beadle. Let any one say that somebody is "a perfect Learoyd," as he would say "a perfect Pecksniff." Let any one write a comic paragraph for a halfpenny paper, and allude to Mrs. Hawksbee instead of to Mrs. Gamp. He will soon discover that the modern world has forgotten its own fiercest booms more completely than it has forgotten this formless tradition from its fathers. The mere dregs of it come to more than any contemporary excitement; the gleaning of the grapes of "Pickwick" is more than the whole vintage of "Soldiers Three." There is one instance, and I think only one, of an exception to this generalization; there is one figure in our popular literature which would really be recognized by the populace. Ordinary men would understand you if you referred currently to Sherlock Holmes. Sir Arthur Conan Doyle would no doubt be justified in rearing his head to the stars, remembering that Sherlock Holmes is the only really familiar figure in modern fiction. But let him droop that head again with a gentle sadness, remembering that if Sherlock Holmes is the only familiar figure in modern fiction, Sherlock Holmes is also the only familiar figure in the Sherlock Holmes tales. Not many people could say offhand what was the name of the owner of Silver Blaze, or whether Mrs. Watson was dark or fair. But if Dickens had written the Sherlock Holmes stories, every character in them would have been equally arresting and memorable. A Sherlock Holmes would have cooked the dinner for Sherlock Holmes; a Sherlock Holmes would have driven his cab. If Dickens brought in a man merely to carry a letter, he had time for a touch or two, and made him a giant. Dickens not only conquered the world, he conquered it with minor characters. Mr. John Smauker, the servant of Mr. Cyrus Bantam, though he merely passes across the stage, is almost as vivid to us as Mr. Samuel Weller, the servant of Mr. Samuel Pickwick. The young man with the lumpy forehead, who only says "Esker" to Mr. Podsnap's foreign gentleman, is as good as Mr. Podsnap himself. They appear only for a fragment of time, but they belong to eternity. We have them only for an instant, but they have us for ever.

In dealing with Dickens, then, we are dealing with a man whose public success was a marvel and almost a monstrosity. And here I perceive that my friend, the purely artistic critic, primed with Flaubert and Turgenev, can contain himself no longer. He leaps to his feet, upsetting his cup of cocoa, and asks contemptuously what all this has to do with criticism. "Why begin your study of an author," he says, "with trash about popularity? Boothby is popular, and Le Queux is popular, and Mother Siegel is popular. It Dickens was even more popular, it may only mean that Dickens was even worse. The people like bad literature. If your object is to show that Dickens was good literature, you should rather apologize for his popularity, and try to explain it away. You should seek to show that Dickens's work was good literature, although it was popular. Yes, that is your task, to prove that Dickens was admirable, although he was admired!"

I ask the artistic critic to be patient for a little and to believe that I have a serious reason for registering this historic popularity. To that we shall come presently. But as a manner of approach I may perhaps ask leave to examine this actual and fashionable statement, to which I have supposed him to have recourse—the statement that the people like bad literature, and even like literature because it is bad. This way of stating the thing is an error, and in that error lies matter of much import to Dickens and his destiny in letters. The public does not like bad literature. The public likes a certain kind of literature and likes that kind of literature even when it is bad better than another kind of literature even when it is good. Nor is this unreasonable; for the line between different types of literature is as real as the line between tears and laughter; and to tell people who can only get bad comedy that you have some first-class tragedy is as irrational as to offer a man who is shivering over weak warm coffee a really superior sort of ice.

Ordinary people dislike the delicate modern work, not because it is good or because it is bad, but because it is not the thing that they asked for. If, for instance, you find them pent in sterile streets and hungering for adventure and a violent secrecy, and if you then give them their choice between "A Study in Scarlet," a good detective story, and "The Autobiography of Mark Rutherford," a good psychological monologue, no doubt they will prefer "A Study in Scarlet." But they will not do so because "The Autobiography of Mark Rutherford" is a very good monologue, but because it is evidently a very poor detective story. They will be indifferent to "Les Aveugles," not because it is good drama, but because it is bad melodrama. They do not like good introspective sonnets; but neither do they like bad introspective sonnets, of which there are many. When they walk behind the brass of the Salvation Army band instead of listening to harmonies at Queen's Hall, it is always assumed that they prefer bad music. But it may be merely that they prefer military music, music marching down the open street, and that if Dan Godfrey's band could be smitten with salvation and lead them, they would like that even better. And while they might easily get more satisfaction out of a screaming article in *The War Cry* than out of a page of Emerson about the Oversoul, this would not be because the page of Emerson is another and superior kind of literature. It would be because the page of Emerson is another (and inferior) kind of religion.

Dickens stands first as a defiant monument of what happens when a great literary genius has a literary taste akin to that of the community. For this kinship was deep and spiritual. Dickens was not like our ordinary demagogues and journalists. Dickens did not write what the people wanted. Dickens wanted what the people wanted. And with this was connected that other fact which must never be forgotten, and which I have more than once insisted on, that Dickens and his school had a hilarious faith in democracy and thought of the service of it as a sacred priesthood. Hence there was this vital point in his popularism, that there was no condescension in it. The belief that the rabble will only read rubbish can be read between the lines of all our contemporary writers, even of those writers whose rubbish the rabble reads. Mr. Fergus Hume has no more respect for the populace than Mr. George Moore. The only difference lies between those writers who will consent to talk down to the people, and those writers who will not consent to talk down to the people. But Dickens never talked down to the people. He talked up to the people. He approached the people like a deity and poured out his riches and his blood. This is what makes the immortal bond between him and the masses of men. He had not merely produced something they could understand, but he took it seriously, and toiled and agonized to produce it. They were not only enjoying one of the best writers, they were enjoying the best he could do. His raging and sleepless nights, his wild walks in the darkness, his note-books crowded, his nerves in rags, all this extraordinary output was but a fit sacrifice to the ordinary man. He climbed towards the lower classes. He panted upwards on weary wings to reach the heaven of the poor.

His power, then, lay in the fact that he expressed with an energy and brilliancy quite uncommon the things close to the common mind. But with this mere phrase, the common mind, we collide with a current error. Commonness and the common mind are now generally spoken of as meaning in some manner inferiority and the inferior mind; the mind of the mere mob. But the common mind means the mind of all the artists and heroes; or else it would not be common. Plato had the common mind; Dante had the common mind; or that mind was not common. Commonness means the quality common to the saint and the sinner, to the philosopher and the fool; and it was this that Dickens grasped and developed. In everybody there is a certain thing that loves babies, that fears death, that likes sunlight: that thing enjoys Dickens. And everybody does not mean uneducated crowds; everybody means everybody: everybody means Mrs. Meynell. This lady, a cloistered and fastidious writer, has written one of the best eulogies of Dickens that exist, an essay in praise of his pungent perfection of epithet. And when I say that everybody understands Dickens I do not mean that he is suited to the untaught intelligence. I mean that he is so plain that even scholars can understand him.

The best expression of the fact, however, is to be found in noting the two things in which he is most triumphant. In order of artistic value, next after his humour, comes his horror. And both his humour and his horror are of a kind strictly to be called human; that is, they belong to the basic part of us, below the lowest roots of our variety. His horror for instance is a healthy churchyard horror, a fear of the grotesque defamation called death: and this every man has, even if he also has the more delicate and depraved fears that come of an evil spiritual outlook. We may be afraid of a fine shade with Henry James; that is, we may be afraid of the world. We may be afraid of a taut silence with Maeterlinck; that is, we may be afraid of our own souls. But every one will certainly be afraid of a Cock Lane Ghost, including Henry James and Maeterlinck. This latter is literally a mortal fear, a fear of death; it is not the immortal fear, or fear of damnation, which belongs to all the more refined intellects of our day. In a word, Dickens does, in the exact sense, make the flesh creep; he does not, like the decadents, make the soul crawl. And the creeping of the flesh on being reminded of its fleshly failure is a strictly universal thing which we can all feel, while some of us are as yet uninstructed in the art of spiritual crawling. In the same way the Dickens mirth is a part of man and universal. All men can laugh at broad humour, even the subtle humourists. Even the modern *flâneur*, who can smile at a particular combination of green and yellow, would laugh at Mr. Lammle's request for Mr. Fledgeby's nose. In a word—the common things are common—even to the uncommon people.

These two primary dispositions of Dickens, to make the flesh creep and to make the sides ache, were a sort of twins of his spirit; they were never far apart and the fact of their affinity is interestingly exhibited in the first two novels.

Generally he mixed the two up in a book and mixed a great many other things with them. As a rule he cared little if he kept six stories of quite different colours running in the same book. The effect was sometimes similar to that of playing six tunes at once. He does not mind the coarse tragic figure of Jonas Chuzzlewit crossing the mental stage which is full of the allegorical pantomime of Eden, Mr. Chollop and *The Watertoast Gazette*, a scene which is as much of a satire as "Gulliver," and nearly as much of a fairy tale. He does not mind binding up a rather pompous sketch of prostitution in the same book with an adorable impossibility like Bunsby. But "Pickwick" is so far a coherent thing that it is coherently comic and consistently rambling. And as a consequence his next book was, upon the whole, coherently and consistently horrible. As his natural turn for terrors was kept down in "Pickwick," so his natural turn for joy and laughter is kept down in "Oliver Twist." In "Oliver Twist" the smoke of the thieves' kitchen hangs over the whole tale, and the shadow of Fagin falls everywhere. The little lamp-lit rooms of Mr. Brownlow and Rose Maylie are to all appearance purposely kept subordinate, a mere foil to the foul darkness without. It was a strange and appropriate accident that Cruikshank and not "Phiz" should have illustrated this book. There was about Cruikshank's art a kind of cramped energy which is almost the definition of the criminal mind. His drawings have a dark strength: yet he does not only draw morbidly, he draws meanly. In the doubled-up figure and frightful eyes of Fagin in the condemned cell there is not only a baseness of subject; there is a kind of baseness in the very technique of it. It is not drawn with the free lines of a free man; it has the half-witted secrecies of a hunted thief. It does not look merely like a picture of Fagin; it looks like a picture by Fagin. Among these dark and detestable plates there is one which has with a kind of black directness, the dreadful poetry that does inhere in the story, stumbling as it often is. It represents Oliver asleep at an open window in the house of one of his humaner patrons. And outside the window, but as big and close as if they were in the room, stand Fagin and the foul-faced Monk, staring at him with dark monstrous visages and great, white wicked eyes, in the style of the simple deviltry of the draughtsman. The very *naïveté* of the horror is horrifying: the very woodenness of the two wicked men seems to make them worse than mere men who are wicked. But this picture of big devils at the window-sill does express, as has been suggested above, the thread of poetry in the whole thing; the sense, that is, of the thieves as a kind of army of devils compassing earth and sky, crying for Oliver's soul and besieging the house in he is barred for safety. In this matter there is, I think, a difference between the author and the illustrator. In Cruikshank there was surely something morbid; but, sensitive and sentimental as Dickens was, there was nothing morbid in him. He had, as Stevenson had, more of the mere boy's love of suffocating stories of blood and darkness; of skulls, of gibbets, of all the things, in a word, that are sombre without being sad. There is a ghastly joy in remembering our boyish reading about Sikes and his flight; especially about the voice of that unbearable pedlar which went on in a monotonous and maddening sing-song, "will wash out grease-stains, mud-stains, blood-stains," until Sikes fled almost screaming. For this boyish mixture of appetite and repugnance there is a good popular phrase, "supping on horrors." Dickens supped on horrors as he supped on Christmas pudding. He supped on horrors because he was an optimist and could sup on anything. There was no saner or simpler schoolboy than Traddles, who covered all his books with skeletons.

"Oliver Twist" had begun in Bentley's *Miscellany*, which Dickens edited in 1837. It was interrupted by a blow that for the moment broke the author's spirit and seemed to have broken his heart. His wife's sister, Mary Hogarth, died suddenly. To Dickens his wife's family seems to have been like his own; his affections were heavily committed to the sisters, and of this one he was peculiarly fond. All his life, through much conceit and sometimes something bordering on selfishness, we can feel the redeeming note of an almost tragic tenderness; he was a man who could really have died of love or sorrow. He took up the work of "Oliver Twist" again later in the year, and finished it at the end of 1838. His work was incessant and almost bewildering. In 1838 he had already brought out the first number of "Nicholas Nickleby." But the great popularity went booming on; the whole world was roaring for books by Dickens, and more books by Dickens, and Dickens was labouring night and day like a factory. Among other things he edited the "Memoirs of Grimaldi." The incident is only worth mentioning for the sake of one more example of the silly ease with which Dickens was drawn by criticism and the clever ease with which he managed, in these small squabbles, to defend himself. Somebody mildly suggested that, after all, Dickens had never known Grimaldi. Dickens was down on him like a thunderbolt, sardonically asking how close an intimacy Lord Braybrooke had with Mr. Samuel Pepys.

"Nicholas Nickleby" is the most typical perhaps of the tone of his earlier works. It is in form a very rambling, old-fashioned romance, the kind of romance in which the hero is only a convenience for the frustration of the villain. Nicholas is what is called in theatricals a stick. But any stick is good enough to beat a Squeers with. That strong thwack, that simplified energy is the whole object of such a story; and the whole of this tale is full of a kind of highly picturesque platitude. The wicked aristocrats, Sir Mulberry Hawk, Lord Frederick Verisopht and the rest are inadequate versions of the fashionable profligate. But this is not (as some suppose) because Dickens in his vulgarity could not comprehend the refinement of patrician vice. There is no idea more vulgar or more ignorant than the notion that a gentleman is generally what is called refined. The error of the Hawk conception is that, if anything, he is too refined. Real aristocratic blackguards do not swagger and rant so well. A real fast baronet would not have defied Nicholas in the tavern with so much oratorical dignity. A real fast baronet would probably have been choked with apoplectic embarrassment and said nothing at all. But Dickens read into this aristocracy a grandiloquence and a natural poetry which, like all melodrama, is really the precious jewel of the poor.

But the book contains something which is much more Dickensian. It is exquisitely characteristic of Dickens that the truly great achievement of the story is the person who delays the story. Mrs. Nickleby with her beautiful mazes of memory does her best to prevent the story of Nicholas Nickleby from being told. And she does well. There is no particular necessity that we should know what happens to Madeline Bray. There is a desperate and crying necessity that we should know that Mrs. Nickleby once had a foot-boy who had a wart on his nose and a driver who had a green shade over his left eye. If Mrs. Nickleby is a fool, she is one of those fools who are wiser than the world. She stands for a great truth which we must not forget; the truth that experience is not in real life a saddening thing at all. The people who have had misfortunes are generally the people who love to talk about them. Experience is really one of the gaieties of old age, one of its dissipations. Mere memory becomes a kind of debauch. Experience may be disheartening to those who are foolish enough to try to co-ordinate it and to draw deductions from it. But to those happy souls, like Mrs. Nickleby, to whom relevancy is nothing, the whole of their past life is like an inexhaustible fairyland. Just as we take a rambling walk because we know that a whole district is beautiful, so they indulge a rambling mind because they know that a whole existence is interesting. A boy does not plunge into his future more romantically and at random, than they plunge into their past.

Another gleam in the book is Mr. Mantalini. Of him, as of all the really great comic characters of Dickens, it is impossible to speak with any critical adequacy. Perfect absurdity is a direct thing, like physical pain, or a strong smell. A joke is a fact. However indefensible it is it cannot be attacked. However defensible it is it cannot be defended. That Mr. Mantalini should say in praising the "outline" of his wife, "The two Countesses had no outlines, and the Dowager's was a demd outline," this can only be called an unanswerable absurdity. You may try to analyze it, as Charles Lamb did the indefensible joke about the hare; you may dwell for a moment on the dark distinctions between the negative disqualification of the Countesses and the positive disqualification of the Dowager, but you will not capture the violent beauty of it in any way. "She will be a lovely widow; I shall be a body. Some handsome women will cry; she will laugh demnedly." This vision of demoniac heartlessness has the same defiant finality. I mention the matter here, but it has to be remembered in connection with all the comic masterpieces of Dickens. Dickens has greatly suffered with the critics precisely through this stunning simplicity in his best work. The critic is called upon to describe his sensations while enjoying Mantalini and Micawber, and he can no more describe them than he can describe a blow in the face. Thus Dickens, in this self-conscious, analytical and descriptive age, loses both ways. He is doubly unfitted for the best modern criticism. His bad work is below that criticism. His good work is above it.

But gigantic as were Dickens's labours, gigantic as were the exactions from him, his own plans were more gigantic still. He had the type of mind that wishes to do every kind of work at once; to do everybody's work as well as its own. There floated before him a vision of a monstrous magazine, entirely written by himself. It is true that when this scheme came to be discussed, he suggested that other pens might be occasionally employed; but, reading between the lines, it is sufficiently evident that he thought of the thing as a kind of vast multiplication of himself, with Dickens as editor, opening letters, Dickens as leader-writer writing leaders, Dickens as reporter reporting meetings, Dickens as reviewer reviewing books, Dickens, for all I know, as office-boy, opening and shutting doors. This serial, of which he spoke to Messrs. Chapman and Hall, began and broke off and remains as a colossal fragment bound together under the title of "Master Humphrey's Clock." One characteristic thing he wished to have in the periodical. He suggested an Arabian Nights of London, in which Gog and Magog, the giants of the city, should give forth chronicles as enormous as themselves. He had a taste for these schemes or frameworks for many tales. He made and abandoned many; many he half-fulfilled. I strongly suspect that he meant Major Jackman, in "Mrs. Lirriper's Lodgings" and "Mrs. Lirriper's Legacy," to start a series of studies of that lady's lodgers, a kind of history of No. 81 Norfolk Street, Strand. "The Seven Poor Travellers" was planned for seven stories; we will not say seven poor stories. Dickens had meant, probably, to write a tale for each article of "Somebody's Luggage": he only got as far as the hat and the boots. This gigantesque scale of literary architecture, huge and yet curiously cosy, is characteristic of his spirit, fond of size and yet fond of comfort. He liked to have story within story, like room within room of some labyrinthine but comfortable castle. In this spirit he wished "Master Humphrey's Clock" to begin, and to be a big frame or bookcase for numberless novels. The clock started; but the clock stopped.

In the prologue by Master Humphrey reappear Mr. Pickwick and Sam Weller, and of that resurrection many things have been said, chiefly expressions of a reasonable regret. Doubtless they do not add much to their author's reputation, but they add a great deal to their author's pleasure. It was ingrained in him to wish to meet old friends. All his characters are, so to speak, designed to be old friends; in a sense every Dickens character is an old friend, even when he first appears. He comes to us mellow out of many implied interviews, and carries the firelight on his face. Dickens was simply pleased to meet Pickwick again, and being pleased, he made the old man too comfortable to be amusing.

But "Master Humphrey's Clock" is now scarcely known except as the shell of one of the well-known novels. "The Old Curiosity Shop" was published in accordance with the original "Clock" scheme. Perhaps the most typical thing about it is the title. There seems no reason in particular, at the first and most literal glance, why the story should be called after the Old Curiosity Shop. Only two of the characters have anything to do with such a shop, and they leave us for ever in the first few pages. It is as if Thackeray had called the whole novel of "Vanity Fair" "Miss Pinkerton's Academy." It is as if Scott had given the whole story of "The Antiquary" the title of "The Hawes Inn." But when we feel the situation with more fidelity we realize that this title is something in the nature of a key to the whole Dickens romance. His tales always started from some splendid hint in the streets. And shops, perhaps the most poetical of all things, often set off his fancy galloping. Every shop, in fact, was to him the door of romance. Among all the huge serial schemes of which we have spoken, it is a matter of wonder that he never started an endless periodical called "The Street," and divided it into shops. He could have written an exquisite romance called "The Baker's Shop"; another called "The Chemist's Shop"; another called "The Oil Shop," to keep company with "The Old Curiosity Shop." Some incomparable baker he invented and forgot. Some gorgeous chemist might have been. Some more than mortal oilman is lost to us for ever. This Old Curiosity Shop he did happen to linger by: its tale he did happen to tell.

Around "Little Nell," of course, a controversy raged and rages; some implored Dickens not to kill her at the end of the story: some regret that he did not kill her at the beginning. To me the chief interest in this young person lies in the fact that she is an example, and the most celebrated example of what must have been, I think, a personal peculiarity, perhaps a personal experience of Dickens. There is, of course, no paradox at all in saying that if we find in a good book a wildly impossible character it is very probable indeed that it was copied from a real person. This is one of the commonplaces of good art criticism. For although people talk of the restraints of fact and the freedom of fiction, the case for most artistic purposes is quite the other way. Nature is as free as air: art is forced to look probable. There may be a million things that do happen, and yet only one thing that convinces us as likely to happen. Out of a million possible things there may be only one appropriate thing. I fancy, therefore, that many stiff, unconvincing characters are copied from the wild freak-show of real life. And in many parts of Dickens's work there is evidence of some peculiar affection on his part for a strange sort of little girl; a little girl with a premature sense of responsibility and duty; a sort of saintly precocity. Did he know some little girl of this kind? Did she die, perhaps, and remain in his memory in colours too ethereal and pale? In any case there are a great number of them in his works. Little Dorrit was one of them, and Florence Dombey with her brother, and even Agnes in infancy; and, of course, Little Nell. And, in any case, one thing is evident; whatever charm these children may have they have not the charm of childhood. They are not little children: they are "little mothers." The beauty and divinity in a child lie in his not being worried, not being conscientious, not being like Little Nell. Little Nell has never any of the sacred bewilderment of a baby. She never wears that face, beautiful but almost half-witted, with which a real child half understands that there is evil in the universe.

As usual, however, little as the story has to do with the title, the splendid and satisfying pages have even less to do with the story. Dick Swiveller is perhaps the noblest of all the noble creations of Dickens. He has all the overwhelming absurdity of Mantalini, with the addition of being human and credible, for he knows he is absurd. His high-falutin is not done because he seriously thinks it right and proper, like that of Mr. Snodgrass, nor is it done because he thinks it will serve his turn, like that of Mr. Pecksniff, for both these beliefs are improbable; it is done because he really loves high-falutin, because he has a lonely literary pleasure in exaggerative language. Great draughts of words are to him like great draughts of wine—pungent and yet refreshing, light and yet leaving him in a glow. In unerring instinct for the perfect folly of a phrase he has no equal, even among the giants of Dickens. "I am sure," says Miss Wackles, when she had been flirting with Cheggs, the market-gardener, and reduced Mr. Swiveller to Byronic renunciation, "I am sure I'm very sorry if—" "Sorry," said Mr. Swiveller, "sorry in the possession of a Cheggs!" The abyss of bitterness is unfathomable. Scarcely less precious is the pose of Mr. Swiveller when he imitates the stage brigand. After crying, "Some wine here! Ho!" he hands the flagon to himself with profound humility, and receives it haughtily. Perhaps the very best scene in the book is that between Mr. Swiveller and the single gentleman with whom he endeavours to remonstrate for having remained in bed all day: "We cannot have single gentlemen coming into the place and sleeping like double gentlemen without paying extra.... An equal amount of slumber was never got out of one bed, and if you want to sleep like that you must pay for a double-bedded room." His relations with the Marchioness are at once purely romantic and purely genuine; there is nothing even of Dickens's legitimate exaggerations about them. A shabby, larky, good-natured clerk would, as a matter of fact, spend hours in the society of a little servant girl if he found her about the house. It would arise partly from a dim kindliness, and partly from that mysterious instinct which is sometimes called, mistakenly, a love of low company—that mysterious instinct which makes so many men of pleasure find something soothing in the society of uneducated people, particularly uneducated women. It is the instinct which accounts for the otherwise unaccountable popularity of barmaids.

And still the pot of that huge popularity boiled. In 1841 another novel was demanded, and "Barnaby Rudge" supplied. It is chiefly of interest as an embodiment of that other element in Dickens, the picturesque or even the pictorial. Barnaby Rudge, the idiot with his rags and his feathers and his raven, the bestial hangman, the blind mob—all make a picture, though they hardly make a novel. One touch there is in it of the richer and more humorous Dickens, the boy-conspirator, Mr. Sim Tappertit. But he might have been treated with more sympathy—with as much sympathy, for instance, as Mr. Dick Swiveller; for he is only the romantic guttersnipe, the bright boy at the particular age when it is most fascinating to found a secret society and most difficult to keep a secret. And if ever there was a romantic guttersnipe on earth it was Charles Dickens. "Barnaby Rudge" is no more an historical novel than Sim's secret league was a political movement; but they are both beautiful creations. When all is said, however, the main reason for mentioning the work here is that it is the next bubble in the pot, the next thing that burst out of that whirling, seething head. The tide of it rose and smoked and sang till it boiled over the pot of Britain and poured over all America. In the January of 1842 he set out for the United States.

GEORGE ORWELL

Dickens's Radicalism, Plausibility, and His Image of the Working Man

It is not merely a coincidence that Dickens never writes about agriculture and writes endlessly about food. He was a cockney, and London is the centre of the earth in rather the same sense that the belly is the centre of the body. It is a city of consumers, of people who are deeply civilised but not primarily useful. A thing that strikes one when one looks below the surface of Dickens's books is that, as nineteenth-century novelists go, he is rather ignorant. He knows very little about the way things really happen. At first sight this statement looks flatly untrue, and it needs some qualification.

Dickens had had vivid glimpses of "low life"—life in a debtor's prison, for example—and he was also a popular novelist and able to write about ordinary people. So were all the characteristic English novelists of the nineteenth century. They felt at home in the world they lived in, whereas a writer nowadays is so hopelessly isolated that the typical modern novel is a novel about a novelist. Even when Joyce, for instance, spends a decade or so in patient efforts to make contact with the "common man", his "common man" finally turns out to be a Jew, and a bit of a highbrow at that. Dickens at least does not suffer from this kind of thing. He has no difficulty in introducing the common motives, love, ambition, avarice, vengeance and so forth. What he does not noticeably write about, however, is *work*.

From *Collected Essays*, Penguin Classics. © 2000 Penguin. First Published in 1939.

In Dickens's novels anything in the nature of work happens offstage. The only one of his heroes who has a plausible profession is David Copperfield, who is first a shorthand writer and then a novelist, like Dickens himself. With most of the others, the way they earn their living is very much in the background. Pip, for instance, "goes into business" in Egypt; we are not told what business, and Pip's working life occupies about half a page of the book. Clennam has been in some unspecified business in China, and later goes into another barely specified business with Doyce. Martin Chuzzlewit is an architect, but does not seem to get much time for practising. In no case do their adventures spring directly out of their work. Here the contrast between Dickens and, say, Trollope is startling. And one reason for this is undoubtedly that Dickens knows very little about the professions his characters are supposed to follow. What exactly went on in Gradgrind's factories? How did Podsnap make his money? How did Merdle work his swindles? One knows that Dickens could never follow up the details of parliamentary elections and Stock Exchange rackets as Trollope could. As soon as he has to deal with trade, finance, industry or politics he takes refuge in vagueness, or in satire. This is the case even with legal processes, about which actually he must have known a good deal. Compare any lawsuit in Dickens with the lawsuit in *Orley Farm*, for instance.

And this partly accounts for the needless ramifications of Dickens's novels, the awful Victorian "plot". It is true that not all his novels are alike in this. *A Tale of Two Cities* is a very good and fairly simple story, and so in its different way is *Hard Times*; but these are just the two which are always rejected as "not like Dickens"—and incidentally they were not published in monthly numbers.[1] The two first-person novels are also good stories, apart from their sub-plots. But the typical Dickens novel, *Nicholas Nickleby*, *Oliver Twist*, *Martin Chuzzlewit*, *Our Mutual Friend*, always exists round a framework of melodrama. The last thing anyone ever remembers about these books is their central story. On the other hand, I suppose no one has ever read them without carrying the memory of individual pages to the day of his death. Dickens sees human beings with the most intense vividness, but he sees them always in private life, as "characters", not as functional members of society; that is to say, he sees them statically. Consequently his greatest success is *The Pickwick Papers*, which is not a story at all, merely a series of sketches; there is little attempt at development—the characters simply go on and on, behaving like idiots, in a kind of eternity. As soon as he tries to bring his characters into action, the melodrama begins. He cannot make the action revolve round their ordinary occupations; hence the crossword puzzle of coincidences, intrigues, murders, disguises, buried wills, long-lost brothers, etc. etc. In the end even people like Squeers and Micawber get sucked into the machinery.

Of course it would be absurd to say that Dickens is a vague or merely melodramatic writer. Much that he wrote is extremely factual, and in the power of evoking visual images he has probably never been equalled. When Dickens has once described something you see it for the rest of your life. But in a way the concreteness of his vision is a sign of what he is missing. For, after all, that is what the merely casual onlooker always sees—the outward appearance, the non-functional, the surfaces of things. No one who is really involved in the landscape ever sees the landscape. Wonderfully as he can describe an *appearance*, Dickens does not often describe a *process*. The vivid pictures that he succeeds in leaving in one's memory are nearly always the pictures of things seen in leisure moments, in the coffee-rooms of country inns or through the windows of a stagecoach; the kind of things he notices are inn-signs, brass door-knockers, painted jugs, the interiors of shops and private houses, clothes, faces and, above all, food. Everything is seen from the consumer-angle. When he writes about Coketown he manages to evoke, in just a few paragraphs, the atmosphere of a Lancashire town as a slightly disgusted southern visitor would see it. "It had a black canal in it, and a river that ran purple with evil smelling dye, and vast piles of buildings full of windows where there was a rattling and a trembling all day long, and where the piston of the steam-engine worked monotonously up and down, like the head of an elephant in a state of melancholy madness." That is as near as Dickens ever gets to the machinery of the mills. An engineer or a cotton-broker would see it differently; but then neither of them would be capable of that impressionistic touch about the heads of the elephants.

In a rather different sense his attitude to life is extremely unphysical. He is a man who lives through his eyes and ears rather than through his hands and muscles. Actually his habits were not so sedentary as this seems to imply. In spite of rather poor health and physique, he was active to the point of restlessness; throughout his life he was a remarkable walker, and he could at any rate carpenter well enough to put up stage scenery. But he was not one of those people who feel a need to use their hands. It is difficult to imagine him digging at a cabbage-patch, for instance. He gives no evidence of knowing anything about agriculture, and obviously knows nothing about any kind of game or sport. He has no interest in pugilism, for instance. Considering the age in which he was writing, it is astonishing how little physical brutality there is in Dickens's novels. Martin Chuzzlewit and Mark Tapley, for instance, behave with the most remarkable mildness towards the Americans who are constantly menacing them with revolvers and bowie-knives. The average English or American novelist would have had them handing out socks on the jaw and exchanging pistol-shots in all directions. Dickens is too decent for that; he sees the stupidity of violence, and also he belongs to a cautious urban class which does not deal in socks on the jaw, even in theory. And his attitude towards sport is mixed up with social feelings. In England, for mainly geographical reasons, sport, especially field-sports, and snobbery are inextricably mingled. English Socialists are often flatly incredulous when told that Lenin, for instance, was devoted to shooting. In their eyes shooting, hunting, etc. are simply snobbish observances of the landed gentry; they forget that these things might appear differently in a huge virgin country like Russia. From Dickens's point of view almost any kind of sport is at best a subject for satire. Consequently one side of nineteenth-century life—the boxing, racing, cock-fighting, badger-digging, poaching, rat-catching side of life, so wonderfully embalmed in Leech's illustrations to Surtees—is outside his scope.

What is more striking, in a seemingly "progressive" radical, is that he is not mechanically minded. He shows no interest either in the details of machinery or in the things machinery can do. As Gissing remarks, Dickens nowhere describes a railway journey with anything like the enthusiasm he shows in describing journeys by stage-coach. In nearly all of his books one has a curious feeling that one is living in the first quarter of the nineteenth century, and in fact, he does tend to return to this period. *Little Dorrit*, written in the middle 'fifties, deals with the late 'twenties; *Great Expectations* (1861) is not dated, but evidently deals with the 'twenties and 'thirties. Several of the inventions and discoveries which have made the modern world possible (the electric telegraph, the breech-loading gun, india-rubber, coal gas, wood-pulp paper) first appeared in Dickens's lifetime, but he scarcely notes them in his books. Nothing is queerer than the vagueness with which he speaks of Doyce's "invention" in *Little Dorrit*. It is represented as something extremely ingenious and revolutionary, "of great importance to his country and his fellow-creatures", and it is also an important minor link in the book; yet we are never told what the "invention" is! On the other hand, Doyce's physical appearance is hit off with the typical Dickens touch; he has a peculiar way of moving his thumb, a way characteristic of engineers. After that, Doyce is firmly anchored in one's memory; but, as usual, Dickens has done it by fastening on something external.

There are people (Tennyson is an example) who lack the mechanical faculty but can see the social possibilities of machinery. Dickens has not this stamp of mind. He shows very little consciousness of the future. When he speaks of human progress it is usually in terms of *moral* progress—men growing better; probably he would never admit that men are only as good as their technical development allows them to be. At this point the gap between Dickens and his modern analogue, H.G. Wells, is at its widest. Wells wears the future round his neck like a millstone, but Dickens's unscientific cast of mind is just as damaging in a different way. What it does is to make any *positive* attitude more difficult for him. He is hostile to the feudal, agricultural past and not in real touch with the industrial present. Well, then, all that remains is the future (meaning science, "progress" and so forth), which hardly enters into his thoughts. Therefore, while attacking everything in sight, he has no definable standard of comparison. As I have pointed out already, he attacks the current educational system with perfect justice, and yet, after all, he has no remedy to offer except kindlier schoolmasters. Why did he not indicate what a school *might* have been? Why did he not have his own sons educated according to some plan of his own, instead of sending them to public schools to be stuffed with Greek? Because he lacked that kind of imagination. He has an infallible moral sense, but very little intellectual curiosity. And here one comes upon something which really is an enormous deficiency in Dickens, something that really does make the nineteenth century seem remote from us—that he has no ideal of *work*.

With the doubtful exception of David Copperfield (merely Dickens himself), one cannot point to a single one of his central characters who is primarily interested in his job. His heroes work in order to make a living and to marry the heroine, not because they feel a passionate interest in one particular subject. Martin Chuzzlewit, for instance, is not burning with zeal to be an architect; he might just as well be a doctor or a barrister. In any case, in the typical Dickens novel, the *deus ex machina* enters with a bag of gold in the last chapter and the hero is absolved from further struggle. The feeling, "This is what I came into the world to do. Everything else is uninteresting. I will do this even if it means starvation", which turns men of differing temperaments into scientists, inventors, artists, priests, explorers and revolutionaries—this motif is almost entirely absent from Dickens's books. He himself, as is well known, worked like a slave and believed in his work as few novelists have ever done. But there seems to be no calling except novel-writing (and perhaps acting) towards which he can imagine this kind of devotion. And, after all, it is natural enough, considering his rather negative attitude towards society. In the last resort there is nothing he admires except common decency. Science is uninteresting and machinery is cruel and ugly (the heads of the elephants). Business is only for ruffians like Bounderby. As for politics—leave that to the Tite Barnacles. Really there is no objective except to marry the heroine, settle down, live solvently and be kind. And you can do that much better in private life.

Here, perhaps, one gets a glimpse of Dickens's secret imaginative background. What did he think of as the most desirable way to live? When Martin Chuzzlewit had made it up with his uncle, when Nicholas Nickleby had married money, when John Harmon had been enriched by Boffin—what did they *do?*

The answer evidently is that they did nothing. Nicholas Nickleby invested his wife's money with the Cheerybles and "became a rich and prosperous merchant", but as he immediately retired into Devonshire, we can assume that he did not work very hard. Mr and Mrs Snodgrass "purchased and cultivated a small farm, more for occupation than profit". That is the spirit in which most of Dickens's books end—a sort of radiant idleness. Where he appears to disapprove of young men who do not work (Harthouse, Harry Gowan, Richard Carstone, Wrayburn before his reformation), it is because they are cynical and immoral or because they are a burden on somebody else; if you are "good", and also self-supporting, there is no reason why you should not spend fifty years in simply drawing your dividends. Home life is always enough. And, after all, it was the general assumption of his age. The "genteel sufficiency", the "competence", the "gentleman of independent means" (or "in easy circumstances")—the very phrases tell one all about the strange, empty dream of the eighteenth- and nineteenth-century middle bourgeoisie. It was a dream of *complete idleness.* Charles Reade conveys its spirit perfectly in the ending of *Hard Cash*. Alfred Hardie, hero of *Hard Cash*, is the typical nineteenth-century novel hero (public-school style), with gifts which Reade describes as amounting to "genius". He is an old Etonian and a scholar of Oxford, he knows most of the Greek and Latin classics by heart, he can box with prizefighters and win the Diamond Sculls at Henley. He goes through incredible adventures in which, of course, he behaves with faultless heroism, and then, at the age of twenty-five, he inherits a fortune, marries his Julia Dodd and settles down in the suburbs of Liverpool, in the same house as his parents-in-law:

> They all lived together at Albion Villa, thanks to Alfred.... Oh, you happy little villa! You were as like Paradise as any mortal dwelling can be. A day came, however, when your walls could no longer hold all the happy inmates. Julia presented Alfred with a lovely boy; enter two nurses and the villa showed symptoms of bursting. Two months more, and Alfred and his wife overflowed into the next villa. It was but twenty yards off; and there was a double reason for the migration. As often happens after a long separation, Heaven bestowed on Captain and Mrs Dodd another infant to play about their knees, etc. etc. etc.

This is the type of the Victorian happy ending—a vision of a huge, loving family of three or four generations, all crammed together in the same house and constantly multiplying, like a bed of oysters. What is striking about it is the utterly soft, sheltered, effortless life that it implies. It is not even a violent idleness, like Squire Western's. That is the significance of Dickens's urban background and his non-interest in the blackguardly-sporting-military side of life. His heroes, once they had come into money and "settled down", would not only do no work; they would not even ride, hunt, shoot, fight duels, elope with actresses or lose money at the races. They would simply live at home in feather-bed respectability, and preferably next door to a blood-relation living exactly the same life:

> The first act of Nicholas, when he became a rich and prosperous merchant, was to buy his father's old house. As time crept on, and there came gradually about him a group of lovely children, it was altered and enlarged; but none of the old rooms were ever pulled down, no old tree was ever rooted up, nothing with which there was any association of bygone times was ever removed or changed.

> Within a stone's-throw was another retreat enlivened by children's pleasant voices too; and here was Kate ... the same true, gentle creature, the same fond sister, the same in the love of all about her, as in her girlish days.

It is the same incestuous atmosphere as in the passage quoted from Reade. And evidently this is Dickens's ideal ending. It is perfectly attained in *Nicholas Nickleby*, *Martin Chuzzlewit* and *Pickwick*, and it is approximated to in varying degrees in almost all the others. The exceptions are *Hard Times* and *Great Expectations*—the latter actually has a "happy ending", but it contradicts the general tendency of the book, and it was put in at the request of Bulwer-Lytton.

The ideal to be striven after, then, appears to be something like this: a hundred thousand pounds, a quaint old house with plenty of ivy on it, a sweetly womanly wife, a horde of children, and no work. Everything is safe, soft, peaceful and, above all, domestic. In the moss-grown churchyard down the road are the graves of the loved ones who passed away before the happy ending happened. The servants are comic and feudal, the children prattle round your feet, the old friends sit at your fireside, talking of past days, there is the endless succession of enormous meals, the cold punch and sherry negus, the feather beds and warming-pans, the Christmas parties with charades and blind man's buff; but nothing ever happens, except the yearly childbirth. The curious thing is that it is a genuinely happy picture, or so

Dickens is able to make it appear. The thought of that kind of existence is satisfying to him. This alone would be enough to tell one that more than a hundred years have passed since Dickens's first book was written. No modern man could combine such purposelessness with so much vitality.

V

By this time anyone who is a lover of Dickens, and who has read as far as this, will probably be angry with me.

I have been discussing Dickens simply in terms of his "message", and almost ignoring his literary qualities. But every writer, especially every novelist, *has* a "message", whether he admits it or not, and the minutest details of his work are influenced by it. All art is propaganda. Neither Dickens himself nor the majority of Victorian novelists would have thought of denying this. On the other hand, not all propaganda is art. As I said earlier, Dickens is one of those writers who are felt to be worth stealing. He has been stolen by Marxists, by Catholics and, above all, by Conservatives. The question is, What is there to steal? Why does anyone care about Dickens? Why do *I* care about Dickens?

That kind of question is never easy to answer. As a rule, an aesthetic preference is either something inexplicable or it is so corrupted by non-aesthetic motives as to make one wonder whether the whole of literary criticism is not a huge network of humbug. In Dickens's case the complicating factor is his familiarity. He happens to be one of those "great authors" who are ladled down everyone's throat in childhood. At the time this causes rebellion and vomiting, but it may have different after-effects in later life. For instance, nearly everyone feels a sneaking affection for the patriotic poems that he learned by heart as a child, "Ye Mariners of England", "The Charge of the Light Brigade" and so forth. What one enjoys is not so much the poems themselves as the memories they call up. And with Dickens the same forces of association are at work. Probably there are copies of one or two of his books lying about in an actual majority of English homes. Many children begin to know his characters by sight before they can even read, for on the whole Dickens was lucky in his illustrators. A thing that is absorbed as early as that does not come up against any critical judgement. And when one thinks of this, one thinks of all that is bad and silly in Dickens—the cast-iron "plots", the characters who don't come off, the *longueurs*, the paragraphs in blank verse, the awful pages of "pathos". And then the thought arises, when I say I like Dickens, do I simply mean that I like thinking about my childhood? Is Dickens merely an institution?

If so, he is an institution that there is no getting away from. How often one really thinks about any writer, even a writer one cares for, is a difficult thing to decide; but I should doubt whether anyone who has actually read Dickens can go a week without remembering him in one context or another. Whether you approve of him or not, he is *there*, like the Nelson Column. At any moment some scene or character, which may come from some book you cannot even remember the name of, is liable to drop into your mind. Micawber's letters! Winkle in the witness box! Mrs Gamp! Mrs Wititterly and Sir Tumley Snuffim! Todger's! (George Gissing said that when he passed the Monument it was never of the Fire of London that he thought, always of Todgers's.) Mrs Leo Hunter! Squeers! Silas Wegg and the Decline and Fall-off of the Russian Empire! Miss Mills and the Desert of Sahara! Wopsle acting Hamlet! Mrs Jellyby! Mantalini! Jerry Cruncher! Barkis! Pumblechook! Tracy Tupman! Skimpole! Joe Gargery! Pecksniff!—and so it goes on and on. It is not so much a series of books, it is more like a world. And not a purely comic world either, for part of what one remembers in Dickens is his Victorian morbidness and necrophilia and the blood-and-thunder scenes—the death of Sikes, Krook's spontaneous combustion, Fagin in the condemned cell, the women knitting round the guillotine. To a surprising extent all this has entered even into the minds of people who do not care about it. A music-hall comedian can (or at any rate could quite recently) go on the stage and impersonate Micawber or Mrs Gamp with a fair certainty of being understood, although not one in twenty of the audience had ever read a book of Dickens's right through. Even people who affect to despise him quote him unconsciously.

Dickens is a writer who can be imitated, up to a certain point. In genuinely popular literature—for instance, the Elephant and Castle version of *Sweeney Todd*—he has been plagiarised quite shamelessly. What has been imitated, however, is simply a tradition that Dickens himself took from earlier novelists and developed, the cult of "character", i.e. eccentricity. The thing that cannot be imitated is his fertility of invention, which is invention not so much of characters, still less of "situations", as of turns of phrase and concrete details. The outstanding, unmistakable mark of Dickens's writing is the *unnecessary detail*. Here is an example of what I mean. The story given below is not particularly funny, but there is one phrase in it that is as individual as a fingerprint. Mr Jack Hopkins, at Bob Sawyer's party, is telling the story of the child who swallowed its sister's necklace:

> Next day, child swallowed two beads; the day after that, he treated himself to three, and so on, till in a week's time he had got through the necklace—five-and-twenty beads in all. The sister, who was an industrious girl and seldom treated herself to a bit of

finery, cried her eyes out at the loss of the necklace; looked high and low for it; but I needn't say, didn't find it. A few days afterwards, the family were at dinner—baked shoulder of mutton and potatoes under it—the child, who wasn't hungry, was playing about the room, when suddenly there was heard the devil of a noise, like a small hailstorm. "Don't do that, my boy," says the father. "I ain't a-doin' nothing," said the child. "Well, don't do it again," said the father. There was a short silence, and then the noise began again, worse than ever. "If you don't mind what I say, my boy," said the father, "you'll find yourself in bed, in something less than a pig's whisper." He gave the child a shake to make him obedient, and such a rattling ensued as nobody ever heard before. "Why, dam' me, it's *in* the child," said the father; "he's got the croup in the wrong place!" "No, I haven't, father," said the child, beginning to cry, "it's the necklace; I swallowed it, father." The father caught the child up, and ran with him to the hospital, the beads in the boy's stomach rattling all the way with the jolting; and the people looking up in the air, and down in the cellars, to see where the unusual sound came from. "He's in the hospital now," said Jack Hopkins, "and he makes such a devil of a noise when he walks about, that they're obliged to muffle him in a watchman's coat, for fear he should wake the patients."

As a whole, this story might come out of any nineteenth-century comic paper. But the unmistakable Dickens touch, the thing nobody else would have thought of, is the baked shoulder of mutton and potatoes under it. How does this advance the story? The answer is that it doesn't. It is something totally unnecessary, a florid little squiggle on the edge of the page; only, it is by just these squiggles that the special Dickens atmosphere is created. The other thing one would notice here is that Dickens's way of telling a story takes a long time. An interesting example, too long to quote, is Sam Weller's story of the obstinate patient in Chapter XLIV of *The Pickwick Papers*. As it happens, we have a standard of comparison here, because Dickens is plagiarising, consciously or unconsciously. The story is also told by some ancient Greek writer. I cannot now find the passage, but I read it years ago as a boy at school, and it runs more or less like this:

A certain Thracian, renowned for his obstinacy, was warned by his physician that if he drank a flagon of wine it would kill him. The Thracian thereupon drank the flagon of wine and immediately jumped off the house-top and perished. "For," said he, "in this way I shall prove that the wine did not kill me."

As the Greek tells it, that is the whole story—about six lines. As Sam Weller tells it, it takes round about a thousand words. Long before getting to the point we have been told all about the patient's clothes, his meals, his manners, even the newspapers he reads, and about the peculiar construction of the doctor's carriage, which conceals the fact that the coachman's trousers do not match his coat. Then there is the dialogue between the doctor and the patient. "'Crumpets is wholesome, sir,' said the patient. 'Crumpets is *not* wholesome, sir,' says the doctor, wery fierce," etc. etc. In the end the original story has been buried under the details. And in all of Dickens's most characteristic passages it is the same. His imagination overwhelms everything, like a kind of weed. Squeers stands up to address his boys, and immediately we are hearing about Bolder's father who was two pounds ten short, and Mobbs's stepmother who took to her bed on hearing that Mobbs wouldn't eat fat and hoped Mr Squeers would flog him into a happier state of mind. Mrs Leo Hunter writes a poem, "Expiring Frog"; two full stanzas are given. Boffin takes a fancy to pose as a miser, and instantly we are down among the squalid biographies of eighteenth century misers, with names like Vulture Hopkins and the Rev. Blewberry Jones, and chapter headings like "The Story of the Mutton Pies" and "The Treasures of a Dunghill". Mrs Harris, who does not even exist, has more detail piled on to her than any three characters in an ordinary novel. Merely in the middle of a sentence we learn, for instance, that her infant nephew has been seen in a bottle at Greenwich Fair, along with the pink-eyed lady, the Prussian dwarf and the living skeleton. Joe Gargery describes how the robbers broke into the house of Pumblechook, the corn and seed merchant—"and they took his till, and they took his cashbox, and they drinked his wine, and they partook of his wittles, and they slapped his face, and they pulled his nose, and they tied him up to his bedpust, and they give him a dozen, and they stuffed his mouth full of flowering annuals to perwent his crying out." Once again the unmistakable Dickens touch, the flowering annuals; but any other novelist would only have mentioned about half of these outrages. Everything is piled up and up, detail on detail, embroidery on embroidery. It is futile to object that this kind of thing is rococo—one might as well make the same objection to a wedding-cake. Either you like it or you do not like it. Other nineteenth-century writers, Surtees, Barham, Thackeray, even Marryat, have something of Dickens's profuse, overflowing quality, but none of them on anything like the same scale. The appeal of all these writers now depends partly on period-flavour, and though Marryat is still officially a "boys' writer" and Surtees has a sort of legendary fame among hunting men, it is probable that they are read mostly by bookish people.

Significantly, Dickens's most successful books (not his *best* books) are *The Pickwick Papers*, which is not a novel, and *Hard Times* and *A Tale of Two Cities*, which are not funny. As a novelist his natural fertility greatly hampers him, because the burlesque which he is never able to resist is constantly breaking into what ought to be serious situations. There is a good example of this in the opening chapter of *Great Expectations*. The escaped convict, Magwitch, has just captured the six-year-old Pip in the churchyard. The scene starts terrifyingly enough, from Pip's point of view. The convict, smothered in mud and with his chain trailing from his leg, suddenly starts up among the tombs, grabs the child, turns him upside down and robs his pockets. Then he begins terrorising him into bringing food and a file:

> He held me by the arms in an upright position on the top of the stone, and went on in these fearful terms:
>
> "You bring me, tomorrow morning early, that file and them wittles. You bring the lot to me, at that old Battery over yonder. You do it, and you never dare to say a word or dare to make a sign concerning your having seen such a person as me, or any person sumever, and you shall be let to live. You fail, or you go from my words in any partickler, no matter how small it is, and your heart and liver shall be tore out, roasted and ate. Now, I ain't alone, as you may think I am. There's a young man hid with me, in comparison with which young man I am a Angel. That young man hears the words I speak. That young man has a secret way pecooliar to himself, of getting at a boy, and at his heart, and at his liver. It is in wain for a boy to attempt to hide himself from that young man. A boy may lock his door, may be warm in bed, may tuck himself up, may draw the clothes over his head, may think himself comfortable and safe, but that young man will softly creep and creep his way to him and tear him open. I am keeping that young man from harming you at the present moment, but with great difficulty. I find it wery hard to hold that young man off of your inside. Now, what do you say?"

Here Dickens has simply yielded to temptation. To begin with, no starving and hunted man would speak in the least like that. Moreover, although the speech shows a remarkable knowledge of the way in which a child's mind works, its actual words are quite out of tune with what is to follow. It turns Magwitch into a sort of pantomime wicked uncle, or, if one sees him through the child's eyes, into an appalling monster. Later in the book he is to be represented as neither, and his exaggerated gratitude, on which the plot turns, is to be incredible because of just this speech. As usual, Dickens's imagination has overwhelmed him. The picturesque details were too good to be left out. Even with characters who are more of a piece than Magwitch he is liable to be tripped up by some seductive phrase. Mr Murdstone, for instance, is in the habit of ending David Copperfield's lessons every morning with a dreadful sum in arithmetic. "If I go into a cheesemonger's shop, and buy five thousand double-Gloucester cheeses at fourpence halfpenny each, present payment," it always begins. Once again the typical Dickens detail, the double-Gloucester cheeses. But it is far too human a touch for Murdstone; he would have made it five thousand cashboxes. Every time this note is struck, the unity of the novel suffers. Not that it matters very much, because Dickens is obviously a writer whose parts are greater than his wholes. He is all fragments, all details—rotten architecture, but wonderful gargoyles—and never better than when he is building up some character who will later on be forced to act inconsistently.

Of course it is not usual to urge against Dickens that he makes his characters behave inconsistently. Generally he is accused of doing just the opposite. His characters are supposed to be mere "types", each crudely representing some single trait and fitted with a kind of label by which you recognise him. Dickens is "only a caricaturist"—that is the usual accusation, and it does him both more and less than justice. To begin with, he did not think of himself as a caricaturist, and was constantly setting into action characters who ought to have been purely static. Squeers, Micawber, Miss Mowcher,[2] Wegg, Skimpole, Pecksniff and many others are finally involved in "plots" where they are out of place and where they behave quite incredibly. They start off as magic-lantern slides and they end by getting mixed up in a third-rate movie. Sometimes one can put one's finger on a single sentence in which the original illusion is destroyed. There is such a sentence in *David Copperfield*. After the famous dinner-party (the one where the leg of mutton was underdone), David is showing his guests out. He stops Traddles at the top of the stairs:

> "Traddles," said I, "Mr Micawber don't mean any harm, poor fellow: but if I were you I wouldn't lend him anything."
> "My dear Copperfield," returned Traddles smiling, "I haven't got anything to lend."
> "You have got a name, you know," I said.

At the place where one reads it this remark jars a little, though something of the kind was inevitable sooner or later. The story is a fairly realistic one, and David is growing up; ultimately he is bound to see Mr Micawber for what he is, a cadging scoundrel. Afterwards, of course, Dickens's sentimentality overcomes him and Micawber is made to turn over a new leaf. But from then on the original Micawber is never quite recaptured, in spite of desperate efforts. As a rule, the "plot" in which Dickens's characters get entangled is not particularly credible, but at least it makes some pretence at reality, whereas the world to which they belong is a never-never land, a kind of eternity. But just here one sees that "only a caricaturist" is not really a condemnation. The fact that Dickens is always thought of as a caricaturist, although he was constantly trying to be something else, is perhaps the surest mark of his genius. The monstrosities that he created are still remembered as monstrosities, in spite of getting mixed up in would-be probable melodramas. Their first impact is so vivid that nothing that comes afterwards effaces it. As with the people one knew in childhood, one seems always to remember them in one particular attitude, doing one particular thing. Mrs Squeers is always ladling out brimstone and treacle, Mrs Gummidge is always weeping, Mrs Gargery is always banging her husband's head against the wall, Mrs Jellyby is always scribbling tracts while her children fall into the area—and there they all are, fixed for ever like little twinkling miniatures painted on snuff-box lids, completely fantastic and incredible, and yet somehow more solid and infinitely more memorable than the efforts of serious novelists. Even by the standards of his time Dickens was an exceptionally artificial writer. As Ruskin said, he "chose to work in a circle of stage fire." His characters are even more distorted and simplified than Smollett's. But there are no rules in novel writing, and for any work of art there is only one test worth bothering about—survival. By this test Dickens's characters have succeeded, even if the people who remember them hardly think of them as human beings. They are monsters, but at any rate they *exist*.

But all the same there is a disadvantage in writing about monsters. It amounts to this, that it is only certain moods that Dickens can speak to. There are large areas of the human mind that he never touches. There is no poetic feeling anywhere in his books, and no genuine tragedy, and even sexual love is almost outside his scope. Actually his books are not so sexless as they are sometimes declared to be, and considering the time in which he was writing, he is reasonably frank. But there is not a trace in him of the feeling that one finds in *Manon Lescaut, Salammbô, Carmen, Wuthering Heights*. According to Aldous Huxley, D. H. Lawrence once said that Balzac was "a gigantic dwarf", and in a sense the same is true of Dickens. There are whole worlds which he either knows nothing about or does not wish to mention. Except in a rather roundabout way, one cannot *learn* very much from Dickens. And to say this is to think almost immediately of the great Russian novelists of the nineteenth century. Why is it that Tolstoy's grasp seems to be so much larger than Dickens's—why is it that he seems able to tell you so much more *about yourself*? It is not that he is more gifted, or even, in the last analysis, more intelligent. It is because he is writing about people who are growing. His characters are struggling to make their souls, whereas Dickens's are already finished and perfect. In my own mind Dickens's people are present far more often and far more vividly than Tolstoy's, but always in a single unchangeable attitude, like pictures or pieces of furniture. You cannot hold an imaginary conversation with a Dickens character as you can with, say, Pierre Bezukhov. And this is not merely because of Tolstoy's greater seriousness, for there are also comic characters that you can imagine yourself talking to—Bloom, for instance, or Pécuchet, or even Wells's Mr Polly. It is because Dickens's characters have no mental life. They say perfectly the thing that they have to say, but they cannot be conceived as talking about anything else. They never learn, never speculate. Perhaps the most meditative of his characters is Paul Dombey, and his thoughts are mush. Does this mean that Tolstoy's novels are "better" than Dickens's? The truth is that it is absurd to make such comparisons in terms of "better" and "worse". If I were forced to compare Tolstoy with Dickens, I should say that Tolstoy's appeal will probably be wider in the long run, because Dickens is scarcely intelligible outside the English-speaking culture; on the other hand, Dickens is able to reach simple people, which Tolstoy is not. Tolstoy's characters can cross a frontier, Dickens's can be portrayed on a cigarette card.[3] But one is no more obliged to choose between them than between a sausage and a rose. Their purposes barely intersect.

VI

If Dickens had been *merely* a comic writer, the chances are that no one would now remember his name. Or at best a few of his books would survive in rather the same way as books like *Frank Fairleigh*, *Mr Verdant Green* and *Mrs Caudle's Curtain Lectures*,[4] as a sort of hangover of the Victorian atmosphere, a pleasant little whiff of oysters and brown stout. Who has not felt sometimes that it was "a pity" that Dickens ever deserted the vein of *Pickwick* for things like *Little Dorrit* and *Hard Times*? What people always demand of a popular novelist is that he shall write the same book over and over again, forgetting that a man who would write the same book twice could not even write it once. Any writer who is not utterly lifeless moves upon a kind of parabola, and the downward curve is implied in the upward one. Joyce has to start with the frigid competence of *Dubliners* and end with the dream-language of *Finnegans Wake*, but *Ulysses* and *Portrait of the Artist* are part of the trajectory. The thing that drove Dickens forward into a form of art for which he was not really suited, and at the same time caused us to remember him, was simply the fact that he was a moralist, the consciousness of "having something to say". He is always preaching a sermon, and that is the final secret of his inventiveness. For you can only create if you can *care*. Types like Squeers and Micawber could not have been produced by a hack writer looking for something to be funny about. A joke worth laughing at always has an idea behind it, and usually a subversive idea. Dickens is able to go on being funny because he is in revolt against authority, and authority is always there to be laughed at. There is always room for one more custard pie.

His radicalism is of the vaguest kind, and yet one always knows that it is there. That is the difference between being a moralist and a politician. He has no constructive suggestions, not even a clear grasp of the nature of the society he is attacking, only an emotional perception that something is wrong. All he can finally say is, "Behave decently," which, as I suggested earlier, is not necessarily so shallow as it sounds. Most revolutionaries are potential Tories, because they imagine that everything can be put right by altering the *shape* of society; once that change is effected, as it sometimes is, they see no need for any other. Dickens has not this kind of mental coarseness. The vagueness of his discontent is the mark of its permanence. What he is out against is not this or that institution, but, as Chesterton put it, "an expression on the human face". Roughly speaking, his morality is the Christian morality, but in spite of his Anglican upbringing he was essentially a Bible-Christian, as he took care to make plain when writing his will. In any case he cannot properly be described as a religious man. He "believed", undoubtedly, but religion in the devotional sense does not seem to have entered much into his thoughts.[5] Where he is Christian is in his quasi-instinctive siding with the oppressed against the oppressors. As a matter of course he is on the side of the underdog, always and everywhere. To carry this to its logical conclusion one has got to change sides when the underdog becomes an upperdog, and in fact Dickens does tend to do so. He loathes the Catholic Church, for instance, but as soon as the Catholics are persecuted (*Barnaby Rudge*) he is on their side. He loathes the aristocratic class even more, but as soon as they are really overthrown (the revolutionary chapters in *A Tale of Two Cities*) his sympathies swing round. Whenever he departs from this emotional attitude he goes astray. A well-known example is at the ending of *David Copperfield*, in which everyone who reads it feels that something has gone wrong. What is wrong is that the closing chapters are pervaded, faintly but noticeably, by the cult of success. It is the gospel according to Smiles, instead of the gospel according to Dickens. The attractive, out-at-elbow characters are got rid of, Micawber makes a fortune, Heep gets into prison—both of these events are flagrantly impossible—and even Dora is killed off to make way for Agnes. If you like, you can read Dora as Dickens's wife and Agnes as his sister-in-law, but the essential point is that Dickens has "turned respectable" and done violence to his own nature. Perhaps that is why Agnes is the most disagreeable of his heroines, the real legless angel of Victorian romance, almost as bad as Thackeray's Laura.

No grown-up person can read Dickens without feeling his limitations, and yet there does remain his native generosity of mind, which acts as a kind of anchor and nearly always keeps him where he belongs. It is probably the central secret of his popularity. A good-tempered antinomianism rather of Dickens's type is one of the marks of western popular culture. One sees it in folk-stories and comic songs, in dream-figures like Mickey Mouse and Popeye the Sailor (both of them variants of Jack the Giant-Killer), in the history of working-class Socialism, in the popular protests (always ineffective but not always a sham) against imperialism, in the impulse that makes a jury award excessive damages when a rich man's car runs over a poor man; it is the feeling that one is always on the side of the underdog, on the side of the weak against the strong. In one sense it is a feeling that is fifty years out of date. The common man is still living in the mental world of Dickens, but nearly every modern intellectual has gone over to some or other form of totalitarianism. From the Marxist or Fascist point of view, nearly all that Dickens stands for can be written off as "bourgeois morality". But in moral outlook no one could be more "bourgeois" than the English working classes. The ordinary people in the western countries have never entered, mentally, into the world of "realism" and power politics. They may do so before long, in which case Dickens will be as out of date as the cab-horse. But in his own age and ours he has been popular chiefly because he was able to express in a comic, simplified and therefore memorable form the native decency of the common man. And it is important that from this point of view people of very different types can be described as "common". In a country like England, in spite of its class-structure there does exist a certain cultural unity. All through the Christian ages, and especially since the French Revolution, the western world has been haunted by the idea of freedom and equality; it is only an *idea*, but it has penetrated to all ranks of society. The most atrocious injustices, cruelties, lies, snobberies exist everywhere, but there are not many people who can regard these things with the same indifference as, say, a Roman slave-owner. Even the millionaire suffers from a vague sense of guilt, like a dog eating a stolen leg of mutton. Nearly everyone, whatever his actual conduct may be, responds emotionally to the idea of human brotherhood. Dickens voiced a code which was and on the whole still is believed in, even by people who violate it. It is difficult otherwise to explain why he could be both read by working people (a thing that has happened to no other novelist of his stature) and buried in Westminster Abbey.

When one reads any strongly individual piece of writing, one has the impression of seeing a face somewhere behind the page. It is not necessarily the actual face of the writer. I feel this very strongly with Swift, with Defoe, with Fielding, Stendhal, Thackeray, Flaubert, though in several cases I do not know what these people looked like and do not want to know. What one sees is the face that the writer *ought* to have. Well, in the case of Dickens I see a face that is not quite the face of Dickens's photographs, though it resembles it. It is the face of a man of about forty, with a small beard and a high colour. He is laughing, with a touch of anger in his laughter, but no triumph, no malignity. It is the face of a man who is always fighting against something, but who fights in the open and is not frightened, the face of a man who is *generously angry*—in other words, of a nineteenth-century liberal, a free intelligence, a type hated with equal hatred by all the smelly little orthodoxies which are now contending for our souls.

Written 1939

I.T.W. (slightly revised) *Cr.E.*; *D.D.*; C.E.

NOTES

1. *Hard Times* was published as a serial in *Household Words* and *Great Expectations* and *A Tale of Two Cities* in *All the Year Round*. Forster says that the shortness of the weekly installments made it "much more difficult to get sufficient interest into each." Dickens himself complained of the lack of "elbow-room". In other words, he had to stick more closely to the story. [Author's footnote.]

2. Dickens turned Miss Mowcher into a sort of heroine because the real woman whom he had caricatured had read the earlier chapters and was bitterly hurt. He had previously meant her to play a villainous part. But *any* action by such a character would seem incongruous. [Author's footnote.]

3. Messrs John Player and Sons issued two series of cigarette cards entitled "Characters from Dickens" in 1913; they reissued them as a single series in 1923.

4. *Frank Fairleigh* by F.E. Smedley, 1850; *The Adventures of Mr Verdant Green* by Cuthbert Bede (pseud. of Edward Bradley), 1853; *Mrs Caudle's Curtain Lectures* by Douglas Jerrold (reprinted from *Punch*, 1846).

5. From a letter to his youngest son (in 1868): "You will remember that you have never at home been harassed about religious observances, or mere formalities. I have always been anxious not to weary my children with such things, before they are old enough to form opinions respecting them. You will therefore understand the better that I now most solemnly impress upon you the truth and beauty of the Christian Religion, as it came from Christ Himself, and the impossibility of your going far wrong if you humbly but heartily respect it.... Never abandon the wholesome practice of saying your own private prayers, night and morning. I have never abandoned it myself, and I know the comfort of it." [Author's footnote.]

GEORGE BERNARD SHAW

Introduction to
Great Expectations

'GREAT EXPECTATIONS' is the last of the three full-length stories written by Dickens in the form of an autobiography. Of the three, *Bleak House*, as the autobiography of Miss Esther Summerson, is naturally the least personal, as Esther is not only a woman but a maddening prig, though we are forced to admit that such paragons exist and are perhaps worthy of the reverent admiration with which Dickens regarded them. Ruling her out, we have *David Copperfield* and *Great Expectations*. David was, for a time at least, Dickens's favourite child, perhaps because he had used him to express the bitterness of that episode in his own experience which had wounded his boyish self-respect most deeply. For Dickens, in spite of his exuberance, was a deeply reserved man: the exuberance was imagination and acting (his imagination was ceaseless, and his outward life a feat of acting from beginning to end); and we shall never know whether in that immensely broadened outlook and knowledge of the world which began with *Hard Times* and *Little Dorrit*, and left all his earlier works behind, he may not have come to see that making his living by sticking labels on blacking bottles and rubbing shoulders with boys who were not gentlemen, was as little shameful as being the genteel apprentice in the office of Mr. Spenlow, or the shorthand writer recording the unending twaddle of the House of Commons and electioneering bunk on the hustings of all the Eatanswills in the country.

From *Great Expectations*. © 1947 The Novel Library.

That there was a tragic change in his valuations can be shown by contrasting Micawber with William Dorrit, in which light Micawber suddenly becomes a mere marionette pantaloon with a funny bag of tricks which he repeats until we can bear no more of him, and Dorrit a portrait of the deadliest and deepest truth to nature. Now contrast David with Pip; and believe, if you can, that there was no revision of his estimate of the favorite child David as a work of art and even as a vehicle of experience. The adult David fades into what stage managers call a walking gentleman. The reappearance of Mr. Dickens in the character of a blacksmith's boy may be regarded as an apology to Mealy Potatoes.

Dickens did in fact know that *Great Expectations* was his most compactly perfect book. In all the other books, there are episodes of wild extravagance, extraordinarily funny if they catch you at the right age, but recklessly grotesque as nature studies. Even in *Little Dorrit*, Dickens's masterpiece among many masterpieces, it is impossible to believe that the perfectly authentic Mr. Pancks really stopped the equally authentic Mr. Casby in a crowded street in London and cut his hair; and though Mr. F.'s aunt is a first-rate clinical study of senile deficiency in a shrewd old woman, her collisions with Arthur Clennam are too funny to be taken seriously. We cannot say of Casby, Pancks, and the aunt, as we can say of Sam Weller, that such people never existed; for most of us have met their counterparts in real life; but we can say that Dickens's sense of fun ran away with him over them. If we have absolutely no fun in us we may even state gravely that there has been a lapse from the artistic integrity of the tragic picture of English society which is the subject of the book.

In *Great Expectations* we have Wopsle and Trabb's boy; but they have their part and purpose in the story and do not overstep the immodesty of nature. It is hardly decent to compare Mr. F.'s aunt with Miss Havisham; but as contrasted studies of madwomen they make you shudder at the thought of what Dickens might have made of Miss Havisham if he had seen her as a comic personage. For life is no laughing matter in *Great Expectations*; the book is all of one piece and consistently truthful as none of the other books are, not even the compact *Tale of Two Cities*, which is pure sentimental melodrama from beginning to end, and shockingly wanting in any philosophy of history in its view of the French Revolution.

Dickens never regarded himself as a revolutionist, though he certainly was one. His implacable contempt for the House of Commons, founded on his experience as a parliamentary reporter, never wavered from the account of the Eatanswill election and of Nicholas Nickleby's interview with Pugstyles to the Veneering election in *Our Mutual Friend*, his last book (*Edwin Drood* is only a gesture by a man three-quarters dead). And this was not mere satire, of which there had been plenty. Dickens was the first writer to perceive and state definitely that the House of Commons, working on the Party system, is an extraordinarily efficient device for dissipating all our reforming energy and ability in Party debate and when anything urgently needs to be done, finding out 'how not to do it.' It took very little time to get an ineffective Factory Act. It took fifty years to make it effective, though the labour conditions in the factories and mines were horrible. After Dickens's death, it took thirty years to pass an Irish Home Rule Bill, which was promptly repudiated by the military plutocracy, leaving the question to be settled by a competition in slaughter and house burning, just as it would have been between two tribes of savages. Liberty under the British parliamentary system means slavery for nine-tenths of the people, and slave exploitation or parasitic idolatry and snobbery for the rest. Parliament men—one cannot call them statesmen—and even historians, keep declaring that the British parliamentary system is one of the greatest blessings British political genius has given to the world; and the world has taken it at its self-valuation and set up imitations of it all over Europe and America, always with the same result: political students outside Parliament exposing the most frightful social evils and prescribing their remedies, and Parliament ignoring them as long as possible and then engulfing their disciples and changing them from reformers into partisans with time for nothing but keeping their party in power or opposing the Government, rightly or wrongly ('it is the duty of the Opposition to oppose'), as the case might be. In the middle of the nineteenth century Dickens saw this and said it. He had to be ignored, as he would not stand for Parliament and be paralyzed.

Europe has had to learn from hard experience what it would not learn from Dickens. The Fascist and Communist revolutions which swept the great parliamentary sham into the dustbin after it had produced a colossal Anarchist war, made no mention of Dickens; but on the parliamentary point he was as much their prophet as Marx was the economic prophet of the Soviets. Yet a recent reactionist against Dickens worship declares that he 'never went ahead of his public.'

Marx and Dickens were contemporaries living in the same city and pursuing the same profession of literature; yet they seem to us like creatures of a different species living in different worlds. Dickens, if he had ever become conscious of Karl Marx, would have been classed with him as a revolutionist. The difference between a revolutionist and what Marx called a bourgeois is that the bourgeois regards the existing social order as the permanent and natural order of human society, needing reforms now and then and here and there, but essentially good and sane and right and respectable and proper and everlasting. To the revolutionist it is transitory, mistaken, objectionable, and pathological: a social disease to be cured, not to be endured. We have only to compare Thackeray and Trollope with Dickens to perceive this contrast. Thackeray reviled the dominant classes with a savagery which would have been unchivalrous in Dickens: he denied to his governing class characters even the common good qualities and accomplishments of ladies and gentleman, making them mean, illiterate, dishonest, ignorant, sycophantic to an inhuman degree, whilst Dickens, even when making his aristocrats ridiculous and futile, at least made gentlemen of them. Trollope, who regarded Thackeray as his master and exemplar, had none of his venom, and has left us a far better balanced and more truthful picture of Victorian well-off society, never consciously whitewashing it, though allowing it its full complement of black sheep of both sexes. But Trollope's politics were those of the country house and the hunting field just as were Thackeray's. Accordingly, Thackeray and Trollope were received and approved by fashionable society with complete confidence. Dickens, though able to fascinate all classes, was never so received or approved except by quite good-natured or stupid ladies and gentlemen who were incapable of criticizing anyone who could make them laugh and cry. He was told that he could not describe a gentleman and that *Little Dorrit* is twaddle. And the reason was that in his books the west-end heaven appears as a fool's paradise that must pass away instead of being an indispensable preparatory school for the New Jerusalem of Revelation. A leading encyclopedia tells us that Dickens had 'no knowledge of country gentlemen.' It would have been nearer the mark to say that Dickens knew all that really mattered about Sir Leicester Dedlock and that Trollope knew nothing that really mattered about him. Trollope and Thackeray could see Chesney Wold; but Dickens could see through it. And this was no joke to Dickens. He was deeply concerned about it, and understood how revolutions begin with burning the chateaux.

The difference between Marx and Dickens was that Marx knew that he was a revolutionist whilst Dickens had not the faintest suspicion of that part of his calling. Compare the young Dickens looking for a job in a lawyer's office and teaching himself shorthand to escape from his office stool to the reporters' gallery, with the young Trotsky, the young Lenin, quite deliberately facing disreputable poverty and adopting revolution as their profession with every alternative of bourgeois security and respectability much more fully open to them than to Dickens.

And this brings us to Dickens's position as a member of the educated and cultured classes who had neither education nor culture. This was fortunate for him and for the world in one way, as he escaped the school and university routine which complicates cultural Philistinism with the mentality of a Red Indian brave. Better no schooling at all than the schooling of Rudyard Kipling and Winston Churchill. But there are homes in which a mentally acquisitive boy can make contact with the fine arts. I myself learnt nothing at school, but gained in my home an extensive and highly educational knowledge of music. I had access to illustrated books on painting which sent me to the National Gallery; so that I was able to support myself as a critic of music and painting as Dickens supported himself by shorthand. I devoured books on science and on the religious controversies of the day. It is in this way, and not in our public schools and universities that such culture as there is in England is kept alive.

Now the Dickenses seem to have been complete barbarians. Dickens mentions the delight with which he discovered in an attic a heap of eighteenth-century novels. But Smollett was a grosser barbarian than Dickens himself; and *Don Quixote* and *The Arabian Nights*, though they gave the cue to his eager imagination, left him quite in the dark as to the philosophy and art of his day. To him a philosopher, an intellectual, was a figure of fun. Count Smorltork is the creation of a street Arab: Dickens did not even know that the Count's method of studying Chinese metaphysics by studying metaphysics and China and 'combining tine information' was not only sensible and correct, but the only possible method. To Dickens as to most Victorian Englishmen metaphysics were ridiculous, useless, unpractical, and the mark of a fool. He was musical enough to have a repertory of popular ballads which he sang all over the house to keep his voice in order; and he made Tom Pinch play the organ in church as an amiable accomplishment; but I cannot remember hearing that he ever went to a classical concert, or even knew of the existence of such entertainments. The articles on the National Gallery in *All the Year Round*, though extremely funny in their descriptions of 'The Apotheosis' of 'William the Silent' (the title alone would make a cat laugh), and on some profane points sensible enough, are those of a complete Philistine. One cannot say that he disliked all painters in the face of his friendship with Maclise and Clarkson Stanfield; but it was not a cultural friendship: Stanfield was a scene painter who appealed to that English love of landscape which is so often confused with a love of art; and Maclise was a pictorial anecdotist who presented scenes from Shakespear's plays exactly as they were presented on the stage. When Dickens introduced in his stories a character whom he intensely disliked he chose an artistic profession for him. Henry Gowan in *Little Dorrit* is a painter. Pecksniff is an architect. Harold Skimpole is a musician. There is real hatred in his treatment of them.

Now far be it from me to imply that they are false to nature. Artists are often detestable human beings; and the famous Anti-Scrape, officially The

Society for the Protection of Ancient Buildings, was founded by William Morris and his friends to protect ancient buildings from architects. What is more, the ultra-artistic sets, the Pre-Raphaelites and the aesthetes grouped round Rossetti and Morris and Ruskin, were all Dickens worshippers who made a sort of cult of Trabb's boy and would have regarded me as a traitor if they had read what I am now writing. They knew better than anyone else that Leigh Hunt deserved all he got as Harold Skimpole, that Gowan's shallow sort of painting was a nuisance, and that architecture was just the right profession for a parasite on Salisbury Cathedral like Pecksniff. But all their Dickensian enthusiasm, and all the truth to life of Dickens's portraiture cannot extenuate the fact that the cultural side of art was as little known to Dickens as it is possible for a thing so public to remain to a man so apprehensive. You may read the stories of Dickens from beginning to end without ever learning that he lived through a period of fierce revivals and revolutionary movements in art, in philosophy, in sociology, in religion: in short, in culture: Dean Inge's remark that 'the number of great subjects in which Dickens took no interest whatever is amazing' hits the nail exactly on the head. As to finding such a person as Karl Marx among his characters, one would as soon look for a nautilus in a nursery.

Yet *Little Dorrit* is a more seditious book than *Das Kapital*. All over Europe men and women are in prison for pamphlets and speeches which are to *Little Dorrit* as red pepper to dynamite. Fortunately for social evolution Governments never know where to strike. Barnacle and Stiltstalking were far too conceited to recognize their own portraits. Parliament, wearying its leaders out in a few years in the ceaseless drudgery of fording out how not to do it, and smothering it in talk, could not conceive that its heartbreaking industry could have any relation to the ridiculous fiction of the Coodle-Doodle discussions in Sir Leicester Dedlock's drawingroom. As to the Circumlocution Office, well, perhaps the staffs, owing their posts to patronage and regarding them as sinecures, were a bit too insolent to the public, and would be none the worse for a little chaff from a funny fellow like Dickens; but their inefficiency as a public service was actually a good thing, as it provided a standing object lesson in the superiority of private enterprise. Mr. Sparkler was not offended: he stuck to his job and never read anything. *Little Dorrit* and *Das Kapital* were all the same to him: they never entered his world; and to him that world was the whole world.

The mass of Dickens readers, finding all these people too funny to be credible, continued to idolize Coodle and Doodle as great statesmen, and made no distinction between John Stuart Mill at the India Office and Mr. Sparkler. In fact the picture was not only too funny to be credible: it was too truthful to be credible. But the fun was no fun to Dickens: the truth was too bitter. When you laugh at Jack Bunsby, or at The Orfling when the handle of her corkscrew came off and smote her on the chin, you have no doubt that Dickens is laughing with you like a street boy, despite Bunsby's tragic end. But whilst you laugh at Sparkler or young Barnacle, Dickens is in deadly earnest: he means that both of them must go into the dustbin if England is to survive.

And yet Dickens never saw himself as a revolutionist. It never occurred to him to found a Red International, as Marx did, not even to join one out of the dozens of political reform societies that were about him. He was an English gentleman of the professional class, who would not allow his daughter to go on the stage because it was not respectable. He knew so little about revolutionists that when Mazzini called on him and sent in his card, Dickens, much puzzled, concluded that the unknown foreign gentleman wanted money, and very kindly sent him down a sovereign to get rid of him. He discovered for himself all the grievances he exposed, and had no sense of belonging to a movement, nor any desire to combine with others who shared his subversive views. To educate his children religiously and historically he wrote *A Child's History of England* which had not even the excuse of being childish, and a paraphrase of the gospel biography which is only a belittling of it for little children. He had much better have left the history to Little Arthur and Mrs. Markham and Goldsmith, and taken into account the extraordinary educational value of the Authorized Version as a work of literary art. He probably thought as seldom of himself as a literary artist as of himself as a revolutionist; and he had his share in the revolt against the supernatural pretensions of the Bible which was to end in the vogue of Agnosticism and the pontificate of Darwin. It blinded that generation to the artistic importance of the fact that at a moment when all the literary energy in England was in full eruption, when Shakespear was just dead and Milton just born, a picked body of scholars undertook the task of translating into English what they believed to be the words of God himself. Under the strain of that conviction they surpassed all their normal powers, transfiguring the original texts into literary masterpieces of a splendor that no merely mortal writers can ever again hope to achieve. But the nineteenth century either did not dare think of the Bible in that way, it being fetish, or else it was in such furious reaction against the fetishism that it would not allow the so-called Holy Scriptures even an artistic merit. At all events Dickens thought his Little Nell style better for his children than the English of King James's inspired scribes. He took them (for a time at least) to churches of the Unitarian persuasion, where they could be both sceptical and respectable; but it is hard to say what Dickens believed or did not believe metaphysically or metapolitically, though he left us in no doubt as to his opinion of the Lords, the Commons, and the ante-Crimean Civil Service.

On the positive side he had nothing to say. Marxism and Darwinism came too late for him. He might have been a Comtist—perhaps ought to have been a Comtist, but was not. He was an independent Dickensian, a sort of unphilosophic Radical, with a complete disbelief in government by the people and an equally complete hostility to government in any other interest than theirs. He exposed many abuses and called passionately on the rulers of the people to remedy them; but he never called on the people themselves. He would as soon have thought of calling on them to write their own novels.

Meanwhile he overloaded himself and his unfortunate wife with such a host of children that he was forced to work himself to death prematurely to provide for them and for the well-to-do life he led. The reading public cannot bear to think of its pet authors as struggling with the economic pressures that often conflict so cruelly with the urge of genius. This pressure was harder on Dickens than on many poorer men. He had a solid bourgeois conscience which made it impossible for him to let wife and children starve whilst he followed the path of destiny. Marx let his wife go crazy with prolonged poverty whilst he wrote a book which changed the mind of the world. But then Marx had been comfortably brought up and thoroughly educated in the German manner. Dickens knew far too much of the horrors of impecuniosity to put his wife through what his mother had gone through, or have his children pasting labels on blacking bottles. He had to please his public or lapse into that sort of poverty. Under such circumstances the domestic conscience inevitably pushes the artistic conscience into the second place. We shall never know how much of Dickens's cheery optimism belied his real outlook on life. He went his own way far enough to make it clear that when he was not infectiously laughing he was a melancholy fellow. Arthur Clennam is one of the Dismal Jemmies of literature. For any gaiety of heart we have to turn to the impossible Dick Swiveller, who by the way, was designed as a revoltingly coarse fortune hunter, and still appears in that character in the single scene which precedes his sudden appeal to Dickens's sense of fun, and consequent transformation into a highly entertaining and entirely fantastic clown. This was a genuine conversion and not a concession to public taste; but the case of Walter Gay in *Dombey and Son*, whose high spirits were planned as a prelude to his degeneration and ruin, is a flagrant case of a manufactured happy ending to save a painful one. *Martin Chuzzlewit* begins as a study in selfishness and ends nowhere. Mr. Boffin, corrupted by riches, gets discharged without a stain on his character by explaining that he was only pretending for benevolent purposes, but leaves us with a feeling that some of his pretences were highly suspicious. Jarndyce, a violently good man, keeps on doing generous things, yet ends by practising a heartlessly cruel and indelicate deception on Esther Summerson for the sake of giving her a pleasant melodramatic surprise. I will not go so far as to say that Dickens's novels are full of melancholy intentions which he dares not carry through to their unhappy conclusions; but he gave us no vitally happy heroes and heroines after Pickwick (begun, like Don Quixote, as a contemptible butt). Their happy endings are manufactured to make the books pleasant. Nobody who has endured the novels of our twentieth-century emancipated women, enormously cleverer and better informed than the novels of Dickens, and ruthlessly calculated to leave their readers hopelessly discouraged and miserable, will feel anything but gratitude to Dickens for his humanity in speeding his parting guests with happy faces by turning from the world of destiny to the world of accidental good luck; but as our minds grow stronger some of his consolations become unnecessary and even irritating. And it happens that it is with just such a consolation that *Great Expectations* ends.

It did not always end so. Dickens wrote two endings, and made a mess of both. In the first ending, which Bulwer-Lytton persuaded him to discard, Pip takes little Pip for a walk in Piccadilly and is stopped by Estella, who is passing in her carriage. She is comfortably married to a Shropshire doctor, and just says how d'y'do to Pip and kisses the little boy before they both pass on out of one another's lives. This, though it is marred by Pip's pious hope that her husband may have thrashed into her some understanding of how much she has made him suffer, is true to nature. But it is much too matter-of-fact to be the right ending to a tragedy. Piccadilly was impossible in such a context; and the passing carriage was unconsciously borrowed from *A Day's Ride: A Life's Romance*, the novel by Lever which was so unpopular that *Great Expectations* had to be written to replace it in *All The Year Round*. But in Lever's story it is the man who stops the carriage, only to be cut dead by the lady. Dickens must have felt that there was something wrong with this ending; and Bulwer's objection confirmed his doubt. Accordingly, he wrote a new ending, in which he got rid of Piccadilly and substituted a perfectly congruous and beautifully touching scene and hour and atmosphere for the meeting. He abolished the Shropshire doctor and left out the little boy. So far the new ending was in every way better than the first one.

Unfortunately, what Bulwer wanted was what is called a happy ending, presenting Pip and Estella as reunited lovers who were going to marry and live happily ever after; and Dickens, though he could not bring himself to be quite so explicit in sentimental falsehood, did, at the end of the very last line, allow himself to say that there was 'no shadow of parting' between them. If Pip had said 'Since that parting I have been able to think of her without the old unhappiness; but I have never tried to see her again, and I know I never shall' he would have been left with at least the prospect of a bearable life. But the notion that he could ever have been happy with Estella: indeed that anyone could ever have been happy with Estella, is positively unpleasant. I can remember when the Cowden Clarks ventured to hint a doubt whether Benedick and Beatrice had a very delightful union to look forward to; but that did not greatly matter, as Benedick and Beatrice have none of the reality of Pip and Estella. Shakespear could afford to trifle with *Much Ado About Nothing*, which is avowedly a potboiler; but *Great Expectations* is a different matter. Dickens put nearly all his thought into it. It is too serious a book to be a trivially happy one. Its beginning is unhappy; its middle is unhappy; and the conventional happy ending is an outrage on it.

Estella is a curious addition to the gallery of unamiable women painted by Dickens. In my youth it was commonly said that Dickens could not draw women. The people who said this were thinking of Agnes Wickfield and Esther Summerson, of Little Dorrit and Florence Dombey, and thinking of them as ridiculous idealizations of their sex. Gissing put a stop to that by asking whether shrews like Mrs. Raddle, Mrs. Macstinger, Mrs. Gargery, fools like Mrs. Nickleby and Flora Frothing, warped spinsters like Rosa Dartle and Miss Wade, were not masterpieces of woman drawing. And they are all unamiable. But for Betsy Trotwood, who is a very lovable fairy godmother and yet a genuine nature study, and an old dear like Mrs. Boffin, one would be tempted to ask whether Dickens had ever in his life met an amiable female. The transformation of Dora into Flora is diabolical, but frightfully true to nature. Of course Dickens with his imagination could invent amiable women by the dozen; but somehow fie could not or would not bring them to life as he brought the others. We doubt whether he ever knew a little Dorrit; but Fanny Dorrit is from the life unmistakably. So is Estella. She is a much more elaborate study than Fanny, and, I should guess, a recent one.

Dickens, when he let himself go in *Great Expectations*, was separated from his wife and free to make more intimate acquaintances with women than a domesticated man can. I know nothing of his adventures in this phase of his career, though I daresay a good deal of it will be dug out by the little sect of anti-Dickensites whose fanaticism has been provoked by the Dickens Fellowships. It is not necessary to suggest a love affair; for Dickens could get from a passing glance a hint which he could expand into a full-grown character. The point concerns us here only because it is the point on which the ending of *Great Expectations* turns: namely, that Estella is a born tormentor. She deliberately torments Pip all through for the fun of it; and in the little we hear of her intercourse with others there is no suggestion of a moment of kindness: in fact her tormenting of Pip is almost affectionate in contrast to the cold disdain of her attitude towards the people who were not worth tormenting. It is not surprising that the unfortunate Bentley Drummle, whom she marries in the stupidity of sheer perversity, is obliged to defend himself from her clever malice with his fists: a consolation to us for Pip's broken heart, but not altogether a credible one; for the real Estellas can usually intimidate the real Bentley Druimmles. At all events the final sugary suggestion of Estella redeemed by Bentley's thrashings and waste of her money, and living happily with Pip for ever after, provoked even Dickens's eldest son to rebel against it, most justly.

Apart from this the story is the most perfect of Dickens's works. In it he does not muddle himself with the ridiculous plots that appear like vestiges of the stone age in many of his books, from *Oliver Twist* to the end. The story is built round a single and simple catastrophe: the revelation to Pip of the source of his great expectations. There is, it is true, a trace of the old plot superstition in Estella turning out to be Magwitch's daughter; but it provides a touchingly happy ending for that heroic Warmint. Who could have the heart to grudge it to him?

As our social conscience expands and makes the intense class snobbery of the nineteenth century seem less natural to us, the tragedy of *Great Expectations* will lose some of its appeal. I have already wondered whether Dickens himself ever came to see that his agonizing sensitiveness about the blacking bottles and his resentment of his mother's opposition to his escape from them was not too snobbish to deserve all the sympathy he claimed for it. Compare the case of H. G. Wells, our nearest to a twentieth-century Dickens. Wells hated being a draper's assistant as much as Dickens hated being a warehouse boy; but he was not in the least ashamed of it, and did not blame his mother for regarding it as the summit of her ambition for him. Fate having imposed on that engaging cricketer Mr. Wells's father an incongruous means of livelihood in the shape of a small shop, shopkeeping did not present itself to the young Wells as beneath him, whereas to the genteel Dickens being a warehouse boy was an unbearable comedown. Still, I cannot help speculating on whether if Dickens had not killed himself prematurely to pile up money for that excessive family of his, he might not have reached a stage at which he could have got as much fun out of the blacking bottles as Mr. Wells got out of his abhorred draper's counter.

Dickens never reached that stage; and there is no prevision of it in *Great Expectations*; for in it he never raises the question why Pip should refuse Magwitch's endowment and shrink from him with such inhuman loathing. Magwitch no doubt was a Warmint from the point of view of the genteel Dickens family and even from his own; but Victor Hugo would have made him a magnificent hero, another Valjean. Inspired by an altogether noble fixed idea, he had lifted himself out of his rut of crime and honestly made a fortune for the child who had fed him when he was starving. If Pip had no objection to be a parasite instead of an honest blacksmith, at least he had a better claim to be a parasite on Magwitch's earnings than, as he imagined, on Miss Havisham's property. It is curious that this should not have occurred to Dickens; for nothing could exceed the bitterness of his exposure of the futility of Pip's parasitism. If all that came of sponging on Miss Havisham (as he thought was the privilege of being one of the Finches of the Grove, he need not have felt his dependence on Magwitch to be incompatible with his entirely baseless self-respect. But Pip—and I am afraid Pip must be to this extent identified with Dickens—could not see Magwitch as an animal of the same species as himself or Miss Havisham. His feeling is true to the nature of snobbery; but his creator says no word in criticism of that ephemeral limitation.

The basic truth of the situation is that Pip, like his creator, has no culture and no religion. Joe Gargery, when Pip tells a monstrous string of lies about Miss Havisham, advises him to say a repentant word about it in his prayers; but Pip never prays; and church means nothing to him but Mr. Wopsle's orotundity. In this he resembles David Copperfield, who has gentility but neither culture nor religion. Pip's world is therefore a very melancholy place, and his conduct, good or bad, always helpless. This is why Dickens worked against so black a background after he was roused from his ignorant middle-class cheery optimism by Carlyle. When he lost his belief in bourgeois society and with it his lightness of heart he had neither an economic Utopia nor a credible religion to hitch on to. His world becomes a world of great expectations cruelly disappointed. The Wells world is a world of greater and greater expectations continually being fulfilled. This is a huge improvement. Dickens never had time to form a philosophy or define a faith; and his later and greater books are saddened by the evil that is done under the sun; but at least he preserved his intellectual innocence sufficiently to escape the dismal pseudo-scientific fatalism that was descending on the world in his latter days, founded on the preposterous error as to causation in which the future is determined by the present, which has been determined by the past. The true causation, of course, is always the incessant irresistible activity of the evolutionary appetite.

LIONEL TRILLING

Little Dorrit

*L*ittle *Dorrit* is one of the three great novels of Dickens' great last period, but of the three it is perhaps the least established with modern readers. When it first appeared—in monthly parts from December 1855 to June 1857—its success was even more decisive than that of *Bleak House*, but the suffrage of later audiences has gone the other way, and of all Dickens' later works it is *Bleak House* that has come to be the best known. As for *Our Mutual Friend*, after having for some time met with adverse critical opinion among the enlightened—one recalls that the youthful Henry James attacked it for standing in the way of art and truth—it has of recent years been regarded with overgrowing admiration. But *Little Dorrit* seems to have retired to the background and shadow of our consciousness of Dickens.

This does not make an occasion for concern or indignation. With a body of works as large and as enduring as that of Dickens, taste and opinion will never be done. They will shift and veer as they have shifted and veered with the canon of Shakespeare, and each generation will have its special favorites and make its surprised discoveries. *Little Dorrit*, one of the most profound of Dickens' novels and one of the most significant works of the nineteenth century, will not fail to be thought of as speaking with a peculiar and passionate intimacy to our own time.

From *The Dickens Critics*, George H. Ford, and Lauriat Lane, Jr., ed. © 1961 Cornell University Press.

Little Dorrit is about society, which certainly does not distinguish it from the rest of Dickens' novels unless we go on to say, as we must, that it is *more* about society than any other of the novels, that it is about society in its very essence. This essential quality of the book has become apparent as many of the particular social conditions to which it refers have passed into history. Some of these conditions were already of the past when Dickens wrote, for although imprisonment for debt was indeed not wholly given up until 1869, yet imprisonment for small debts had been done away with in 1844, the prison of the Marshalsea had been abolished in 1842 and the Court of the Marshalsea in 1849. Bernard Shaw said of Little Dorrit that it converted him to socialism; it is not likely that any contemporary English reader would feel it appropriate to respond to its social message in the same way. The dead hand of outworn tradition no longer supports special privilege in England. For good or bad, in scarcely any country in the world can the whole art of government be said to be How Not To Do It. Mrs. General cannot impose the genteel discipline of Prunes and Prisms, and no prestige whatever attaches to "the truly refined mind" of her definition—"one that will seem to be ignorant of the existence of anything that is not perfectly proper, placid, and pleasant." At no point, perhaps, do the particular abuses and absurdities upon which Dickens directed his terrible cold anger represent the problems of social life as we now conceive them.

Yet this makes Little Dorrit not less but more relevant to our sense of things. As the particulars seem less immediate to our case, the general force of the novel becomes greater, and Little Dorrit is seen to be about a problem which does not yield easily to time. It is about society in relation to the individual human will. This is certainly a matter general enough—general to the point of tautology, were it not for the bitterness with which the tautology is articulated, were it not for the specificity and the subtlety and the boldness with which the human will is anatomized.

The subject of Little Dorrit is borne in upon us by the symbol, or emblem, of the book, which is the prison. The story opens in a prison in Marseilles. It goes on to the Marshalsea, which in effect it never leaves. The second of the two parts of the novel begins in what we are urged to think of as a sort of prison, the monastery of the Great St. Bernard. The Circumlocution Office is the prison of the creative mind of England. Mr. Merdle is shown habitually holding himself by the wrist, taking himself into custody, and in a score of ways the theme of incarceration is carried out, persons and classes being imprisoned by their notions of their predestined fate or their religious duty, or by their occupations, their life schemes, their ideas of themselves, their very habits of language.

Symbolic or emblematic devices are used by Dickens to one degree or another in several of the novels of his late period, but nowhere to such good effects as in *Little Dorrit*. The fog of *Bleak House*, the dust heap and the river of *Our Mutual Friend* are very striking, but they scarcely equal in force the prison image which dominates *Little Dorrit*. This is because the prison is an actuality before it is ever a symbol;[1] its connection with the will is real, it is the practical instrument for the negation of man's will which the will of society has contrived. As such, the prison haunted the mind of the nineteenth century, which may be said to have had its birth at the fall of the Bastille. The genius of the age, conceiving itself as creative will, naturally thought of the prisons from which it must be freed, and the trumpet call of the "Leonore" overture sounds through the century, the signal for the opening of the gates, for a general deliverance, although it grows fainter as men come to think of the prison not as a political instrument merely but as the ineluctable condition of life in society. "Most men in a brazen prison live"—the line in which Matthew Arnold echoes Wordsworth's "shades of the prison-house begin to close / Upon the growing boy," might have served as the epigraph of *Little Dorrit*. In the mind of Dickens himself the idea of the prison was obsessive, not merely because of his own boyhood experience of prison life through his father's three months in the Marshalsea (although this must be given great weight in our understanding of his intense preoccupation with the theme), but because of his own consciousness of the force and scope of his will.

If we speak of the place which the image of the prison occupied in the mind of the nineteenth century, we ought to recollect a certain German picture of the time, inconsiderable in itself but made significant by its use in a famous work of the early twentieth century. It represents a man lying in a medieval dungeon; he is asleep, his head pillowed on straw, and we know that he dreams of freedom because the bars on his window are shown being sawed by gnomes. This picture serves as the frontispiece of Freud's *Introductory Lectures on Psychoanalysis*—Freud uses it to make plain one of the more elementary ideas of his psychology, the idea of the fulfillment in dream or fantasy of impulses of the will that cannot be fulfilled in actuality. His choice of this particular picture is not fortuitous; other graphic representations of wish-fulfillment exist which might have served equally well his immediate didactic purpose, but Freud's general conception of the mind does indeed make the prison image peculiarly appropriate. And Freud is in point here because in a passage of *Little Dorrit* Dickens anticipates one of Freud's ideas, and not one of the simplest but nothing less bold and inclusive than the essential theory of the neurosis.

The brief passage to which I make reference occurs in the course of Arthur Clennam's pursuit of the obsessive notion that his family is in some way guilty, that its fortune, although now greatly diminished, has been built on injury done to someone. And he conjectures that the injured person is William Dorrit, who has been confined for debt in the Marshalsea for twenty years. Clennam is not wholly wrong in his supposition—there is indeed guilt in the family, incurred by Arthur's mother, and it consists in part of an injury done to a member of the Dorrit family. But he is not wholly right, for Mr. Dorrit has not been imprisoned through the wish or agency of Mrs. Clennam. The reasoning by which Arthur reaches his partly mistaken conclusion is of the greatest interest. It is based upon the fact that his mother, although mentally very vigorous, has lived as an invalid for many years. She has been imprisoned in a single room of her house, confined to her chair, which she leaves only for her bed. And her son conjectures that her imprisoning illness is the price she pays for the guilty gratification of keeping William Dorrit in *his* prison—that is, in order to have the right to injure another, she must unconsciously injure herself in an equivalent way: "A swift thought shot into [Arthur Clennam's] mind. In that long imprisonment here [i.e., Mr. Dorrit's] and in her long confinement to her room, did his mother find a balance to be struck? I admit that I was accessory to that man's captivity. I have suffered it in kind. He has decayed in his prison; I in mine. I have paid the penalty."

I have dwelt on this detail because it suggests, even more than the naked fact of the prison itself, the nature of the vision of society of *Little Dorrit*. One way of describing Freud's conception of the mind is to say that it is based upon the primacy of the will, and that the organization of the internal life is in the form, often fantastically parodic, of a criminal process in which the mind is at once the criminal, the victim, the police, the judge, and the executioner. And this is a fair description of Dickens' own view of the mind, as, having received the social impress, it becomes in turn the matrix of society.

In emphasizing the psychological aspects of the representation of society of *Little Dorrit* I do not wish to slight those more immediate institutional aspects of which earlier readers of the novel were chiefly aware. These are of as great importance now as they ever were in Dickens' career. Dickens is far from having lost his sense of the cruelty and stupidity of institutions and functionaries, his sense of the general rightness of the people as a whole and of the general wrongness of those who are put in authority over them. He certainly has not moved to that specious position in which all injustice is laid at the door of the original Old Adam in each of us, not to be done away with until we shall all, at the same moment, become the new Adam. The Circumlocution Office is a constraint upon the life of England which nothing can justify. Mr. Dorrit's sufferings and the injustice done to him are not denied or mitigated by his passionate commitment to some of the worst aspects of the society which deals with him so badly.

Yet the emphasis on the internal life and on personal responsibility is very strong in *Little Dorrit*. Thus, to take but one example, in the matter of the Circumlocution Office Dickens is at pains to remind us that the responsibility for its existence lies even with so good a man as Mr. Meagles. In the alliance against the torpor of the Office which he has made with Daniel Doyce, the engineer and inventor, Mr. Meagles has been undeviatingly faithful. Yet Clennam finds occasion to wonder whether there might not be "in the breast of this honest, affectionate, and cordial Mr. Meagles, any microscopic portion of the mustard-seed that had sprung up into the great tree of the Circumlocution Office." He is led to this speculation by his awareness that Mr. Meagles feels "a general superiority to Daniel Doyce, which seemed to be founded, not so much on anything in Doyce's personal character, as on the mere fact of [Doyce's] being an originator and a man out of the beaten track of other men."

Perhaps the single best index of the degree of complexity with which Dickens views society in *Little Dorrit* is afforded by the character of Blandois and his place in the novel. Blandois is wholly wicked, the embodiment of evil; he is, indeed, a devil. One of the effects of his presence in *Little Dorrit* is to complicate our response to the theme of the prison, to deprive us of the comfortable, philanthropic thought that prisons are nothing but instruments of injustice. Because Blandois exists, prisons are necessary. The generation of readers that preceded our own was inclined, I think, to withhold credence from Blandois—they did not believe in his aesthetic actuality because they did not believe in his moral actuality, the less so because they could not account for his existence in specific terms of social causation. But events have required us to believe that there really are people who seem entirely wicked, and almost unaccountably so; the social causes of their badness lie so far back that they can scarcely be reached, and in any case causation pales into irrelevance before the effects of their actions; our effort to "understand" them becomes a mere form of thought.

In this novel about the will and society, the devilish nature of Blandois is confirmed by his maniac insistence upon his gentility, his mad reiteration that it is the right and necessity of his existence to be served by others. He is the exemplification of the line in *Lear*: "The prince of darkness is a gentleman." The influence of Dickens upon Dostoevski is perhaps nowhere exhibited in a more detailed way than in the similarities between Blandois and the shabby-genteel devil of *The Brothers Karamazov*, and also between him and Smerdyakov of the same novel. It is of consequence to Dickens as to Dostoevski that the evil of the unmitigated social will should own no country, yet that the flavor of its cosmopolitanism should be "French"—that is, rationalistic and subversive of the very assumption of society. Blandois enfolds himself in the soiled tatters of the revolutionary pathos. So long as he can play the game in his chosen style, he is nature's gentleman dispossessed of his rightful place, he is the natural genius against whom the philistine world closes its dull ranks. And when the disguise, which deceives no one, is off, he makes use of the classic social rationalization: Society has made him what he is; he does in his own person only what society does in its corporate form and with its corporate self-justification. "Society sells itself and sells me: and I sell society."[2]

Around Blandois are grouped certain characters of the novel of whose manner of life he is the pure principle. In these people the social will, the will to status, is the ruling faculty. To be recognized, deferred to, and served—this is their master passion. Money is of course of great consequence in the exercise of this passion, yet in *Little Dorrit* the desire for money is subordinated to the desire for deference. The Midas figure of Mr. Merdle must not mislead us on this point—should, indeed, guide us aright, for Mr. Merdle, despite his destructive power, is an innocent and passive man among those who live by the social will. It is to be noted of all these people that they justify their insensate demand for status by some version of Blandois's pathos; they are confirmed in their lives by self-pity, they rely on the great modern strategy of being the insulted and injured. Mr. Dorrit is too soft a man for his gentility mania ever to be quite diabolical, but his younger daughter Fanny sells herself to the devil, damns herself entirely, in order to torture the woman who once questioned her social position. Henry Gowan, the cynical, incompetent gentleman-artist who associates himself with Blandois in order to *épater* society, is very nearly as diabolical as his companion. From his mother—who must dismiss once and for all any lingering doubt of Dickens' ability to portray what Chesterton calls the delicate or deadly in human character—he has learned to base his attack on society upon the unquestionable rightness of wronged gentility. Miss Wade lives a life of tortured self-commiseration which gives her license to turn her hatred and her hand against everyone, and she imposes her principle of judgment and conduct upon Tattycoram.

In short, it is part of the complexity of this novel which deals so bitterly with society that those of its characters who share its social bitterness are by that very fact condemned. And yet—so much further does the complexity extend—the subversive pathos of self-pity is by no means wholly dismissed, the devil has not wholly lied. No reader of *Little Dorrit* can possibly conclude that the rage of envy which Tattycoram feels is not justified in some degree, or that Miss Wade is wholly wrong in pointing out to her the insupportable ambiguity of her position as the daughter-servant of Mr. and Mrs. Meagles and the sister-servant of Pet Meagles. Nor is it possible to read Miss Wade's account of her life, "The History of a Self Tormentor," without an understanding that amounts to sympathy. We feel this the more—Dickens meant us to feel it the more—because the two young women have been orphaned from infancy, and are illegitimate. Their bitterness is seen to be the perversion of the desire for love. The self-torture of Miss Wade—who becomes the more interesting if we think of her as the exact inversion of Esther Summerson of *Bleak House*—is the classic maneuver of the child who is unloved, or believes herself to be unloved; she refuses to be lovable, she elects to be hateful. In all of us the sense of injustice precedes the sense of justice by many years. It haunts our infancy, and even the most dearly loved of children may conceive themselves to be oppressed. Such is the nature of the human will, so perplexed is it by the disparity between what it desires and what it is allowed to have. With Dickens as with Blake, the perfect image of injustice is the unhappy child, and, like the historian Burckhardt, he connects the fate of nations with the treatment of children. It is a commonplace of the biography and criticism of Dickens that this reflects his own sense of having been unjustly treated by his parents, specifically in ways which injured his own sense of social status, his own gentility; the general force of Dickens' social feelings derives from their being rooted in childhood experience, and something of the special force of *Little Dorrit* derives from Dickens' having discovered its matter in the depths of his own social will.

At this point we become aware of the remarkable number of false and inadequate parents in *Little Dorrit*. To what pains Dickens goes to represent delinquent parenthood, with what an elaboration of irony he sets it forth! "The Father of the Marshalsea"—this is the title borne by Mr. Dorrit, who, preoccupied by the gratification of being the First Gentleman of a prison, is unable to exercise the simplest paternal function; who corrupts two of his children by his dream of gentility; who will accept any sacrifice from his saintly daughter Amy, Little Dorrit, to whom he is the beloved child to be cherished and forgiven. "The Patriarch"—this is the name bestowed upon Mr. Casby, who stands as a parody of all Dickens' benevolent old gentlemen from Mr. Pickwick through the Cheerybles to John Jarndyce, an astounding unreality of a man who, living only to grip and grind, has convinced the world by the iconography of his dress and mien that he is the repository of all benevolence. The primitive appropriateness of the strange—the un-English!—punishment which Mr. Pancks metes out to this hollow paternity, the cutting off of his long hair and the broad brim of his hat, will be understood by any reader with the least tincture of psychoanalytical knowledge. Then the Meagles, however solicitous of their own daughter, are, as we have seen, but indifferent parents to Tattycoram. Mrs. Gowan's rearing of her son is the root of his corruption. It is Fanny Dorrit's complaint of her enemy, Mrs. Merdle, that she refuses to surrender the appearance of youth, as a mother should. And at the very center of the novel is Mrs. Clennam, a false mother in more ways than one; she does not deny love but she perverts and prevents it by denying all that love feeds on—liberty, demonstrative tenderness, joy, and, what for Dickens is the guardian of love in society, art. It is her harsh rearing of her son that has given him cause to say in his fortieth year, "I have no will."

Some grace—it is, of course, the secret of his birth, of his being really a child of love and art—has kept Arthur Clennam from responding to the will of his mother with a bitter, clenched will of his own. The alternative he has chosen has not, contrary to his declaration, left him no will at all. He has by no means been robbed of his ethical will, he can exert energy to help others, and for the sake of Mr. Dorrit or Daniel Doyce's invention he can haunt the Circumlocution Office with his mild, stubborn, "I want to know...." But the very accent of that phrase seems to forecast the terrible "I prefer not to" of Bartleby the Scrivener in Melville's great story of the will in its ultimate fatigue.

It is impossible, I think, not to find in Arthur Clennam the evidence of Dickens' deep personal involvement in *Little Dorrit*. If we ask what Charles Dickens has to do with poor Clennam, what The Inimitable has to do with this sad depleted failure, the answer must be: nothing, save what is implied by Clennam's consciousness that he has passed the summit of life and that the path from now on leads downward, by his belief that the pleasures of love are not for him, by his "I want to know ... ," by his wish to negate the will in death. Arthur Clennam is that mode of Dickens' existence at the time of *Little Dorrit* which makes it possible for him to write to his friend Macready, "However strange it is never to be at rest, and never satisfied, and ever trying after something that is never reached, and to be always laden with plot and plan and care and worry, how clear it is that it must be, and that one is driven by an irresistible might until the journey is worked out." And somewhat earlier and with a yet more poignant relevance: "Why is it, that as with poor David, a sense always comes crushing upon me now, when I fall into low spirits, as of one happiness I have missed in life, and one friend and companion I have never made?"

If we become aware of an autobiographical element in *Little Dorrit*, we must of course take notice of the fact that the novel was conceived after the famous incident of Maria Beadnell, who, poor woman, was the original of Arthur Clennam's Flora Finching. She was the first love of Dickens' proud, unfledged youth; she had married what Dickens has taught us to call Another, and now, after twenty years, she had chosen to come back into his

life. Familiarity with the story cannot diminish our amazement at it—
Dickens was a subtle and worldly man, but his sophistication was not proof
against his passionate sentimentality, and he fully expected the past to come
back to him, borne in the little hands of the adorable Maria. The actuality
had a quite extreme effect upon him, and Flora, fat and foolish, is his
monument to the discovered discontinuity between youth and middle age;
she is the nonsensical spirit of the anticlimax of the years. And if she is in
some degree forgiven, being represented as the kindest of foolish women, yet
it is not without meaning that she is everywhere attended by Mr. F's Aunt,
one of Dickens' most astonishing ideas, the embodiment of senile rage and
spite, flinging to the world the crusts of her buttered toast. "He has a proud
stomach, this chap," she cries when poor Arthur hesitates over her dreadful
gift. "Give him a meal of chaff!" It is the voice of one of the Parcae.

It did not, of course, need the sad comedy of Maria Beadnell for
Dickens to conceive that something in his life had come to an end. It did not
even need his growing certainty that, after so many years and so many
children, his relations with his wife were insupportable—this realization was
as much a consequence as it was a cause of the sense of termination. He was
forty-three years old and at the pinnacle of a success unique in the history of
letters. The wildest ambitions of his youth could not have comprehended the
actuality of his fame. But the last infirmity of noble mind may lead to the first
infirmity of noble will. Dickens, to be sure, never lost his love of fame, or of
whatever of life's goods his miraculous powers might bring him, but there
came a moment when the old primitive motive could no longer serve, when
the joy of impressing his powers on the world no longer seemed delightful in
itself, and when the first, simple, honest, vulgar energy of desire no longer
seemed appropriate to his idea of himself.

We may say of Dickens that at the time of *Little Dorrit* he was at a crisis
of the will which is expressed in the characters and forces of the novel, in the
extremity of its bitterness against the social will, in its vision of peace and
selflessness. This moral crisis is most immediately represented by the
condition of Arthur Clennam's will, by his sense of guilt, by his belief that he
is unloved and unlovable, by his retirement to the Marshalsea as by an act of
choice, by his sickness unto death. We have here the analogy to the familiar
elements of a religious crisis. This is not the place to raise the question of
Dickens' relation to the Christian religion, which was a complicated one. But
we cannot speak of *Little Dorrit* without taking notice of its reference to
Christian feeling, if only because this is of considerable importance in its
effect upon the aesthetic of the novel.

It has been observed of *Little Dorrit* that certain of Dickens'
characteristic delights are not present in their usual force. Something of his

gusto is diminished in at least one of its aspects. We do not have the amazing thickness of fact and incident that marks, say, *Bleak House* or *Our Mutual Friend*—not that we do not have sufficient thickness, but we do not have what Dickens usually gives us. We do not have the great population of characters from whom shines the freshness of their autonomous life. Mr. Pancks and Mrs. Plornish and Flora Finching and Flintwinch are interesting and amusing, but they seem to be the fruit of conscious intention rather than of free creation. This is sometimes explained by saying that Dickens was fatigued. Perhaps so, but if we are aware that Dickens is here expending less of one kind of creative energy, we must at the same time be aware that he is expending more than ever before of another kind. The imagination of *Little Dorrit* is marked not so much by its powers of particularization as by its powers of generalization and abstraction. It is an imagination under the dominion of a great articulated idea, a moral idea which tends to find its full development in a religious experience. It is an imagination akin to that which created *Piers Plowman* and *Pilgrim's Progress*. And, indeed, it is akin to the imagination of *The Divine Comedy*. Never before has Dickens made so full, so Dantean, a claim for the virtue of the artist, and there is a Dantean pride and a Dantean reason in what he says of Daniel Doyce, who, although an engineer, stands for the creative mind in general and for its appropriate virtue: "His dismissal of himself [was] remarkable. He never said, I discovered this adaptation or invented that combination; but showed the whole thing as if the Divine Artificer had made it, and he had happened to find it. So modest was he about it, such a pleasant touch of respect was mingled with his quiet admiration of it, and so calmly convinced was he that it was established on irrefragable laws." Like much else that might be pointed to, this confirms us in the sense that the whole energy of the imagination of *Little Dorrit* is directed to the transcending of the personal will, to the search for the Will in which shall be our peace.

We must accept—and we easily do accept, if we do not permit critical cliché to interfere—the aesthetic of such an imagination, which will inevitably tend toward a certain formality of pattern and toward the generalization and the abstraction we have remarked. In a novel in which a house falls physically to ruins from the moral collapse of its inhabitants, in which the heavens open over London to show a crown of thorns, in which the devil has something like an actual existence, we quite easily accept characters named nothing else than Bar, Bishop, Physician. And we do not reject, despite our inevitable first impulse to do so, the character of Little Dorrit herself. Her untinctured goodness does not appall us or make us misdoubt her, as we expected it to do. This novel at its best is only incidentally realistic; its finest power of imagination appears in the great general images whose abstractness is their actuality, like Mr. Merdle's dinner parties, or the Circumlocution Office itself, and in such a context we understand Little Dorrit to be the Beatrice of the *Comedy*, the Paraclete in female form. Even the physical littleness of this grown woman, an attribute which is insisted on and which seems likely to repel us, does not do so, for we perceive it to be the sign that she is not only the Child of the Marshalsea, as she is called, but also the Child of the Parable, the negation of the social will.

NOTES

1. Since writing this, I have had to revise my idea of the actuality of the symbols of *Our Mutual Friend*. Professor Johnson's biography of Dickens has taught me much about the nature of dust heaps, including their monetary value, which was very large, quite large enough to represent a considerable fortune: I had never quite believed that Dickens was telling the literal truth about this. From Professor Dodd's *The Age of Paradox* I have learned to what an extent the Thames was visibly the sewer of London, of how pressing was the problem of the sewage in the city as Dickens knew it, of how present to the mind was the sensible and even the tangible evidence that the problem was not being solved. The moral *disgust* of the book is thus seen to be quite adequately comprehended by the symbols which are used to represent it.

2. This is in effect the doctrine of Balzac's philosophical-anarchist criminal, Vautrin. But in all other respects the difference between Blandois and Vautrin is extreme. Vautrin is a "noble" and justified character; for all his cynicism, he is on the side of virtue and innocence. He is not corrupted by the social injustices he has suffered and perceived, by the self-pity to which they might have given rise; his wholesomeness may be said to be the result of his preference for power as against the status which Blandois desires. The development of Blandois from Vautrin—I do not know whether Dickens's creation was actually influenced by Balzac's—is a literary fact which has considerable social import.

ANGUS WILSON

The Heroes and Heroines of Dickens

To examine the heroes and heroines of Dickens is to dwell on his weaknesses and failures. Only a strong conviction of Dickens's extraordinary greatness can make such an examination either worth while or decorous; since the literary critic, unlike the reviewer, can always choose his fields and should seek surely to appreciate rather than to disparage. Even in the weak field of his heroes and heroines, Dickens made remarkable advances, for though he matured—or, to use a less evaluating word, changed—late both as a man and as an artist, his immense energy drove him on through the vast field of his natural genius to attempt the conquest of the territory that lay beyond. The development of the heroes and heroines of his novels is indeed a reflection of this change or maturing, and a measure of his success in going beyond the great domain he had so easily mastered. Some of the dilemmas that lay at the root of his difficulties were personal to him; but others were historical, and some perhaps will never be solved by any novelist.

In general, the subject of Dickens's heroes has not received much attention from serious critics. Admirers have preferred to dwell on his excellencies; detractors had found more positive qualities to excite their antipathy. The child heroes and heroines brought tears to the eyes of contemporary readers, and have found equal portions of admiration and dislike in later times. There has been some general recognition that the now

From *Dickens and the Twentieth Century*, John Gross and Gabriel Pearson, ed. © 1962 Routledge & Kegan Paul Ltd.

highly acclaimed late novels owe something of their declared superior merit to a greater depth in the portrayal of the heroes and the heroines.

I shall not here discuss the child heroes and heroines, except to suggest that as Dickens matured he found them inadequate centres for the complex social and moral structures he was trying to compose. The children too gained in realism by being removed from the centre. The peripheral Jo has a deeply moving realism that is not there in the necessarily falsely genteel Little Nell or Oliver. It is also perhaps worth noticing as a mark of Dickens's rich genius that he could be prodigal with his gifts, making masterly child portraits of Paul, David, and Pip serve merely as fractions of a large structure. Most post-Jamesian novelists would have exhausted their total energies in such portrayals of the childhood vision.

It is, however, the adult heroes and heroines with whom I am concerned. Let me first suggest the limitations which I believe hampered Dickens in successfully creating central figures in his works, and then, by analysis of the development of the heroes and heroines through his novels, throw some light perhaps upon how far he overcame or could overcome these limitations.

The historical limitations of the Victorian novelists are too well known to be worth more than a mention. The happy ending is an unfortunate distortion in Dickens's work as it is in that of the other great Victorians, but, despite the change made to *Great Expectations*, it goes deeper than a mere capitulation to the whims of readers. With Dickens as with Thackeray, though for different reasons, the contemporary idea of domestic happiness as the resolution of, or perhaps more fairly one should say, the counterpoise to social evil, was a strongly held personal conviction. Even more vital to Dickens was the idea of pure love as the means of redemption of flawed, weak, or sinful men. Neither of these beliefs can properly take the weight that he imposed upon them; though the latter, at any rate, is not such a psychological falsity perhaps as many twentieth-century critics have thought. The main destructive effort of this exaggerated view of love as a moral solvent falls upon those characters in the novels who, under any view, could be regarded as heroes and heroines. Closely allied to the popular prejudice in favour of wedding bells and the patter of tiny feet is the contemporary absolute demand for sexual purity. There has been a recent tendency to play down the effects of this on the Victorian novel. True, these effects have so often been discussed as now to be trite, but that does not unfortunately diminish them. This censorship did, in fact, reduce the great Victorian novelists in the sexual sphere to a childish status beside their continental contemporaries. It is surprising how often they can get past the ban by suggestion; it is surprising how often the ban does not matter to an imaginative reader; again, our freedom is only relative and has its own danger of absurdity; all this is true—yet the fact remains that our great Victorian novelists were forced at times to devices that are false, ridiculous, or blurred. And these faults occur too often at the moral heart of their work. In English fashion, and with reason, we may take pride in the degree to which our Victorian novelists achieved greatness in spite of this—but we can't efface it. No characters, of course, suffer so greatly as the heroes and heroines. Once again, however, I would suggest that Dickens had a special personal relationship to this sexual censorship—and that, while it sometimes led him into exceptionally absurd devices, it also produced a characteristically powerful effect. The sexual life of Charles Dickens, like that of most Victorians, has become a shop-soiled subject, but one may briefly say four things of it—he was a strongly sensual man, he had a deep social and emotional need for family life and love, he had a compensating claustrophobic dislike of the domestic scene, and he woke up to these contradictions in his sexual make-up very late. Surely the distressing feature about the famous letter to the press upon the break-up of his marriage is not so much the tasteless publicity, but the tasteless publicity sought by a man of Dickens's years and standing. He acted at best like a young man blinded by new fame. His emotional life, in fact, for all his many children, was by most standards immature. Thackeray, very percipient where his dislike of Dickens was concerned, hit the right note, when he said of Kate, 'the poor matron'. Dickens behaved not as a middle-aged man but as a young fool or as an old fool.

The contemporary censorship, in fact, went along with, rather than against, Dickens's natural inclinations. His submerged, but fierce, sensuality was to run some strange courses from the days of John Chester until it came to light in the diverging streams of Wrayburn and Headstone. Seduction withheld, deferred, foiled—at any rate never accomplished—produced many interesting and complex characters, who would not have been born in a fiction that reflected the real world where men are more resolute and women are weaker.

Perhaps even more important in its effect on his heroes and heroines than the imperfect view of love and the impossible view of sex that Dickens shared with his readers was the ambiguous view of Victorian society that he shared with so many of the artists and intellectuals of his age. Broadly speaking, one could say that the young Dickens aspired to a respectable middle-class radicalism attacking particular social evils, and ended as a middle-aged revolutionary with a peculiar hostility to the middle classes. Such an evolution in a man not given to intellectual self-analysis inevitably produced ambiguities in his portrayal of every social class at one time or another. And in no group of characters is this unconscious evolution with its accompanying contradictions more clearly displayed than in the young men who stand at the heroic centre of his books. This uneven course in his social opinions, now veering, now tacking, yet for all its changes moving in one final direction, affected his attitude to the future and to the past, to all classes, to education, to money, to ambition, to work, to play, to conformity, and to rebellion. This strange and complex pattern of life may be observed working out in various ways among his heroes and heroines.

Any account of Dickens must start with *Pickwick Papers*, the novel which announces an age of innocence before the course has begun. Perhaps Dickens never produced so satisfactory a hero as Mr. Pickwick again—a man who, like his author, imperceptibly changes; but not from hope to despair, rather from nullity to positive goodness. None of the problems of Dickens are met in this book: Mr. Pickwick developed in the garden of Eden before the fall, the next step from him was to Oliver and Nell—children, at least, have their measure of original sin. Yet no article on Dickens's heroes should fail to salute the perfection of Mr. Pickwick before it goes on to the real story.

Apart from the children, the first group of heroes may be seen leading up to the self-portrait of David Copperfield. Like Mr. Pickwick, this 'walking gentleman', genteel hero group begins in near nullity: one cannot discuss Harry Maylie or Edward Chester, for they are not there. Nicholas and Martin advance us a few steps: they are haters of hypocrisy, cant, and cruelty; sharp-tongued and humorous; hot-tempered; inclined to selfishness; a bit weak and spoilt; pale reflections, with their eye for the absurd, of the unintrospective young Dickens as he saw himself. Martin, with Jonas and Chevy Slyme for his relations, can hardly claim gentility; but Nicholas is a born gentleman of a somewhat ill-defined kind, although his uncle is a money-lender. The young, socially unsure Dickens had need not only of false gentility and of hatred of the aristocracy, he needed also a suffused and vague love of the past—a mark of the genteel. So Nicholas's first act, when he became a rich and prosperous merchant, was to buy his father's 'old house ... none of the old rooms were ever pulled down, no old tree was ever rooted up, nothing with which there was any association of bygone times was ever removed or changed'.

It is something of the same undefined traditional gentility which so endears to David Copperfield Dr. Strong's vaguely traditional old school and the aroma of scholarship given off by his improbable dictionary. David is the culmination, in fact, of these purely genteel heroes for whom Pip was later to atone. Of course, being a self-portrait, David has more life, but, after childhood, it is a feeble ray. To begin with, who can believe that he is a novelist? Indeed, although he is said to be a model of hard work, we never have any sense of it except in his learning shorthand. Dickens was far too extrovert in those days to analyse the qualities in himself that made for his genius. It is notable that David is no more than 'advanced in fame and fortune', where Dickens was advanced in literary skill and imaginative power. It is also notable that after childhood, nothing happened to David himself except the passion of his love for Dora and the shock of her death—and these, which should be poignant, are somehow made less so by being smiled back upon through the tears as part of youth's folly and life's pageant. *David Copperfield* is technically a very fine novel of the sentimental education genre, but the mood of mellow, wise reflection is surely too easily held; and, when we think of Dickens's age at the time of its writing, held all too prematurely. 'Advanced in fortune and fame', as a result, has inevitably a smug sound, and 'my domestic joy was perfect' seems to demand the Nemesis that was to come in real life.

Nor is this smug, genteel, conformist quality of David helped by Agnes. A successful novelist guided by her 'deep wisdom' would surely become a smug, insensitive, comfortable old best seller of the worst kind. Agnes, indeed, is the first of the group of heroines who mark the least pleasing, most frumpy, and smug vision of ideal womanhood that he produced. Agnes, in fact, is betrayed by Esther Summerson, when Dickens in his next book so unwisely decided to speak through his heroine's voice. It is not surprising that this wise, womanly, housekeeping, moralizing, self-congratulating, busy little creature should have needed a good dose of childlikeness, a dose of Little Nell to keep her going when she reappears as Little Dorrit. If we cannot believe in the child-woman Little Dorrit, at least we are not worried as we are by Agnes or Esther Summerson about her complete lack of a physical body—a deficiency so great that Esther's smallpox-spoilt face jars us because she has no body upon which a head could rest.

But if nothing happens to David himself after Mr. Murdstone goes off the scene, something does happen in the novel, about which David (Dickens) uses language that suggests that there lies the real drama—as well he may, for with Steerforth's seduction of Em'ly, and indeed with Steerforth himself, we are at the beginning of all those twists and turns by which Dickens eventually transforms a somewhat stagy villain into a new sort of full-sized hero. From Steerforth to Eugene Wrayburn is the road of self-discovery. Of all the would-be seducers in Dickens's novels, James Steerforth alone gets his prey; yet he is the only one, until Wrayburn, whom Dickens seems to have wished to redeem. If we look at the facts of Steerforth's character, it may be difficult to see why. From the moment that he so revoltingly gets Mr. Mell dismissed at Creakle's school until his carefully planned seduction of Em'ly he *does* nothing to commend himself. Yet David (and surely Dickens) uses language that would save if it could—'But he slept—let me think of him so again—as I had often seen him sleep at school; and thus, in this silent hour I left him. Never more, oh God forgive you, Steerforth, to touch that passive hand in love and friendship. Never, never more!' ... 'Yes, Steerforth, long removed from the scenes of this poor history! My sorrow may bear involuntary witness against you at the Judgement Throne; but my angry thoughts or reproaches never will, I know.' And at the last—'among the ruins of the home he had wronged, I saw him lying with his hand upon his arm, as I had often seen him lie at school'. If Dickens could have redeemed Steerforth he surely would have done so. And, indeed, he did; for Eugene Wrayburn is as much a redemption of Steerforth as Pip is a scapegoat for the falsities in David. On the whole, as I suggest, redemption through Wrayburn is a somewhat arbitrary business; but before that redemption came about, the figure of Steerforth had suffered under many guises and, in the course of his translation to hero, had borne witness to many changes in Dickens's social and moral outlook, had even assisted in the birth of a heroine more adequate to Dickens's mature outlook than either Little Nell or Agnes, or indeed the strange hybrid figure of Little Dorrit.

To trace these changes we should perhaps go back before Steerforth to earlier seductions in the novels. At the start the seducer is a cynical rake or libertine—John Chester or Sir Mulberry Hawk. He stands full square for the aristocratic dandy whom the middle-class radical Dickens detests as the source of outdated arbitrary power. Yet we have only to look at Boz in his early pictures to see the beringed and ringleted dandy—or is it the 'gent'? Dick Swiveller is kindly treated. In his adolescence surely it was among the would-be swells of Dick Swiveller's world that Dickens moved—the direct butt, no doubt, of any real dandy's contempt and laughter. The seducer, then, up to *Dombey*, is a crude class symbol.

Dombey and Son brings us farther forward. Carker has some genuine sensuality, of the cold, calculating, rather epicene imitation-Byron kind that the early nineteenth century must often have bred. True, he is vulgar, hypocritical, and apparently subservient—but then, unlike Steerforth, he has to scheme and work for his living. Like Steerforth, his Byronic professional seducing spills over into, other sorts of pleasure-loving—a somewhat ornately comfortable villa. There are four things in which Steerforth differs from him, apart from age: Steerforth despises the world, he puts other values above work, he sometimes wishes that he was not wasting his life, he has the vestige of a power to love or at any rate to want to be loved. It is not very much luggage, yet it proves enough to make the long journey to Eugene Wrayburn. Carker fails in his seduction, but then in Edith Dombey he has a

much more difficult job than little Em'ly presents to Steerforth. There were
two roads open for the Dickensian seducer—glamour (it was presumably this
that Steerforth used, though little Em'ly's last note to Peggotty shows small
evidence that she has felt it) or boredom. Boredom and self-distaste, these
were the marks of the woman who had already sold herself into loveless
marriage—Edith, Louisa Bounderby, Honoria Dedlock, if she had not
already been seduced before the novel began. Pride saves Edith Dombey;
pride would have saved Lady Dedlock; pride and an instinct of self-
preservation saved Louisa. Yet it is hardly a fair contest—Mr. Carker emits
his faint ray of vulgar sensuality, James Harthouse his rather superior brand
of Steerforth's worldly charm. But, if it only takes one to make a rape, it takes
two to make a seduction; and there is nothing in Edith or Louisa to respond.
They are looking for flight from a desperate situation and indeed they take
it; but they are not looking for any species of sexual love. The female
equivalent to the sort of professional minor Byronism that Steerforth and
Harthouse and Gowan, no doubt, in his relations with Miss Wade, offer, is
the minor, rather half-hearted coquetry that is touched on in Dolly Vardon,
punished in Fanny Dorrit and Estella, and finally redeemed in Bella Wilfer.
But Estella and Bella are more than coquettes, they are proud, frozen,
unhappy women anxious to be free of desperate homes, they combine in fact
the nearest approach that Dickens gets to a sensually alive woman with the
proud cold beauties—Edith, Louisa, and Honoria. *Our Mutual Friend*, in
fact, contains the developed hero and the most developed heroine in
Dickens's fiction. The one has come a long journey from the seducer-villain;
and the other, almost as long a journey from the coquette and the runaway
wife. Even so they remain separate, each is reclaimed by a nullity, John
Harmon and Lizzie Hexam. Yet in them Dickens had admitted to the saved
a degree of sexual reality that argues well for the future.

We may leave Bella on one side; she has brought some frailty, some
liveliness and some sexual warmth to Dickens's heroines; but she plays little
part in the evolution of Dickens's social or moral outlook—it was not a
woman's role to do so.

Eugene Wrayburn is a far more interesting case. His salvation is really
immensely arbitrary. Even after he has left Lizzie for the last time before
Headstone's murderous attack, he has not given up his ideas of seduction
entirely—his father's voice tells him, 'You wouldn't marry for some money
and some station, because you were frightfully likely to become bored. Are
you less frightfully likely to become bored marrying for no money and no
station?' It is indeed his rival's blows that save him. Yet we have seen that
Steerforth had certain pleas to offer; Wrayburn offers all the same pleas and
by this time they have become more urgent to Dickens. First, contempt for

the World and for success—this, once a hidden admiration, is now the centre of Dickens's moral values. Private income, public school, and university education, all these may be forgiven if they produce a despiser of bourgeois society. Dandy insolence, once the mark of an arbitrary, outdated order, is now the badge of rejection of Podsnap. Other values above work and duty? This has been amply confirmed by a rather separate but very successful hero, the sad, Calvinist-destroyed Clennam. Then the vestige of regret for a wasted life has gone through many fires since Steerforth's day; it has been purified by Richard Carstone and above all by Sidney Carton, whom Shrewsbury, gentlemanly bohemianism, and the Bar could not entirely destroy. Above all the need for love has also been through Carton's fire so that Lucie can say to Darnay, 'remember how strong we are in our happiness, and how weak he is in his misery'. Loneliness, failure, pride, bitter rejection of all that made up Victorian progress and Victorian morality, a considered rejection of duty and hard work as moral ends, Dickens comes through to acceptance of these in the person of Eugene Wrayburn. And sensuality? Does he also redeem his own strong sensuality? This, I think, is less certain. The thin, calculated sensuality that runs from the Byronic Steerforth to the Yellow Book Wrayburn is not surely of the obsessive, tortured kind that we suspect in Dickens. Does not this real sensuality peep through in more sinister places? In Pecksniff's scene with Mary Graham, in Jonas's wooing of Mercy, in Uriah's glances at Agnes—there is more real lust there than in all the wiles of Steerforth and Harthouse, in all the brutalities of Gowan. And now the lust comes up again on the wrong side, in slavery to the Victorian doctrines of hard work, of fact, of ambition, and of self-betterment—all things that had played a large part in Dickens's own life and which he had now rejected. The obsessive lust of Bradley Headstone finds no redemption. Yet as he rolls on the ground, after Charlie Hexam has left him, I believe that Dickens feels as strong a pity for him as David had felt for Steerforth. Would Dickens perhaps have left from here on another long pilgrimage deep into the holy places of his own soul? Can Jasper be the next strange step in that new pilgrimage?

WILLIAM ODDIE

Mr. Micawber and the Redefinition of Experience

'Such is "the latent power of Mr. Micawber"', says Professor Hillis
Miller, 'that he can always spiritualize his situation and thus escape it.
Even when he is literally caught and imprisoned, he can spring out in a
minute by a mere redefinition of what has happened ...'[1] Most critics of
Dickens are content to make a ritual obeisance to Mr. Micawber as 'one of
the great triumphs of Dickens's genius' and then retreat to safer pastures:
'it is a deeply felt experience,' says Mr. Cockshut, 'but it is not susceptible
to analytic description.'[2] The attempts of some critics who think, on the
contrary, that Mr. Micawber *can* be usefully subjected to the indignity of
critical examination, do a lot to explain this reluctance; it is difficult,
reading Hillis Millers' account, to imagine him actually *laughing*: his
Micawber, whatever else he is, just is not funny. Nevertheless, he has a
point, which is worth developing. Micawber constantly redefines his own
experience (a procedure which, it might be argued, hardly warrants the
word 'spiritualize'.) Not only this; he is himself a redefinition of an
intimate and sensitive part of the experience of his creator. And the
imaginative process involved here is also one of the most pervasively
discernible processes of the book itself: *David Copperfield* is
autobiographical in two ways: firstly, on a more or less factual level, and

From *The Dickensian* 63, 352 (May 1967). © 1967 by the Dickens Fellowship secondly, on the level which transforms or rationalises fact which cannot, for some reason, be accepted on its own terms.[3] Hence, most obviously, Maria Beadnell becomes Dora. The most fascinating example of this kind of problem can be seen in Dickens's attempt to clarify his ambiguous attitude to his father. The attempt at a fictional reconciliation of John Dickens's responsibility for the blacking warehouse trauma with the real warmth of feeling he inspired in his son as a loveable and affectionate eccentric, could have produced the kind of tension on which the modern novelist thrives. But this was not the kind of literary convention open to him; what was open to him was, in any case, more relevant both to his own peculiar experience and problems, and to the imaginative processes they helped to form:

> It is curious to me how I could ever have consoled myself under my small troubles (which were great troubles to me) by impersonating my favourite characters in them—as I did—and by putting Mr. and Miss Murdstone into all the bad ones which I did too.[4]

The convention of heroes and villains helps Dickens to solve his problem. The process is obvious enough: the part of John Dickens his son could never forgive for the state of neglect and loneliness into which he fell after the departure from Chatham and, later, for the agony of the blacking warehouse becomes, as it were, siphoned off into Murdstone, into a character of black forbidding brow and festering humours, leaving Dickens still with a residual problem, but with a much less tense one.

I

Mr. Micawber, I suggest, poses three related problems. Firstly; how far is he an instrument for Dickens's working out to himself of his father, and how does this reorientation, if it is one, operate? Secondly; what is the source of Micawber's humour? From these two questions follows a third: how far can we relate his capacity for making us laugh to his capacity for redefining painful experience; is the quality simply straightforward comic relief coupled with an assertion of indestructibility, or is there something here more intimately connected with the terrors of the first quarter of the book?

The process of redefinition operates in two directions. We can see something of what is involved by a comparison of a passage from the novel and a group of biographical and autobiographical passages from Forster:

DAVID COPPERFIELD

And now I fell into a state of neglect, which I cannot look back upon without compassion. I fell at once into a solitary condition,— apart from all friendly notice, apart from the society of all other boys of my own age, apart from all companionship but my own spiritless thoughts, which seems to cast its gloom upon this paper as I write.

What would I have given, to have been sent to the hardest school that ever was kept!—to have been taught something, anyhow, anywhere! No such hope dawned upon me. They disliked me; and they sullenly, sternly, steadily overlooked me. I think Mr. Murdstone's means were straitened at about this time; but it is little to the purpose. He could not bear me; and in putting me from him, he tried, as I believe, to put away the notion that I had any claim upon him—and succeeded.

I was not actively ill-used. I was not beaten or starved; but the wrong that was done to me had no intervals of relenting, and was done in a systematic, passionless manner. Day after day, week after week, month after month, I was coldly neglected. I wonder sometimes, when I think of it, what they would have done if I had been taken with an illness; whether I should have lain down in my

FORSTER

Bayham Street was about the poorest part of the London suburbs then, and the house was a mean small tenement, with a wretched little back garden abutting on a squalid court. Here was no place for new acquaintances to him: not a boy was near with whom he might hope to become in any way familiar. A washerwoman lived next door, and a Bow Street officer lived over the way. Many many times has he spoken to me of this, and how he seemed at once to fall into a solitary condition apart from all other boys of his own age, and to sink into a neglected state at home which had always been quite unaccountable to him.

"As I thought," he said on one occasion very bitterly, "in the little back garret in Bayham Street," of all I had lost in losing Chatham, what would I have given, if I had had anything to give, to have been sent back to any other school, to have been taught something anywhere![6]

He never undertook any business, charge or trust that he did not zealously, conscientiously, punctually, honourably discharge ... He was proud of me, in his way, and had a great admiration of the comic singing. But, in the ease of his temper, and the straitness of his means, he appeared to have utterly put from him the notion that I had

DAVID COPPERFIELD	FORSTER
lonely room, and languished through it in my usual solitary way, or whether anybody would have helped me out.[5]	any claim on him, in that regard, whatever.[7]
	I know my father to be as kind-hearted and generous a man as ever lived in the world. Everything that I can remember of his conduct to his wife, or children, or friends, in sickness or affliction, is beyond all praise. By me, as a sick child he has watched night and day, unweariedly and patiently, many nights and days.[8]

This speaks for itself. The difficulty of reconciling his father's neglect with his affection is resolved by turning it into actual active dislike; his father's "ease of temper," the diffuseness which leads to his failure to grasp his son's emotional needs becomes an actual effort of renunciation; straitness of means, instead of being proferred as a partial excuse, is dismissed as irrelevant; his father's watching by him in sickness is transformed into a fantasy of Murdstone's neglecting him in similar circumstances. And in spite of the highly emotional tone of the whole of the passage from *David Copperfield*, its real bitterness is concentrated in the purely fictional area, the area which is a simple reversal of the truth. The impression that Dickens is containing himself in the first part of the passage is confirmed by an examination of his manuscript. Taking into account three separate alterations in the sentence which appears in the published text as "And now I fell into a state of neglect, which I cannot look back upon without compassion," an alternative version can be put together which is very much more revealing:

> And now I fell into a state of *dire* neglect, which *I have never been able to* look back upon without *a kind of agony*.[9]

"A kind of agony" was altered on a re-reading; Dickens changed the colour of his ink after the second paragraph, and this phrase, written in black ink, is scored out, and the word "compassion" substituted, in pale blue. We can similarly deduce that he probably also added the words "and succeeded" on to the end of the second paragraph during the same re-reading, hence strengthening the bitterness of the pure fantasy of the passage at the same time as he emotionally tones down the area which is factually closer to himself.

Dickens, then, can be seen here partially exorcising the neglect of this period of his life by presenting it as the work of fictional malignant beings. But there is more to the process than this. The complete change of scene, from Bayham Street to Blunderstone Rookery, although it must obviously be explained at the same time in terms of the needs of the plot, is not without significance. Dickens, we know, had an intense feeling for the emotional associations of a particular place; once some deeply felt experience had taken place in it, the two were inseparable. Hence (among many instances) his old way home through the borough made him weep after his eldest son could speak. The Blacking Warehouse has naturally attracted more attention as a formative traumatic experience than the Bayham Street period, but the contrast with what had come before must, in its way, have been as great, and it is clear from the passages quoted above that Dickens felt the loneliness of this time bitterly, and associated it in his mind with an actual physical milieu. It is interesting, then, to see the way in which he deals with this milieu in *David Copperfield*. In Chapter XXVII, Tommy Traddles and Micawber reappear, both after a long absence. The place Dickens chooses for their reappearance is clearly identifiable as Bayham Street. Like Bayham Street, it is in Camden Town, and is described in the terms one would expect of "about the poorest part of the London suburbs": "The inhabitants appeared to have a propensity to throw any little trifles they were not in want of into the road: which not only made it rank and sloppy, but untidy too, on account of the cabbage leaves."[10] The identification is clinched by a remark of Micawber's, about "a washerwoman, who exposes hard-bake for sale in her parlour window, dwelling next door, and a Bow Street officer residing over the way."[11] This appearance of a setting which we know had painful associations for Dickens in a part of the book remarkable for what Forster calls a "uniform pleasantness of tone"[12] demonstrates what really needed no demonstration: that underneath the placid surface of this part of the book, there are treacherous cross-currents at work. The loneliness of Bayham Street is dealt with by transferring to it Blunderstone rookery, thus leaving Bayham Street itself free for the habitation of such delightful and apparently uncomplicated beings as Traddles and the Micawbers. But this negative side of the process of redefinition has limits; it can channel off the tenseness, by excising large chunks of painful experience, and placing them elsewhere; but there still remains a lot to be done. It is here that Mr. Micawber steps in:

DAVID COPPERFIELD

At last Mr. Micawber's difficulties came to a crisis, and he was arrested early one morning, and carried over to the King's bench prison in the Borough. He told me, as he went out of the house, that the God of day had gone down upon him—and I really thought his heart was broken and mine too. But I heard, afterwards, that he was seen to play a lively game at skittles, before noon.[13]

Mr. Micawber was waiting for me within the gate, and we went up to his room (top story but one) and cried very much. He solemnly conjured me, I remember, to take warning by by his fate; and to observe that if a man had twenty pounds a year for his income, and spent nineteen pounds nineteen shillings and sixpence, he would be happy, but that if he spent twenty pounds one he would be miserable. After which he borrowed a shilling of me for porter, gave me a written order on Mrs. Micawber for the amount and put away his pocket-handkerchief, and cheered up.

We sat before a little fire, with two bricks put within the rusted grate, one on each side ...[14]

FORSTER

The interval between the sponging-house and the prison was passed by the sorrowful lad in running errands and carrying messages for the prisoner, delivered with swollen eyes and through shining tears; and the last words said to him by his father before he was finally carried to the Marshalsea were to the effect that the sun was set upon him for ever. "I really believed at the time," said Dickens to me, "that they had broken my heart."[15]

"My father was waiting for me in the lodge, and we went up to his room (on the top story but one), and cried very much. And he told me, I remember, to take warning by the Marshalsea, and to observe that if a man had twenty pounds a year, and spent nineteen pounds nineteen shillings and sixpence, he would be happy; but that a shilling spent the other way would make him wretched. I see the fire we sat before now; with two bricks inside the rusted grate, one on each side... "[16]

The strictly biographical or autobiographical passages are totally humourless, and in Forster's version, when Dickens says "I really believed at the time ... that they had broken my heart," he *means* it. The shift of emphasis is achieved by a fairly simple assertion of two of Micawber's characteristic traits. The language is inflated slightly: "the sun was set upon him for ever" becomes "the God of Day had now gone down upon him" and "he told me" becomes 'he solemnly conjured me.' There is a different kind of shift, too, from the Marshalsea to the King's Bench Prison, and the manuscript reveals that this was an afterthought; Dickens originally wrote "Marshalsea" but afterwards scored the word out and wrote in "King's Bench" above. But the most striking thing here is the injection of what we might call the principle of instant recovery. We can see the principle at work throughout the novel, but nowhere so clearly definable as it is here. The idea that, no matter how dark things may seem, there will always come some sudden melting-away of difficulties, is obviously a cardinal shaping principle of Dickens's imagination in this book, and it is clear that an important part of Micawber's function for him is in his continual reassertion of this idea. In a letter to Henry Austin written in September 1857 (nearly seven years after the appearance of the final number of *Copperfield*) about a projected "tour in search of an article," he seems to show this part of his attitude to Micawber: "I am horribly used up! ...", he writes; "low spirits, low pulse, low voice, intense reaction. If I were not like Mr. Micawber, 'falling back for a spring' on Monday, I think I should slink into a corner and cry."[17]

II

Micawber's function as an agent of the principle of instant recovery is embodied in his irresistible power as a humorous creation; it follows that we have to make some kind of attempt to come to grips with his comedy. How can we describe the effect he has on us? The most obvious thing about him is that he exists. He is *there*, and there is no getting away from him. What we feel above all else, reading one of his scenes, is the sense of his sheer physical presence. He is a born actor, and he acts without knowing he is doing it; establishing that he is *en scène* is an unconscious reflex to him:

> "I have discovered my friend Copperfield," said Mr. Micawber
> genteelly and without addressing himself particularly to anyone,
> "not in solitude, but partaking of a social meal ..."[18]

As much and perhaps more than any of Dickens's great comic characters, his visual aura is an insistent part of his appeal, and the little mnemonic ritual that usually ushers him in after an absence—"it was Mr. Micawber, with his eyeglass, and his walking stick, and his shirt collar, and his genteel air, and the condescending roll in his voice, all complete"[19] always strikes us as important, never irritates us as the same device sometimes does in lesser creations; the way he looks, and what he is, overlap completely. The book is full of little cameos of him, brilliantly drawn with a few swift strokes of the pen, like the glimpse David catches of him on the stagecoach, before his first departure from Canterbury, "the very picture of tranquil enjoyment, smiling at Mrs. Micawber's conversation, eating walnuts out of a paper bag, with a bottle sticking out of his breast pocket."[20] Above all, the picture that remains is of Mr. Micawber, eating and, especially, drinking or preparing for drinking, the image of him seen through a cloud of rising steam, making "his face shine with the punch, so that it looked as if it had been varnished all over."[21] He has Dickens's own love of food and drink and good company, and Dickens's own animal magnetism. We are aware of him, not simply as someone we read about, but as someone *there*, a real person, for whom we can feel a kind of personal affection.

This sense that we are dealing with a real, larger than life "character," for whom we feel an instinctive liking is not, in itself, funny; but it does predispose us to laughter. The "fragrance of lemon-peel and sugar, the odour of burning rum"[22] that hang around him like a kind of *charmisma*, his infinite capacity for enjoyment, are irresistibly infectious. His love of performing in public is part of the same extrovert love of life, and this, indirectly, can be associated with the two main themes of his comedy, the humour of the mock tragic-heroic, and the humour of social pretentiousness. We can see both these two sources of comedy separately elsewhere in Dickens, and in at least two cases (for what the point is worth) we can see them embodied by professional actors. We can see Mr. Micawber's love of the tragic set-piece and also the public nature of his lachrymose effusions (he never threatens to cut his throat without an audience) in Vincent Crummles;[23] and we can see something like the shabby-genteel verbal inflation that he inherits from John Dickens[24] in another actor; here, from the other end of Dickens's career, is Mr. Wopsle:

> "You must have observed, gentlemen," said he "an ignorant and a blatant ass, with a rasping throat and a countenance expressive of low malignity, who went through—I will not say sustained—the role (if I may use the French expression) of Claudius, King of Denmark. That is his employer, gentlemen, Such is the profession."[25]

Dickens likes this kind of verbal self-inflation as a source of comedy, and he also likes deflating it. The difference between the speech of Mr. Wopsle and that of Micawber is, that any desire we might have to deflate Micawber's utterance ourselves is always forestalled by him; his peculiar speech pattern depends on the repeated confrontation of unsustained hyperbole with prosaic reality: the words "in short" always herald the bursting of a balloon.

In this respect, his speech is the exact counterpart of his life. The comic conventions that can be seen to contain it rely on the inflation of an idea beyond its natural boundaries, and its inevitable collapse when seen against the prosaic realities of life. This recurrent deflation takes place in two ways, on a social level, and (if the word doesn't itself sound a little self-important in this context) on an existential level. The comic ideas that are the basis for the most of our laughter at Micawber are, firstly the humour involved in the assumption of social attitudes that can't be supported economically, and secondly the humour of the mock tragic-heroic:

> At these times, Mr. Micawber would be transported with grief and mortification, even to the length (as I was once made aware by a scream from his wife) of making motions at himself with a razor, but within half-an-hour afterwards, he would polish up his shoes with extraordinary pains, and go out ...[26]

The comic effect of this is due to its combination of two incompatible ideas about living, the idea that life's *comédie humaine* resolves itself periodically in the form of some kind of tragic or heroic catastrophe which has, in some way, an absolute and definitive significance, and the idea that life is something trivial and repetitive which doesn't resolve itself, but simply goes on going on; for someone to make "motions at himself with a razor" is not, in itself, comic: to do so almost as a matter of daily routine, is.

These two comic ideas interact to form a perpetually self-renewing cycle. The recurring disappointments that come from the inevitable failure of his economic fantasies lead to his mock suicidal posturings, which in their turn are absorbed by a resurgence of his middle-class dream world:

> I have known him come home to supper with a flood of tears, and a declaration that nothing was now left but jail; and go to bed making a calculation of the expense of putting bow-windows to the house, "in case anything turned up ..."[27]

Micawber's bourgeois fantasies represent a recurrent theme in Dickens's comedy, and one to which his attitude is not always so benign as it is here, the idea of the surface appearance and attitudes of life being adopted as a substitute for the reality of life itself:

> I quite believe that Mr. Micawber saw himself, in his judicial minds eye, on the woolsack. He passed his hand complacently over his bald head, and said with ostentatious resignation: "My dear, we will not anticipate the decrees of fortune. If I am reserved to wear a wig, I am at least prepared, externally," in allusion to his baldness, "for that distinction. I do not," said Mr. Micawber, "regret my hair, and I may have been deprived of it for a specific purpose. I cannot say."[28]

This is so sublimely hilarious that to analyse the comic mechanism that makes it work seems Philistine, to say the least. This fact in itself may be significant in considering the function for Dickens of a certain kind of comedy; humour at a certain level not only relies on illogic to cause laughter, but covers its tracks, so to speak, by a kind of built-in anti-analytic bias, that prevents us from probing this breakdown of logical processes too closely; a contrast with the operation of Dickens's satirical humour makes the point clearer. Our laughter at this passage is caused by a simple logical reversal, taken to the extremes of its own illogic; judges wear wigs, therefore anyone who can wear a wig can become a judge; a bald person is more qualified to wear a wig than someone who isn't bald, and is therefore more qualified to be a judge. And this destruction of normal logic is so assured and vital (a quality we don't need to analyse), and our attitude to Micawber personally is such, that we can for the moment accept his substitution of accidentals for substance as a real way of meeting the challenge that life throws out. Mrs. General and the Veneerings attempt precisely the same thing; but we are always intensely and uncharitably aware of their illogicality because for them it is a means of destroying vitality; Mr. Micawber's personal magnetism and sense of life never let us, or himself really focus anything like the same cold, dissecting gaze on what he is actually about.

III

John Dickens, by his fecklessness and failure to understand his son's emotional needs, was directly responsible for the great trauma of his childhood; he is also the clearly recognisable source for what is arguably Dickens's funniest character. What connection between these two facts can we propound? Perhaps Dickens himself gives us the answer:

> Surely nobody supposes that the young mother in the pit who
> falls into fits of laughter when the baby is boiled or sat upon,

would be at all diverted by such an occurrence off the stage ... It always appears to me that the secret of this enjoyment lies in the temporary superiority to the common hazards and misfortunes of life; in seeing casualities, attended when they readily occur with bodily and mental suffering, tears and poverty, happen through a very rough sort of poetry without the least being harm done to anyone ...[29]

This, surely, goes a long way towards explaining both Micawber's humour and, at the same time, how he redefines John Dickens. The creditors howling up the stairs for payment, the recurrent imprisonment for debt, the belligerent milkman cutting off supplies, these give us some of our happiest moments when we are reading *David Copperfield*:

> "I tell you what," said the milkman, looking hard at her for the first time, and taking her by the chin, "are you fond of milk?"
>
> "Yes, I likes it," she replied.
>
> "Good," said the milkman." Then you won't have none tomorrow ...
>
> I thought she seemed, upon the whole, relieved by the prospect of having any today. The milkman ... deposited the usual quantity in the family jug. This done, he went away, muttering, and uttered the cry of his trade next door, in a vindictive shriek.[30]

The fact that this is from the Bayham Street chapter reminds us that, although they seem funny enough to us, for Dickens such incidents were the accompaniment to the sense of loneliness and neglect of the immediate post-Chatham period, and later, to the events that led up to John Dickens's incarceration and to the agony which formed Dickens's imaginative processes so decisively that we can say with near certainty that without it, his novels would be either totally different or non-existent. Nobody supposes that he was "at all diverted" by such incidents "off the stage". Nor, for that matter, would we be. But this thought never once occurs to us when we are reading about Micawber; we might rationalise him later, but, at the time, his "superiority to the common hazards and misfortunes of life" is absolute. And clearly, both of the inclusive comic ideas which I have suggested as being at the root of Micawber's comedy, work to achieve precisely this end. The comedy of the mock tragic, by showing the actions and postures that manifest Micawber's "mental suffering, tears, and poverty" as being absurdly inflated, and then deflating them before our eyes, renders harmless the visible effect of Micawber's distresses, just as his comedy of the shabby-genteel, by presenting the deportment and external attitudes of a certain social level somehow as valid substitutes for its reality, renders harmless the cause; by making the breakdown of normal logic so vital, so convincing on its own terms, Micawber's humour somehow achieves for him the spiritual immunity of the middle classes without its normal stable-mate, their economic immunity.

John Dickens is the source for Mr. Micawber; he also becomes, later, the source for William Dorrit. Perhaps this, more than anything, shows how profoundly Dickens *needed* to write about his father; it seems to suggest, too, something of the relationship between the comic and tragic masks of the Dickensian stage. Much of the subject matter of Mr. Micawber's comedy, although some of it can hardly have the same associations for us as it did for Dickens, has a universal significance: bailiffs, imprisonment, financial embarrassment, are all archetypal comic ideas, and stripped of their comedy are far from pleasant for anyone. We can make the same general point about much of Dickens's comedy—the implications of Sarah Gamp or Wackford Squeers would be hard to look at without flinching, if these characters weren't also hilariously funny. John Dickens presented for his son one of those problems that had to be faced squarely. His first attack on it, through the medium of Micawber's verbal humour, succeeds colossally for us; William Dorrit shows that for Dickens this answer provided at best only a "temporary superiority."

Forster, perhaps, shows us why:

> ... no one could know the elder Dickens without secretly liking him the better for these flourishes of speech, which adapted themselves so readily to his gloom as well as to his cheerfulness, that it was difficult not to fancy they had helped him considerably in both, and had rendered more tolerable to him, if also more possible, the shade and sunshine of his chequered life.[31]

John Dickens himself had already provided the basis for his son's comic transformation of his "chequered life"; and Dickens is too anxious to love his father to accept him, yet, on anything but his terms. Perhaps, during his lifetime, this was all he felt able to do. And so there is no real qualitative readjustment. His father's techniques for living with the reality of his own failures are taken over, extended, and made the basis of Micawber's triumphs. Micawber, for Dickens, turns out to be just as much an evasion of one emotional problem as Agnes is of another.

NOTES

1. J. Hillis Miller, *Charles Dickens, the World of his novels*, Oxford, 1959, p. 151.

2. A. O. J. Cockshut, *The imagination of Charles Dickens*, Collins, 1961, p. 14.

3. For a general discussion of this point, see Edgar Johnson, *Charles Dickens, his triumph and tragedy*, Gollancz, 1953, pp. 677–81. Sylvère Monod, *Dickens Romancier*, 1953, pp. 284–312, also discusses the relation between the real and the imaginary in the novel.

4. *David Copperfield*, Oxford Illustrated Dickens, p. 56. (All references to Dickens's works are to this edition.)

5. *David Copperfield*, Oxford Illustrated Dickens, 149.

6. *The Life of Charles Dickens*, by John Forster, Ed. by J. W. T. Ley, Cecil Palmer, 1928, p. 9.

7. *The Life of Charles Dickens*, by John Forster, Ed. by J. W. T. Ley, Cecil Parker 1928, p. 10.

8. *Ibid.*, p. 10.

9. Material from the MS. of *David Copperfield* is published by permission of the V. & A. Museum. 'Dire' is probably the correct reading, but this is not beyond question. Whatever the deleted word, however, it was certainly an adjective strengthening 'neglect.'

10. *David Copperfield*, p. 400.

11. *Ibid.*, pp. 408–9.

12. Forster, *op. cit.*, p. 553.

13. *David Copperfield*, p. 165.

14. Forster, *op. cit.*, p. 13.

15. *David Copperfield*, p. 165.

16. Forster, *op. cit.*, pp. 13–14.

17. *Letters*, Nonesuch Ed., Vol. II, p. 875.

18. *David Copperfield*, p. 257.

19. *Ibid.*, p. 256.

20. *David Copperfield*, p. 264.

21. *Ibid.*, p. 262.

22. *Ibid.*, p. 412.

23. *Nicholas Nickleby*, p. 39.

24. Forster, *op. cit.*, pp. 551, and K. J. Fielding, "The Making of David Copperfield," *The Listener*, July 19th, 1951.

25. *Great Expectations*, p. 243.

26. *David Copperfield*, p. 159.

27. *Ibid.*, p. 163.

28. *Ibid.*, p. 534.

29. Quoted by E. Wagenknecht, *The Man Charles Dickens*, 1966, p. 22.

30. *David Copperfield*, p. 402.

31. Forster, *op. cit.*, p. 55.

JOHN CAREY

Dickens and Violence

In Dickens' travel book *Pictures from Italy* he describes how on February 21, 1845, he, 31 guides, 6 saddled ponies and a handful of tourists made an ascent of Mount Vesuvius. The local people warned him it was the wrong time of year, especially for a night ascent. Snow and ice lay thick on the summit. Characteristically he ignored the advice of these 'croakers', as he called them. His wife and another lady and gentleman had to be carried in litters. Dickens went on foot. As the party approached the top, blundering in the darkness over the broken ground, half suffocated with sulphurous fumes, Dickens' description of the sheets of fire, and the red-hot stones and cinders flying into the air 'like feathers', becomes more and more excited. 'There is something', he relates, 'in the fire and the roar, that generates an irresistible desire to get nearer to it.' Not that this desire was felt by the others. While Dickens, a guide and the other crawled to the edge of the crater, the rest of the party cowered below in the hot ashes yelling to them of the danger. 'What with their noise,' writes Dickens,

> and what with the trembling of the thin crust of ground, that seems about to open underneath our feet and plunge us in the burning gulf below which is the real danger, if there be any); and what with the flashing of the fire in our faces, and the shower of

From *The Violent Effigy: A Study of Dickens' Imagination.* © John Carey, 1973, 1991.

red hot ashes that is raining down, and the choking smoke and sulphur; we may well feel giddy and irrational, like drunken men. But we contrive to climb up to the brim, and look down, for a moment, into the Hell of boiling fire below. Then, we all three come rolling down; blackened and singed, and scorched, and hot, and giddy: and each with his dress alight in half-a-dozen places.

On the way down one of the tourists falls—'skimming over the white ice, like a cannon-ball'—and almost at the same moment two of the guides come rolling past. Dickens is offended, unreasonably enough, by the cries of dismay the other guides send up. Luckily all three casualties are eventually recovered, none of them badly injured.

The anecdote is typical of Dickens. Typical of his disregard for other people—his 'hard and aggressive' nature, 'impetuous' and 'overbearing', in Forster's words; typical of his enormous and unquenchable desire for activity, for something which would use up his dynamic energies; and typical of his fascination with fire as a beautiful and terrible destroyer, a visible expression of pure violence. In Rome on Easter Sunday he watches St. Peter's stuck all over with fireworks, and records his sense of exultation at seeing great, red fires suddenly burst out from every part of the building, so that the black groundwork of the dome 'seemed to grow transparent as an eggshell'. Railway trains and steamboats excite him as moving fires. In his American travel book he describes the engine which takes them across the country as a thirsty monster, a dragon, yelling and panting along its rails, scattering a shower of sparks in all directions. Crossing the Atlantic on board the *Britannia* in 1840 he was impressed at night by the way light gleamed out from every chink and aperture about the decks 'as though the ship were filled with fire in hiding, ready to burst through any outlet, wild with its resistless power of death and ruin'.

In *Dombey and Son* the railway train becomes a fiery animal with 'red eyes, bleared and dim in the daylight', which smashes Carker when he unwisely steps on its track. It 'struck him limb from limb, and licked his stream of life up with its fiery heat, and cast his mutilated fragments in the air'. But fire had been used to express violence in the novels before this. In *Oliver Twist*, in the scene where Nancy suddenly braves Fagin and Sikes, the signs of human passion—Nancy stamping her foot and going white with rage—are reinforced when she seizes Fagin's club and flings it into the fire, 'with a force', Dickens notes, 'that brought some of the glowing coals whirling out into the room'. It's as if the human actors are inadequate to embody the violence of Dickens' idea, and he has to bring in fire to express it. This scene is recalled when Sikes murders Nancy. Afterwards he lights a fire and thrusts his club into it. Dickens vivifies the moment with an incandescent detail: 'There was hair upon the end, which blazed and shrunk into a light cinder, and, caught by the air, whirled up the chimney.' Running away from his murder, Sikes suddenly comes upon a conflagration:

> The broad sky seemed on fire. Rising into the air with showers of sparks, and rolling one above the other, were sheets of flame, lighting the atmosphere for miles around, and driving clouds of smoke in the direction where he stood.

It is, in fact, a house on fire, and Dickens fills in the circumstances with his usual enthusiasm for such subjects—the 'molten lead and iron' pouring white-hot onto the ground, and so on. The episode seems an arbitrary intrusion, quite redundant so far as the plot is concerned, unless one sees it as a projection of the violence and torment within Sikes. Similarly in Peggotty's abode, when David Copperfield comes upon the lustful Steerforth snarling about 'this Devil's bark of a boat', the malcontent seizes a piece of wood from the fire and strikes out of it 'a train of red-hot sparks that went careering up the little chimney, and roaring out into the air'—just to impress upon the reader the dangerous state he's in. Fire spells peril as well as passion. In *Bleak House*, Esther first comes upon Ada and Richard 'standing near a great, loud-roaring fire' with a screen 'interposed between them and it'. Our sense of destruction reaching towards youth and beauty becomes definite when this fire is given 'red eyes' like a 'Chancery lion'.

The violence of a mob, which always intensely excites Dickens, is repeatedly conveyed through its fiery antics. In *Barnaby Rudge* the molten lead on Bill Sikes' house recurs in the magnificent scene where the rioters burn down Mr. Haredale's mansion:

> There were men who cast their lighted torches in the air, and suffered them to fall upon their heads and faces, blistering their skin with deep unseemly burns. There were men who rushed up to the fire, and paddled in it with their hands as if in water; and others who were restrained by force from plunging in, to gratify their deadly longing. On the skull of one drunken lad—not twenty, by his looks—who lay upon the ground with a bottle to his mouth, the lead from the roof came streaming down in a shower of liquid fire, white-hot; melting his head like wax.

Later in the novel, when Newgate prison is stormed, the mob build a fire against the main gate, and men can be seen in the middle of the flames trying to prise down the red-hot metal with crowbars. The same mob howls and exults as Lord Mansfield's Law library, with its priceless collection of manuscripts, goes up in flames. Seeing the violence directed against a prison and the law should remind us how much Dickens, the Dickens who was to write *Little Dorrit* and *Bleak House*, is imaginatively on the side of the rioters and wreckers, despite the dutiful expressions of dismay with which he surrounds the scene. 'I have let all the prisoners out of Newgate, burnt down Lord Mansfield's, and played the very devil,' he wrote exultingly to Forster, 'I feel quite smoky.' Similarly in *A Tale of Two Cities* the chateau, symbol of aristocratic oppression, is fired in a scene reminiscent of the St. Peter's firework display. At first the chateau begins 'to make itself strangely visible, by some light of its own, as though it were growing luminous'. Soon flames burst out of the windows, rents and splits branch out in the solid walls 'like crystallization', and lead and iron boil in the marble basin of the fountain. The 'illuminated village' rings its bells for joy.

Even when a mob can't actually burn things, Dickens gives it bits of fire to signify its rage and frenzy. The mob which hunts down Sikes is 'a struggling current of angry faces, with here and there a glaring torch to light them up'. Similarly, if a character can't be supplied with a blazing house to symbolize his violence, the fire can be conveyed in the imagery. When, in *Little Dorrit*, Mrs. Clennam is eventually goaded beyond endurance by Rigaud, she defies him, Dickens says, 'with the set expression of her face all torn away by the explosion of her passion, and with a bursting from every rent feature of the smouldering fire so long pent up'. Mrs. Clennam, like the steamship *Britannia*, shows fire at every porthole. Introducing Krook, the villainous rag and bottle dealer in *Bleak House*, Dickens draws attention to 'the breath issuing in visible smoke from his mouth, as if he were on fire within'. Unlike Mrs. Clennam and the *Britannia*, Krook does, of course, literally explode later in the novel, leaving nothing but oily soot on the walls of his room. Dickens regularly spoke of his own industry and his need for strenuous exercise in the same fiery terms. 'I blaze away, wrathful and red-hot,' he reported, at work on *The Chimes*. 'If I couldn't walk fast and far I should just explode.'

Great Expectations is another novel which plays with fire. The blacksmith's furnace, with its red-hot sparks and murky shadows, and its two giants, Joe and Orlick, one good, one bad, is an imaginative touchstone in the book. Walking home at night Pip notices the furnace 'flinging a path of fire across the road'. Out on the marshes the torches of the search party are intensely seen. 'The torches we carried, dropped great blotches of fire upon the track, and I could see those, too, lying smoking and flaring ... Our lights warmed the air about us with their pitchy blaze.' Pip's sister is murderously struck down by a blow on the head at a moment when, Dickens notes, 'her face was turned towards the fire.' Pip sees the face of Estella's mother 'as if it were all disturbed by fiery air', like a face passing behind 'a bowl of flaming spirits in a darkened room'. Dickens intends this as an index, of course, of the criminal passions that lurk within. Miss Havisham goes up in flames, 'shrieking, with a whirl of fire blazing all about her, and soaring at least as many feet above her head as she was high'. She had, of course, tempted providence by becoming so fond of Joe's blacksmith song about fire 'soaring higher', which Pip taught her. The image of her rouged corpse with fire bursting from its head had so strong an appeal, it seems, that Dickens attached it, rather gratuitously, to Magwitch as well. The disguise Magwitch contrives for leaving London includes a 'touch of powder', which suggests to Pip:

> the probable effect of rouge upon the dead; so awful was the manner in which everything in him, that it was most desirable to repress, started through the thin layer of pretence, and seemed to come blazing out at the crown of his head.

Miss Havisham on fire, and the fire of Joe's smithy, fuse in Pip's mind. Delirious, after his own narrow escape from being burned in Orlick's lime-kiln, he dreams of an iron furnace in a corner of his room, and a voice calling that Miss Havisham is burning within. Pip's sick fancy recalls Esther Summerson's dream, striking in one so uninflammable, that she is a bead on a 'flaming necklace' in 'black space', praying to be released from 'the dreadful thing'.

Joe is a good character, of course: the repository of those natural, human affections that Dickens dwells upon with such patronizing approval. His association with fire warns us that in Dickens' imaginative landscape fire is not simply the sign of violence and destruction. It is a leading characteristic of Dickens' mind that he is able to see almost everything from two opposed points of view. In his thinking about society this often makes him look confused and hypocritical, as we have noted. Even a major Dickensian property like the prison is viewed at different times as a hideous deprivation of freedom and as a snug retreat from the world. Some of the prisoners released from Newgate by the mob, creep back and 'lounge about the old place'. For them it's home. So, too, with fire. A violent, though enthralling destroyer on the one hand, it also becomes, in the innumerable cosy Dickensian inn parlours with their blazing logs, a natural accompaniment to comfort and security. The fire of Joe Gargery's forge represents the safety of the childhood home. It flings a path of fire across Pip's road as a friendly, domestic warning to turn him aside from his ruinous ambitions. With something of the same purpose, no doubt, it tries to cremate Miss Havisham, who has done her best to make Pip rebel against the values of home and fireside.

The episode in *The Old Curiosity Shop* where Nell and her grandfather make a brief excursion into the industrial midlands neatly illustrates Dickens' two ways of looking at fire. A lurid glare in the sky hangs over the neighbourhood, and the wanderers meet a factory worker, imagined by Dickens as a sort of smoky goblin, who lets them spend a comfortable night in the ashes beside his furnace. This touching scene is strangely out of key with the way the factory is described. It is said to be full of the 'deafening' noise of hammers. Men move 'like demons' among the flame and smoke, 'tormented by the burning fires', and drag from the white-hot furnace doors sheets of clashing steel, 'emitting an insupportable heat, and a dull deep light like that which reddens in the eyes of savage beasts'. The factory worker proves communicative about his own particular fire. It has been alive, he says, as long as he has. He crawled among its ashes as a baby. It's his 'book' and his 'memory': he sees faces and scenes among its red-hot coals. In Dickens' terms this marks him as a good character. Only virtuous people in the novels practise this species of fire watching. We recall Lizzie Hexam in *Our Mutual Friend* who develops her imagination by looking at red-hot embers, in strong contrast to her selfish brother Charlie who wants to better himself by reading books. The fire in this episode, then, is both nurse and destroyer; the fire of home and the fire of Hell.

Dickens, who saw himself as the great prophet of cosy, domestic virtue, purveyor of improving literature to the middle classes, never seems to have quite reconciled himself to the fact that violence and destruction were the most powerful stimulants to his imagination. To the end of his career he continues to insert the sickly scenes of family fun, and seriously asks us to accept them as the positives in his fiction. The savages and the cynics, the Quilps and the Scrooges, who have all the vitality, are, in the end, tritely punished or improbably converted. His public championship of domestic bliss became so natural to him that he persisted in it even when his own actions wildly belied it. Starting a new magazine in 1859, he seriously proposed to call it *Household Harmony*, despite the fact that he had recently separated from his wife, had personally announced in the newspapers that she was an unsatisfactory mother disliked by all her children, and was himself having an affair with the actress Ellen Ternan. When Forster pointed out that the proposed title would be met with derision, Dickens was surprised and irritated.

With so much of his imaginative self invested in his violent and vicious characters, and so much of the self he approved of vowed to the service of home and family life, Dickens has a particular weakness for villains whose express intention it is to smash up happy homes. Silas Wegg in *Our Mutual Friend* walks to the Boffin house each evening in order to gloat over it like an evil genius, exulting in his power 'to strip the roof off the inhabiting family like the roof of a house of cards'. It was, says Dickens, 'a treat which had a charm for Silas Wegg'. For Dickens too, to judge from the vigour of the image. Steerforth, in *David Copperfield*, smashes the pure Peggotty home by seducing Little Em'ly. The old converted boat in which the Peggottys pursue their blameless existence is blown down on the night of the storm which drowns Steerforth. David finds him next morning, lying appropriately 'among the ruins of the home he had wronged'. Even Gabriel Varden in *Barnaby Rudge* indulges in some miniature home-smashing. Mrs. Varden has been in the habit of putting her voluntary contributions to the Protestant cause in a collecting box shaped like a little red-brick dwelling house with a yellow roof. When the riots show how mistaken her allegiance has been, Gabriel throws the little house on the floor and crushes it with his heel. So much for little houses, militant Protestants and meddling females. Apart from the home, the main haunt of Dickensian snugness is the inn. Of the Maypole Inn in *Barnaby Rudge* he writes 'All bars are snug places, but the Maypole's was the very snuggest, cosiest and completest bar, that ever the wit of man devised.' A rhapsodic description of its neat rows of bottles in oaken pigeonholes, and its snowy loaves of sugar follows. It's appropriate that this veritable temple of snugness and security should be selected by Dickens for one of his wildest home-wrecking scenes. When the mob arrive at the Maypole, equipped with their usual flaring torches, they smash the glass, turn all the liquor taps on, hack the cheeses to bits, break open the drawers, saw down the inn sign and are divided in opinion whether to hang the landlord or burn him alive. Dickens' tone is predominantly comic, and there is no mistaking the pleasure with which he elaborates the details of pillage and destruction.

Early in his career Dickens began to produce narratives in which the figures who are regarded with the most intense fellow feeling are the murderers. He habitually speaks about murderers' mental habits with extraordinary self-confidence, as if he were one himself. The consequences of murder, he asserts in *Bleak House*, are always hidden from the murderer behind a 'gigantic dilation' of his victim, and rush upon him only when the blow is struck. This 'always happens when a murder is done'. Similarly he is adamant that murderers like Sikes, who do not give 'the faintest indication of a better nature', really do exist. 'That the fact is so, I am sure.' From where, we wonder, could he get such certainty? The conformist part of him repudiated his murderers with horror. But the artist delved with fascination into their responses, and particularly into how they feel when hunted down or at bay. In *Master Humphrey's Clock*, for instance, we find a first-person narrative in which Dickens casts himself in the role of a child slayer, telling what it was like to murder his brother's son. He stabs him in a garden, and as he does so he is struck not only by the look in his victim's eyes, but also by the eyes which seem to watch him, even in the drops of water on the leaves. 'There were eyes in everything.' He buries the child in a piece of ground which is to be newly turfed, but when the lawn has been completed over the grave he is haunted by visions of the child's hand or his foot or his head sticking up through the grass. He sits and watches the secret grave all day. 'When a servant walked across it, I felt as if he must sink in; when he had passed, I looked to see that his feet had not worn the edges.' Eventually he has a table set out on the lawn, and puts his chair directly over the grave, so that no one can disturb it. When he is entertaining some friends at this table, though, two great bloodhounds come bounding into the garden and circle about it excitedly, ending up snuffing at the earth directly under his chair. As his friends dragged him away, he says, 'I saw the angry dogs tearing at the earth and throwing it up into the air like water.' Bill Sikes, like this murderer, is haunted by eyes after his slaying of Nancy, and it is his dog's eyes gleaming from behind the chimney pot that send him plunging to his death. '"The eyes again!" he cried in an unearthly screech.' Similarly the elder Mr. Rudge, who has little to occupy himself with in the novel besides galloping furiously through the night, is brought to life for a moment when Dickens shows him remembering the circumstances of the murder he committed. He recalls how his victim's face went stiff, 'and so fell idly down with upturned eyes, like the dead stags' he had often peeped at when a little child: 'shrinking and shuddering ... and clinging to an apron as he looked.' The flash of childhood recollection at the moment of murder is instantly convincing: the one convincing sentence about Mr. Rudge in the entire book. Again, Jonas Chuzzlewit isn't generally a figure we feel Dickens has managed to get inside. He is viewed from above as a vile, cringing specimen with whom we can all feel virtuously disgusted. But in the few pages where he commits murder he suddenly becomes the recipient of Dickens' imaginative sympathy. The details of the blotched; stained, mouldering room with its gurgling water-pipes in which Jonas locks himself are intently conveyed. When he unlocks the long-unused door in order to slink off and murder Montague Tigg, Dickens makes the reader attend to his tiniest movements:

> He put the key into the lock, and turned it. The door resisted for
> a while, but soon came stiffly open; mingling with the sense of

fever in his mouth, a taste of rust, and dust, and earth, and rotting
wood.

We know even what the murderer's mouth tastes like. After the murder,
Jonas keeps fancying himself creeping back through the undergrowth to peer
at the corpse, 'startling the very flies that were thickly, sprinkled all over it,
like heaps of dried currants'. The simile—added in the manuscript—shows
Dickens' imagination entrapped by the scene, like Jonas'. But Jonas has to
commit murder to get promoted from the status of a routine Dickensian
villain and earn himself a page or two of great literature. No other human
experience—least of all the positive human experiences, like being in love—
will arouse Dickens to such intense imaginative sympathy as the experience
of being a murderer. One of his most vivid studies in this mode is Fagin on
trial for his life—a very different matter from Fagin in the death cell a few
pages later, where he is transformed into a gibbering wretch for the unctuous
Oliver to pity. Fagin's sensations in the courtroom are recorded as
scrupulously as Jonas Chuzzlewit's:

> He looked up into the gallery again. Some of the people were
> eating, and some fanning themselves with handkerchiefs; for the
> crowded place was very hot. There was one young man sketching
> his face in a little notebook. He wondered whether it was like,
> and looked on when the artist broke his pencil point, and made
> another with his knife, as any idle spectator might have done ...
> There was an old fat gentleman on the bench, too, who had gone
> out, some half an hour before, and now come back. He wondered
> within himself whether this man had been to get his dinner, what
> he had had, and where he had had it ... He fell to counting the
> iron spikes before him, and wondering how the head of one had
> been broken off, and whether they would mend it or leave it as it
> was.

Here the hypersensitivity, combined with a strange feeling of detachment,
common to people who find themselves at the centre of an accident, are
conveyed by Dickens with absolute seriousness of intent and perfect
artistic honesty. The temptation to use Fagin as the occasion for lofty
moralizing is withstood, though Dickens succumbs to it soon afterwards.
Oliver's reactions after the trial are, by contrast, wholly preposterous:
"'Oh! God forgive this wretched man!'" cried the boy with a burst of
tears.... Oliver nearly swooned after this frightful scene, and was so weak
that for an hour or more, he had not the strength to walk.' Dickens could

furnish this type of saintly confection in unlimited quantities, but the triumphs of his art stick out of it like islands, and there is no difficulty about distinguishing them.

Before Oliver's visit Fagin's mind is seized with the details of how murderers are disposed of: 'With what a rattling noise the drop went down; and how suddenly they changed, from strong and vigorous men to dangling heaps of clothes.' A keen interest in the different methods of executing men, and the precise manner of each, was another aspect of Dickens' preoccupation with violence. The guillotine stands in the foreground of *A Tale of Two Cities*. Charles Darnay, in the condemned cell, realizes he has never seen it, and questions about it keep thrusting themselves into his mind: 'How high it was from the ground, how many steps it had, where he would be stood ... which way his face would be turned.' Dickens could have enlightened him. When in Rome he went to see a man guillotined, and has left a minute account of the whole affair, from the behaviour of the various members of the crowd to the appearance of the scaffold: 'An untidy, unpainted, uncouth, crazy-looking thing ... some seven feet high, perhaps: with a tall, gallows-shaped frame rising above it, in which was the knife, charged with a ponderous mass of iron.' The prisoner appears on the platform, barefoot, hands bound, the collar and neck of his shirt cut away. A young, pale man, with a small dark moustache, and dark brown hair.

> He immediately kneeled down, below the knife. His neck fitting into a hole, made for the purpose, in a cross plank, was shut down, by another plank above; exactly like the pillory. Immediately below him was a leathern bag. And into it his head rolled instantly.
>
> The executioner was holding it by the hair, and walking with it round the scaffold, showing it to the people, before one quite knew that the knife had fallen heavily, and with a rattling sound.

The head is set up on a pole—'a little patch of black and white' for 'the flies to settle on'. The eyes, Dickens notices, are turned up, 'as if he had avoided the sight of the leathern bag'. He stays on to see the scaffold washed down, observing 'There was a great deal of blood,' and to get a closer look at the body.

> A strange appearance was the apparent annihilation of the neck. The head was taken off so close, that it seemed as if the knife had narrowly escaped crushing the jaw, or shaving off the

ear; and the body looked as if there were nothing left above the shoulder.

The eager, graphic brilliance of the writing throughout hardly prepares one for the moral stance Dickens hastily adopts at the end, complaining that the crowd was callous, and that several attempts were made to pick his pocket during the spectacle.

In July 1840 Dickens was one of the 40,000 people who witnessed the hanging of the murderer Courvoisier. Writing of it later he is again hot against the pickpockets, and stigmatizes the disgraceful behaviour of the crowd, whose motives for being there, he leaves us in no doubt, are altogether more reprehensible than his own. Opposed in principle to capital punishment, he plainly cannot admit to himself that he watches it out of curiosity, like everyone else. When Mr. and Mrs. George Manning were hanged together in 1849 on top of the Horsemonger Lane Gaol, Dickens was in attendance again to see them 'turned quivering into the air'. He recalls the curious difference in appearance between the two dangling bodies: 'the man's, a limp, loose suit of clothes as if the man had gone out of them; the woman's, a fine shape, so elaborately corseted and artfully dressed, that it was quite unchanged in its trim appearance as it slowly swung from side to side'. In Switzerland he went to see a man beheaded, and writes an account later in *Household Words*. The victim sits tied to a chair on a scaffold, and the executioner uses a huge sword loaded with quicksilver in the thick part of the blade.

It's plain that Dickens derives a considerable thrill, too, from visiting localities where executions and murders have occurred. The only thing that redeemed the city of Norwich, in his eyes, was its place of execution, 'fit for a gigantic scoundrel's exit'. After a tour of the prison at Venice he writes, 'I had my foot upon the spot, where ... the shriven prisoner was strangled.' In the Tombs Prison in New York he has himself conducted to the yard where prisoners are hanged: 'The wretched creature stands beneath the gibbet on the ground; the rope about his neck; and when the sign is given, a weight at its other end comes running down, and swings him up into the air—a corpse.' Dickens preferred this method to the English—'far less degrading and indecent'. By the time he visited America again, a former acquaintance of his had been able to assess its advantages. This was Professor Webster of Harvard, hanged for murdering a colleague, portions of whose body he had concealed about his lecture room. Dickens eagerly inspected the scene of the crime, sniffed the unpleasant odours of the furnace—'some anatomical broth in it I suppose'—and peered at the 'pieces of sour mortality' standing around in jars. In *Sketches by Boz* he relates how he often wanders into Newgate

Prison 'to catch a glimpse of the whipping place, and that dark building on one side of the yard, in which is kept the gibbet with all its dreadful apparatus'. Dennis the hangman in *Barnaby Rudge* provides Dickens with ample opportunity for anecdotes about the dreadful apparatus and its operation. The first feature of Dennis to which Dickens draws attention is his neck, with its great veins 'swollen and starting'. A neck for stretching, as Dennis himself would say, and at the end of the novel it is stretched—unlike that of the real-life Dennis, who was reprieved. Several aspects of the execution scene show that Dickens' imaginative powers have been aroused: Dennis between two officers, unable to walk for terror, his legs trailing on the ground; the room into which the prisoners are taken to have their irons struck off, so close to the gallows that they can plainly hear people in the crowd outside complaining of the crush; and the gallows itself, its black paint blistering in the sun, and 'its nooses dangling ... like loathsome garlands'.

A form of violence more exotic and, to Dickens' way of thinking, more amusing than capital punishment was cannibalism, and we can see his thoughts straying towards it on several occasions. He was introduced to the subject by his nurse, Mary Weller, who used to take a fiendish delight in terrifying him with the story of a certain Captain Murderer whose practice it was to get his tender young brides to make a piecrust into which he would then chop them up, adding pepper and salt. The resultant pie he would eat, with his teeth filed sharp by the blacksmith for the occasion. He was finally thwarted by a bride who took deadly poison just before he killed her, so that after his meal he began to swell and turn blue, and went on swelling until he blew up with a loud explosion—an early version of Krook in *Bleak House*. The Fat Boy in *Pickwick Papers* has similar tendencies. He is about to consume a meat pie when he notices Mary, the pretty housemaid, sitting opposite. He leans forward, knife and fork in hand, and slowly enunciates: 'I say! How nice you look.' 'There was enough of the cannibal in the young gentleman's eyes', Dickens remarks, 'to render the compliment a double one.' When Hugh in *Barnaby Rudge* has the delicious Dolly Varden and haughty Emma Haredale at his mercy, imprisoned in a closed carriage, he insists on speaking of them as delicate, tender birds, and stares into the carriage, we are told, 'like an ogre into his larder'. Furthermore Dickens is just as excited as Hugh and his confederates at the sight of tempting, helpless femininity, and hardly conceals the fact. 'Poor Dolly! Do what she would, she only looked the better for it, and tempted them the more. When her eyes flashed angrily, and her ripe lips slightly parted, to give her rapid breathing vent, who could resist it?' Not Dickens, we gather, who is evidently salivating freely. It is by far his sexiest scene, which makes the cannibalistic hint more worth noting. Even Pecksniff, in *Martin Chuzzlewit*, has a cannibalistic impulse when forcing his attentions on the maidenly Mary Grant, having first got her alone in a wood, as Hugh does with Dolly Varden. Mary struggles but, Dickens comments, 'she might as well have tried to free herself from the embrace of an affectionate boa-constrictor.' Pecksniff clutches one of her hands, despite her attempts to pull it free, and gazes at it speculatively, 'tracing the course of one delicate blue vein with his fat thumb'. Eventually he holds up her little finger and asks, 'in playful accents', 'Shall I bite it?' But the tearful, trembling Mary doesn't get nibbled after all: Pecksniff kisses the finger and lets her have it back. In both these scenes the flutterings of female distress and the humbling of female pride are evidently so appetizing to Dickens that it is really hypocritical of him to pretend that the two men concerned are thorough rogues with whom he has no sympathy. But as usual he can preserve his moral composure only by foisting his violent imaginings onto another character, whom he then condemns for imagining them. A further edible heroine is Estella—or so it seems to Miss Havisham, who eyes the girl 'with a ravenous intensity', 'as though she were devouring the beautiful creature.' In *Bleak House* the cannibal is the dyspeptic Vholes. Given to regarding Richard 'as if he were making a lingering meal of him', he finally quits the novel with a gasp, suggesting that he has 'swallowed the last morsel of his client'. Opponents of legal reform defend Vholes' livelihood as though he and his relations were 'minor cannibal chiefs' threatened by the abolition of cannibalism. 'Make man-eating unlawful, and you starve the Vholeses!' Pip in *Great Expectations* is likewise an edible hero. Magwitch, on the marsh, is immediately tempted by his plumpness: "'You young dog," said the man, licking his lips, "what fat cheeks you ha' got ... Darn Me if I couldn't eat 'em".' He refrains, however, and instead tells Pip about the young man whom he is with difficulty holding back from tearing out Pip's heart and liver and eating them, roasted. Uncle Pumblechook's mouth seems to water too, at the sight of the succulent boy, and he takes pleasure in informing Pip that if he had been born a pig Dunstable the butcher would have come along and seized him under his arm and taken out his penknife from his waistcoat pocket and killed him for pork. 'He would have shed your blood and had your life.' 'I'm a going to have your life!' declares Orlick, later in the novel, when he has Pip all ready trussed up in the sluice-house on the marsh: 'He leaned forward staring at me, slowly unclenched his hand and drew it across his mouth as if his mouth watered for me.' It's unusual to find a hero who has such difficulty keeping himself out of the stomachs of the other characters.

Dickens' need to express his violent and murderous instincts through his fiction can be seen, of course, as early as *Pickwick Papers*. But there the tales of savagery and slaughter are kept apart from the main narrative and are quite untouched by the humour which pervades it. In the tale called *A Madman's Manuscript*, for example, Dickens tries to imagine himself into a demented wife-slayer: 'Oh! the pleasure of stropping the razor day after day, feeling the sharp edge, and thinking of the gash one stroke of its thin bright edge would make!' Another of the inset tales concerns a man who murderously avenges himself for the imprisonment of himself and his family in the Marshalsea. This, it has been conjectured, may mean that Dickens' resentment against society over his father's imprisonment is one of the roots of his violence. But the *Pickwick* tales, particularly *A Madman's Manuscript*, are forced and melodramatic, because Dickens' sense of humour, his greatest gift as a novelist, simply switches off when he starts to tell them. Not until the writing of *The Old Curiosity Shop* in 1840 did he create an embodiment of his violence who could also express his black and anarchic laughter. This embodiment was Daniel Quilp, a magnificent invention who is able to embrace all the variations of violence Dickens can desire.

Quilp is both dwarf and giant—a dwarf in body, with a giant's head. For teeth he has a few discoloured fangs, and he is so filthy that when he rubs his hands together the dirt drops off in pellets. Much of his time is spent in driving to ludicrous excess the components of Dickensian cheeriness. Conviviality trails a hair-raising image of itself around with it. Food consumption, for instance, is an indispensable accompaniment of Dickensian bliss. Quilp approaches meals with horrible ferocity. He eats hard-boiled eggs shell and all. He devours 'gigantic prawns with the heads and tails on'. He chews tobacco and watercress at the same time, and bites his fork and spoon until they bend. He smokes pipes of hideous strength, and forces his guests to do the same, warning them that otherwise he will put the sealing-waxed end in the fire and rub it red-hot on their tongues. He drinks boiling spirit, bubbling and hissing fiercely, straight from the saucepan. He pinches his wife black and blue, bites her, and keeps her in constant terror of the ingenious punishments he devises. For all this she is utterly infatuated, and tells her lady friends that they would all marry Quilp tomorrow if they had a chance. What's more, Dickens implies that she is right. His corrected proofs show that Quilp was originally meant to have a child by Sally Brass—an earnest of his exceptional virility. When amused, Quilp screams and rolls on the floor. He delights in tormenting animals as well as people. Finding a dog chained up he taunts it with hideous faces, and dances round it snapping his fingers, driving it wild with rage. He keeps a huge wooden figurehead of an admiral, sawn off at the waist, in his room, and diverts himself by driving red-hot pokers through it. He is, in short, a masterpiece of creative energy in comparison with whom Little Nell and her grandfather and all their part of the novel are so much waste paper.

Dickens was never able to create a second Quilp, but bits of him turn up in the other novels. His treatment of his wife is reflected in Flintwinch in *Little Dorrit*, who shakes Mrs. Flintwinch by the throat till she's black in the face, and twists her nose between his thumb and finger with all the 'screw-power of his person'. Cruncher in *A Tale of Two Cities*, who flings boots at his wife because she insists on saying her prayers, has Quilpish quality too. Quilp's taste for boiling spirit is something he shares with the maddened rioters in *Barnaby Rudge*. When a vintner's house catches light they lap up the scorching liquor which flows along the gutters, dropping dead by the dozen, rolling and hissing in a lake of flame, and splashing up liquid fire. Already in *Pickwick Papers*, in the story of the goblins and the sexton, the goblin king had drunk blazing liquor, his cheeks and throat growing transparent as he swallowed it. And the thrill of blistering beverages survives in *Our Mutual Friend*. Jenny Wren, saddled with a sottish parent, invents a short way with drunkards:

> When he was asleep, I'd make a spoon red-hot, and I'd have some boiling liquor bubbling in a saucepan, and I'd take it out hissing, and I'd open his mouth with the other hand—or perhaps he'd sleep with his mouth ready open—and I'd pour it down his throat, and blister it and choke him.

Quilp piercing the admiral with a red-hot poker is recalled in David Copperfield's vindictive fantasies relative to Uriah Heep. When Heep is audacious enough to fall in love with Agnes, David is tempted to seize the red-hot poker from the fire and run him through the body with it. That night he dreams so vividly that he's actually done this that he has to creep into Heep's bedroom to make sure he's still alive. Pip in *Great Expectations* recalls how Orlick drew a red-hot bar from the furnace and 'made at me with it as if he were going to run it through my body'. According to Dickens, one of his nurse's ghoulish tales featured a lady who slew her husband with a heated poker, so his interest in this topic began early.

Quilp is Dickens' way of avenging himself upon the sentimental set-up of *The Old Curiosity Shop*, upon all that part of his nature that revelled in angelic, plaster heroines, the deaths of little children, and touching animals. To aid her in her assault on the readers' hearts, for example, Nell has a little bird in a cage. Quilp threatens to wring its neck. He is salaciously inclined towards Little Nell herself, gloats over her blue veins and transparent skin, and invites her to become the second Mrs. Quilp. Nell trembles violently, much to Quilp's amusement. When he takes over Nell's grandfather's house, he chooses her own little bed to sleep in. Dickens offers violence to his own sexless heroine in these passages, and with aggressive enjoyment. Quilp's reduction of his wife to a mass of bruises gives an outlet to Dickens' punitive feelings towards women, which he felt the need to repress when speaking about them in his own person. In *Martin Chuzzlewit*, reporting that Jonas actually struck his wife, Dickens soars into virtuous indignation and the second person singular—always a bad sign with him: 'Oh woman, God beloved in old Jerusalem! The best among us need deal lightly with thy faults.' After the strain of such noble attitudes Quilp would clearly be a relief.

Both before and after 1840 Dickens attempted to create violent villains, but none ever rivals Quilp, because their violence seems stuck on, not essential to their natures, as Quilp's is. Monks, for instance, in *Oliver Twist*, has fits, writhes on the ground, foams at the mouth, bites his hands and covers them with wounds, and entertains the Bumbles to the accompaniment of thunder and lightning. But he lacks Quilp's humour and energy. On the one occasion he tries to hit Oliver, he falls over. Uriah Heep has an isolated moment of violent power. This is in the scene with David where he tells him he has Agnes' father, Mr. Wickfield, under his thumb:

> 'Un—der—his thumb,' said Uriah, very slowly, as he stretched
> out his cruel-looking hand above my table, and pressed his own
> thumb down upon it, until it shook, and shook the room.

Heep is a boy of 15, and nothing in his cringing gait or starved appearance suggests a figure who could shake a whole room merely by pressing the table with his thumb. In this instant he is about to turn into an altogether different and more violent creation, but Dickens doesn't forget himself again.

Thomas Wright notes that Quilp's mother-in-law Mrs. Jiniwin was modelled on Dickens' mother-in-law Mrs. Hogarth. Quilp was, in a sense, Dickens himself, as seen through his mother-in-law's disapproving eyes. In his last completed novel Dickens drew another violent villain, also to some degree a self-portrait—Bradley Headstone. Headstone's jealous love for Lizzie Hexam is usually taken to reflect Dickens' feelings for his young mistress Ellen Ternan, and the location of Headstone's school, Edgar Johnson has noticed, parallels that of the house, Windsor Lodge, which Dickens had rented for Ellen. Comparing Headstone with Quilp's fine demonic rapture allows us to see how much has been lost over the years. Headstone is presented as a man of terrible passions which lurk beneath a respectable exterior. When moved, his lips quiver uncontrollably, blood gushes from his nose, his face turns 'from burning red to white, and from white back to burning red', and he punches a stone wall until his knuckles are raw and bleeding. When he hears of Lizzie's marriage he throws a fit, and bites and lashes about. As he sleeps, red and blue lightning and palpitating white fire flicker about his bed. On one of his particularly bad nights Dickens shows him sitting in front of the fire, 'the dark lines deepening in his face ... and the very texture and colour of his hair degenerating'. Despite all these alarming physical symptoms, though, Headstone is utterly helpless and ineffective. He has no weapons against Eugene Wrayburn's cool irony, which goads him almost to madness. There is no glimmer of humour about him or his presentation. Compared to Quilp, he is a lamb for the slaughter. He is sexually null too. His desire for Lizzie is a dry, theoretic passion. There is nothing to show he even notices her body, as Quilp does Nell's.

The trouble is that Headstone is only partly a vehicle for Dickens' love for Ellen. He also has to serve as a diagram for certain social developments that Dickens deplores. From humble origins he has raised himself by hard work and is now a schoolmaster. Dickens, formerly a hearty advocate of universal education, now sees it as the breeder of pedantry and social pretensions. Once educated, the lower classes get above themselves. In his decent black coat and waistcoat Headstone looks, Dickens says, like a workman in his holiday clothes. He might have made a good sailor if, when a pauper child, he had taken to the sea instead of to learning. As it is, his learning is merely mechanically acquired. Needless to say, Dickens doesn't explain what the alternative ways of acquiring learning might be. When Headstone has committed, or thinks he has committed, murder, he is made into a model to illustrate another of Dickens' pet social theories: that the murderer is never sorry for his crime. All Headstone can think about is how he might have got rid of Wrayburn more efficiently. Dickens is no longer an opponent of capital punishment. Headstone proves a failure because he is fabricated out of his author's social prejudices, instead of being impelled, as Quilp is, by his author's savage humour, self-criticism and emancipation from the cant and sentimentality that were always threatening to kill Dickens' art.

It would be wrong to conclude that because Headstone is a violent character, and is disapproved of by Dickens, Dickens has grown disillusioned with violence. On the contrary, he retains to the end his perfectly simple faith in a strong right arm. Nicholas Nickleby is the first of the heroes to exercise his virtuous muscles on evil-doers. Though slight in appearance—John Browdie refers to him as a whipper-snapper—he makes an impressive showing when struck across the face by Squeers: 'Nicholas sprang upon him, wrested the weapon from his hand, and pinning him by the throat, beat the ruffian till he roared for mercy.' Mr. Lenville is the next victim: 'Nicholas ... suffered him to approach to within the requisite distance, and then, without the smallest discomposure, knocked him down.' To complete the act Nicholas picks up Mr. Lenville's ash stick, breaks it in half, tosses him the pieces, and makes his exit. There follows a fine dramatic encounter between Nicholas and the dastardly Sir Mulberry Hawk: 'Stand out of the way, dog,' blusters Sir Mulberry. Nicholas shouts that he is the son of a country gentleman, and lays Sir Mulberry's face open from eye to lip. Finally Nicholas confronts the arch villain, Uncle Ralph. '"One word!" cried Ralph, foaming at the mouth.' But Nicholas, distrustful of words, knocks down Ralph's elderly fellow-conspirator Arthur Gride instead, picks up Madeline Bray, and rushes out with, as Dickens puts it, 'his beautiful burden in his arms'. Granted this is a very early novel, but the victory of righteousness is no less physical, and no less theatrical, at the end of *Martin Chuzzlewit*. Old Martin rises against Pecksniff and strikes him to the ground, 'with such a well-directed nervous blow, that down he went, as heavily and true as if the charge of a Life-Guardsman had tumbled him out of the saddle'. The soldierly simile here is, of course, meant to give the violence an especially decent flavour. A similar motive prompts Dickens to remind us, at the end of *Our Mutual Friend*, that John Harmon's 'seafaring hold was like that of a vice', and that he takes a 'sailor-like turn' on Silas Wegg's cravat, preparatory to knocking Silas' head against the wall. There is something healthy and patriotic about a sailor, which makes it all right to assault a cripple. Eventually Wegg and his wooden leg are carried down-stairs and thrown into a muck cart. By such summary means is evil expelled from a Dickens novel.

We notice, in these examples, how the writing deteriorates once the violence becomes virtuous. The military images are shoddy subterfuge. Hopelessly dignified, the good characters brandish their sticks or fists, and the villains tumble. Dickens beams complacently. It is a dutiful, perfunctory business. Riot, murder, savagery have to be there before Dickens' imagination is gripped.

D.A. MILLER

Discipline in Different Voices:
Bureaucracy, Police, Family, and Bleak House

I

Chancery Court in *Bleak House* (1852–53) makes a certain difference in Dickens's representation of social discipline. This representation had hitherto been restricted to places of confinement which, as much as they referred to a disciplinary society committed to the manufacture and diffusion of such enclosures, also carried an even more emphatic allusion to the space between them: a space of freedom or domestic tranquillity that was their "other." The often ferocious architecture that immured the inmates of a carceral institution seemed to immure the operations practiced on them there as well, and if the thick, spiked walls, the multiple gateways, the attendants and the administrators assured the confinement of those within, they seemed equally to provide for the protectedness of those without, including most pertinently the novelist and his readers. Embodied in the prison, the workhouse, the factory, the school, discipline became, quite precisely, a *topic* of Dickensian representation: a site whose redoubtable but all the more easily identified boundaries allowed it to be the target of criticism to the same extent that they isolated it from other, better sites. The topic of the carceral in Dickens—better, the carceral as topic—thus worked to secure the effect of difference between, on the one hand, a confined, institutional space in which power is violently exercised on collectivized

From *Representations* 1, no. 1 (February 1983). © 1983 by the Regents of the University of California. University of California Press, 1983.

subjects, and on the other, a space of "liberal society," generally determined as a free, private, and individual domain and practically specified as the family. Yet clear though the lines of demarcation were, it was alarmingly easy to cross them. After all, what brought carceral institutions into being in the first place were lapses in the proper management of the family: in its failure to constitute itself (the problem of illegitimate or orphaned children and the institutional solution of foundling hospitals and baby farms) or in its failure to sustain itself by means of a self-sufficient domestic economy (the problem of poverty and debt and the institutional responses of workhouses and debtor's prisons). And in the portrayal of its hero in the workhouse, *Oliver Twist* (1837–39) dramatized the shameful facility with which such institutions might mistakenly seize upon what were middle-class subjects to begin with. Still, if to witness the horror of the carceral was always to incur a debt of gratitude for the immunities of middle-class life, then to sense the danger from the carceral was already to learn how this debt had to be acquitted. When Oliver Twist, enchanted by the difference from his previous experience he found in his life at Mr. Brownlow's, begged the latter not to send him back to "the wretched place I came from," Brownlow declared: "You need not be afraid of my deserting you, unless you give me cause." Earlier he had promised Oliver access to the culture represented by the books in his library on similar conditions: "You shall read them, if you behave well."[1] The price of Oliver's deliverance from the carceral (either as the workhouse or as Fagin's gang) would be his absolute submission to the norms, protocols, and regulations of the middle-class family, in which he receives tuition not just from Brownlow but from the Maylies as well. Liberal society and the family were kept free from the carceral institutions that were set up to remedy their failures only by assuming the burden of an immense internal regulation. If discipline was confined to the carceral, then, this was so in order that it might ultimately be extended—in the mode of what was experientially its opposite—to the space outside it.

Chancery Court in *Bleak House* forces upon this representation the necessity of a certain readjustment. In the first place, an essential characteristic of the court is that its operations far exceed the architecture in which it is apparently circumscribed. The distinctive gesture of the carceral—that of locking up—makes little sense here when, at the end of the day, what is locked up is only "the empty court" and not "all the misery it has caused."[2] Though the court is affirmed to be situated "at the very heart of the fog" (2), this literally nebulous information only restates the difficulty of locating it substantially, since there is "fog everywhere" (1). The ultimate unlocalizability of its operations permits them to be in all places at once. "How many people out of the suit, Jarndyce and Jarndyce has stretched forth

its unwholesome hand to spoil and corrupt, would be a very wide question"
(5), but it would perhaps also be a moot one, since nearly all the characters
we meet in the novel are in the cause, either as parties to it or administrators
of it, even those like Esther who seem to have nothing to do with it. And the
suit is as long as it is wide, the immense spatial extension of its filiations being
matched by the long temporal duration that unfolds under its "eternal
heading" (5). Dickens's satire on the inefficiency of the court begins to seem
a feeble, even desperate act of whistling in the dark, for the power organized
under the name of Chancery is repeatedly demonstrated to be all too
effective. Like the fog and dirt that are its first symbols, this power insinuates
itself by virtue of its quasi-alchemical subtlety. To violent acts of penetration
it prefers the milder modes of permeation, and instead of being densely
consolidated into a force prepared to encounter a certain resistance, it is so
finely vaporized—sublimated, we should say, thinking of alchemy and
psychoanalysis together—that every surface it needs to attack is already
porously welcoming it. Unlike, say, the power that keeps order in Dotheboys
Hall in *Nicholas Nickleby* (1838–39), this power does not impose itself by
physical coercion (though, as the case of Gridley reminds us, it does dispose
of carceral sanctions for those who hold it in contempt). Rather, it relies on
being voluntarily assumed by its subjects, who, seduced by it, addicted to it,
internalize the requirements for maintaining its hold. "Fog everywhere."
What Chancery produces, or threatens to do, is an organization of power
which, ceasing entirely to be a *topic*, has become topography itself: a system
of control which can be all-encompassing because it cannot be compassed in
turn. Writing in the nineteenth century, John Forster would not be the last
critic of *Bleak House* to notice how "the great Chancery suit, on which the
plot hinges, on incidents connected with which, important or trivial, all the
passion and suffering turns, is worked into every part of the book."[3] Yet
though we see nothing but the effects of Jarndyce and Jarndyce, everywhere
present, affecting everyone, everything, we never come close to seeing what
the suit is all about, as though this were merely the pretext that allowed for
the disposition and deployment of the elaborate channels, targets, and
techniques of a state bureaucracy. The interminable process of interpretation
to which the original will gives rise, literally maddening to those who bring
to it the demand that it issue in final truths and last judgments, is abandoned
rather than adjudicated. If Chancery thus names an organization of power
that is total but not totalizable, total *because* it is not totalizable, then what is
most radically the matter with being "in Chancery" is not that there may be
no way out of it (a dilemma belonging to the problematic of the carceral),
but, more seriously, that the binarisms of inside/outside, here/elsewhere
become meaningless and the ideological effects they ground impossible.

Furthermore, the nature of Chancery necessarily affects the nature of the resistance to it. Whereas the topic of the carceral, localizing disciplinary practices that thereby seemed to require only local remedies, always implied a feasible politics of reformism, the total social reticulation of Chancery finds its corresponding oppositional practice in the equally total social negation of anarchism. Repeatedly, the court induces in the narration a wish for its wholesale destruction by fire: "If all the injustice it has committed, and all the misery it has caused, could only be locked up with it, and the whole burnt away in a great funeral pyre—why, so much the better for other parties than the parties in Jarndyce and Jarndyce!" (7). Even the elision of agency managed by the passive voice (who, exactly, would burn the court?), stopping short of any subjective assumption of the action, mirrors perfectly the court whose operations are in no one's control. The wish, moreover, may be considered fulfilled (albeit also displaced) when Mr. Krook, who has personified the Chancellor and Chancery from the first, dies of spontaneous combustion. It is as though apocalyptic suddenness were the only conceivable way to put an end to Chancery's meanderings, violent spontaneity the only means to abridge its elaborate procedures, and mere combustion the only response to its accumulation of paperwork. One of the least welcome implications of an all-inclusive system, such as Chancery is implied to be, is that even opposition to it, limited to the specular forms of reflection and inversion, merely intensifies our attachment to the perceptual grid constructed by its practices.

To say so much, of course, is to treat Chancery, if not more radically, then certainly more single-mindedly, than Dickens is ever willing to do. For while a major effort of *Bleak House* is to establish Chancery as an all-pervasive system of domination, another is to refute the fact of this system and recontain the court within a larger spatial organization that would once again permit an elsewhere along with all the ideological effects attaching to it. If Krook's death, for instance, illustrates the apocalyptically anti-social kinds of retribution that are the only adequate responses to Chancery remaining, it can also be seen to reinstate precisely those social and political possibilities that Chancery, as a total order, ought to have made impossible. For insofar as Krook dies, as in certain modern aetiologies of cancer, of his own internal repressions, then Chancery can be safely trusted to collapse from its own refusal to release what is unhealthily accumulating in its system. Alternatively, insofar as Krook's violent end is meant to foreshadow what is in store for the institution he figures, then his death carries a warning to the court to amend its ways or else. In either case, we are reinstalled within the reformist perspectives that Chancery had, we thought, in principle annulled.

Even the omnipresence of the Chancery suit that Forster rightly noted is frequently neutralized by a certain inconsequentiality. John Jarndyce, Ada Clare, and Esther Summerson are all in the suit without being spoiled or corrupted by it—indeed, they constitute the domestic retreat to which the institutional, social space of the court can then be contrasted. Richard Carstone, whose aimlessness internalizes the procedural protractions of the court, makes a better example of Chancery's power to spoil and corrupt. Yet it is also possible to argue, as did an early critic of the novel, under the impression that he was exposing its deficiency, that Richard "is not made reckless and unsteady by his interest in the great suit, but simply expends his recklessness and unsteadiness on it, as he would on something else if it were nonexistent."[4] It is, of course, Dickens's own text that opens up the possibility of this moral explanation in its reluctance to commit itself to social determination:

> 'How much of this indecision of character,' Mr. Jarndyce said to me, 'is chargeable on that incomprehensible heap of uncertainty and procrastination on which he has been thrown from his birth, I don't pretend to say; but that Chancery, among its other sins, is responsible for some of it, I can plainly see. It has engendered or confirmed in him a habit of putting off—and trusting to this, that, and the other chance, without knowing what chance—and dismissing everything as unsettled, uncertain, and confused. The character of much older and steadier people may be even changed by the circumstances surrounding them. It would be too much to expect that a boy's, in its formation, should be the subject of such influences, and escape them.' (167)

Jarndyce kind-heartedly proposes the sociological key to Richard's character in the same breath as he admits its insufficiency. And what is at stake in his hesitation between "engendered" and "confirmed," between the court as cause and the court as occasion, goes beyond the double view of Richard. Ultimately, the text oscillates between two seemingly incompatible sets of assumptions about the nature of Chancery's power—one deriving from the perception of total domination, the other still attached to the topic of the carceral. Thus, just as the satire on the inefficiency of the court contradicts the demonstrated power of such inefficiency, so too the anachronism of Chancery, upheld as "a slow, expensive, British, constitutional sort of thing" (13) by such fossils as Sir Leicester, counters the newness of the phenomenon that Dickens is describing under that name: the expanded development of the Victorian state bureaucracy that is at least as current as the novel's official exhibit of modernity in the Detective Police.[5]

All the evidence of Chancery's totalizing effects—of its productivity as an all-englobing system of power—is equivocal in such ways, as the text at once claims that this system is and isn't efficient, is and isn't everywhere, can and cannot be reformed. In the literal sense of giving utterance to a double discourse, *Bleak House* is a contradictory text. Yet as we continue to consider the operation of such "contradiction" in the text, we should be wary of prejudging it, in a certain Marxist manner, as the "symptom" of an ideological bind, obligingly betrayed to our notice in the text's taken-for-granted "distanciation" from its own program.[6] We need rather to be prepared to find in the source of "incoherence," the very resource on which the text draws for its consistency; in the ideological "conflict," a precise means of addressing and solving it; in the "failure" of intention on the part of the text, a positively advantageous *strategy*.

II

Of all the mysteries that will crop up in *Bleak House*, not the least instructive concerns the curious formal torsion whereby a novel dealing with a civil suit becomes a murder mystery, and whereby the themes of power and social control are passed accordingly from the abyssal filiations of the law into the capable hands of the detective police. By what kinds of logic or necessity is the law thus turned over to the police, and the civil suit turned into the criminal case? For if Jarndyce and Jarndyce provides the ground from which mysteries and the consequent detections originate, it is certainly not because the suit is itself a mystery. In one sense, it is so illegible that we don't even have a sense, as we should with a mystery, of what needs to be explained or, more importantly, of what might constitute either the clues or the cruxes of such an explanation. In another, the suit may be read fully and at leisure: in the reams of dusty warrants, in the tens of thousands of Chancery-folio pages, in the battery of blue bags with their heavy charges of paper—in all the archival litter that has accumulated over the dead letter of the original will. Dickens's presentation offers either too little or else too much to amount to mystery. Besides, nothing about the suit is secret or hidden, unless we count the second will found late in the novel, and this hardly brings us closer to a judgment. All that is even unavailable are the dead legator's intentions.

It would be seriously misleading, however, on the basis of this exception, to deconstruct the suit into an allegory of interpretation as that which, confronting the absence of an immediate meaning effected by the very nature of the sign or text, must unfold as an interminable proliferation of readings.[7] For one thing, if the suit can be thought to give expression to such difficulties of interpretation, this is because, more than merely finding them acceptable, it goes out of its way to manufacture them; and no response would serve Chancery or the logic of its law better than to see this manufacture as inhering in the nature of "textuality" rather than belonging to an institutional practice that seeks to implant and sanction its own technical procedures. For another, it seems willful to see the work of interpretation occurring in what is far more obviously and actually the profitable business of deferring it indefinitely. With its endless referrals, relays, remands, its ecologically terrifying production of papers, minutes, memoranda, Dickens's bureaucracy works positively to elude the project of interpretation that nominally guides it. (And by the time that the Circumlocution Office in *Little Dorrit* [1855–57] avows the principle "HOW NOT TO DO IT," even the nominal commitment seems abandoned.[8]) Esther properly recognizes how "ridiculous" it is to speak of a Chancery suit as "in progress," since the term implies a linear directedness which, while fully suitable to the project that subtends Esther's own narration (indicatively begun under the title of "A Progress"), must be wholly absent from a case which, typically, "seemed to die out of its own vapidity, without coming, or being by anybody expected to come, to any result" (345). Moreover, to see that, in Chancery, the process of decision and interpretation is diverted is also to see that it is diverted *into* Chancery, as an apparatus. It is diverted, in other words, into the work of establishing the very channels for its diversion: channels by means of which a legal establishment is ramified, its points of contact multiplied, and routes of circulation organized for the subjects who are thus recruited under its power.[9]

Yet Chancery can never dispense with the judgments that it also never dispenses. Though the project of interpretation is virtually annulled in the workings of its formalism ("the lantern that has no light in it"), the *promise* of interpretation, as that which initiates and facilitates this formalism, remains absolutely necessary. At the theoretical level of ideology, the promise functions to confer legitimacy on Chancery proceedings: as even poor crazed Miss Flyte, in her confusion of the Last Judgment with the long-delayed judgment in her own case, is capable of revealing, the legal system must appeal for its authority to transcendent concepts of truth, justice, meaning, and ending, even when its actual work will be to hold these concepts in profitable abeyance or to redefine and contain them as functions of its own operations. And at the practical and technical level of such operations, the promise of judgment becomes the lure of advertising, extended by venalities such as Vholes to promote the purchase and exercise of their services.

Perhaps the most interesting effect of all produced by the promise, however, considerably exceeds these theoretical and practical functions. If Chancery exploits the logic of a promise by perpetually maintaining it as *no more than such*, then the suit must obviously produce as much frustration as hopefulness. Accordingly, one consequence of a system that, as it engenders an interpretative project, simultaneously deprives it of all the requirements for its accomplishment is the desire for an interpretative project that would *not* be so balked. This desire is called into being from within the ground of a system that, it bears repeating, resists interpretation on two counts: because it cannot be localized as an object of interpretation, and because it is never willing to become the agency or subject of interpretation. What such a desire effectively seeks, therefore, is a reduced model of the untotalizable system and a legible version of the undecidable suit. What such a desire calls for, in short, both as a concept and as a fact, is the detective story.

The detective story gives obscurity a name and a local habitation: in that highly specific "mystery" whose ultimate uncovering motivates an equally specific program of detection. If the Chancery system includes everything but settles nothing, then one way in which it differs from the detective story is that the latter is, precisely, a *story*: sufficiently selective to allow for the emergence of a narrative and properly committed, once one has emerged, to bringing it to completion. In relation to an organization so complex that it often tempts its subjects to misunderstand it as chaos, the detective story realizes the possibility of an easily comprehensible version of order. And in the face—or facelessness—of a system where it is generally impossible to assign responsibility for its workings to any single person or group of persons, where even the process of victimization seems capricious, the detective story performs a drastic simplification of power as well. For unlike Chancery, the detective story is fully prepared to affirm the efficacy and priority of personal agency, be it that of the criminal figures who do the work of concealment or that of the detective figures who undo it. It is not at all surprising, therefore, that the desire for the detective story first emerges from within the legal community itself, in Tulkinghorn and Guppy, since lawyers, having charge of the system, are most likely to be aware of the extent to which they merely convey a power which is theirs only to hold and not to have. It is entirely suitable that those who continually *exercise* this power—in the root sense, that is, of driving it on—should be the first to dream of *possessing* it, so that the calling of Mr. Tulkinghorn, for instance, "eke solicitor of the High Court of Chancery" (11), becomes "the acquisition of secrets and the holding possession of such power as they give him, with no sharer or opponent in it" (511). At the other end of the legal hierarchy (though not, one may be sure, for long), Mr. Guppy prepares for a similar vocation:

> Mr. Guppy suspects everybody who enters on the occupation of a stool in Kenge and Carboy's office, of entertaining, as a matter of course, sinister designs upon him. He is clear that every such person wants to depose him. If he be ever asked how, why, when, or wherefore, he shuts up one eye and shakes his head. On the strength of these profound views, he in the most ingenious manner takes infinite pains to counter-plot, when there is no plot; and plays the deepest games of chess without any adversary. (272)

Guppy's counter-plotting "when there is no plot" may be seen as the usefully paranoid attempt of an ambitious clerk to grasp the power of the legal system over him by turning everybody in it into his personal enemy. It may also be seen as the desperately fanciful effort of an otherwise bored office worker to overwrite the impersonal and inconsequential tedium of his tasks with lively dramas centered on himself. In either case, it suggests precisely the sense in which the non-narrative system of Chancery generates narratives both to grasp its evasiveness and equally to evade its grasp.

Yet within this perspective, one must register the general failure of the amateur detectives in *Bleak House* to impose a will to truth and power. Anecdotally, their stories all reach a final point of checkmate. Guppy's chance to lay his hands on the decisive evidence goes up in smoke with Krook; Tulkinghorn is murdered before he has quite decided how to make use of his discovery; and even Mrs. Snagsby is still "on the great high road that is to terminate in Mr. Snagsby's full exposure" (734) when Mr. Bucket is obliged to set her straight. These abortive endings, which effectively place the stories under the paradigm of the interminable Chancery suit, also carry "political" rebukes, as the detectives are denied the power to which their knowledge seemed to entitle them. Tulkinghorn's violent death at the hands of a woman over whom he had flaunted his control is the most dramatic example of such chastisement; but another is Guppy's rejection by Esther, the woman who initially inspired his detective work and who he hoped might reward it with her hand; and still another is the gentle but public reprimand that Mrs. Snagsby receives from Mr. Bucket. The profound reason for the anecdotal failure of these stories is that they are undertaken as individual projects. That individuality not only must debilitate the power of the will-to-power, but also qualifies the general validity of the production of truth. Even when the stories have more to go on than Mrs. Snagsby's—exemplary in its forced, false, but flawless coherence—, they are marred by an egocentricity that confers on them the epistemologically suspect tautology of wish-fulfillments. Just as Guppy's detection is part and parcel of his *arrivisme*, an ambitious attempt to enoble the woman of his choice and to win her gratitude for doing so, similarly, Tulkinghorn, who holds that women "are at the bottom of all that goes wrong in [the world]" (222), finds his sexual resentment justified in a story of female error and deceit. Even Mrs. Snagsby's fantasy that Jo has been illegitimately sired by her husband likewise satisfies her need to see herself as wronged, and so consolidates the basis of her domestic tyranny. It is not enough to say that, if the detective story is meant to be an individual rendition of an order and a power that are social and institutional in nature, then a great deal must be lost in the translation. For that loss to be registered as its loss, in its formal incompletion, its cognitive inadequacy, and its political failure, what must also be asserted is the priority assumed by social and institutional categories over the individual projects that they will ultimately reabsorb.

Even as a failure, however, the project of detection enjoys a certain dangerous efficacy. For it fails in every respect except that of catching on. Its weakness as an individual enterprise becomes a demonstrable strength as the number of individuals undertaking it increases and it thereby acquires a certain social distribution and consistency. As a common individual project, detection poses a threat to the social and institutional orders that continue to doom it to failure as a single undertaking. From beginning to end, the project sanctions the unwholesomely deviate erotic desire that inspires it and that it releases into action. The unsavory sexual secrets in which this desire, having been liberated, is ultimately gratified, are themselves subversive of socially given arrangements. Regularly involving a double transgression, of class as well as conjugal boundaries, they give scandal to the twin unities that Dickens puts at the basis of a decent social order, family and station. To disclose these secrets, moreover, exacerbates their scandalous effects, as when what Mrs. Snagsby thinks she knows leads her to seek a marital separation, and what Tulkinghorn tells Lady Dedlock prompts her public flight. In a context where home and family are the chief bulwarks against drifting into the interminable circulations of Chancery Court, the kind of individuality implied and exfoliating in the project of detection must seem ultimately anarchic. Born, as Tulkinghorn's case makes particularly clear, when the law is taken into one's own hands, it gives birth to the familiar rivalrous, *sauve-qui-peut* world of which the tension between Tulkinghorn and Guppy is an early symptom, and in which the murderous personal arrogations of Mademoiselle Hortense are, though shocking, perfectly proper.

We begin to see why the detective narratives require to come under the management of a master-agency charged with the task both of suppressing their successes (in fostering extreme threats to social order) and also of supplying their failures (to provide a widely available, consoling simplification of this order). We begin to understand, in other words, the profound necessity of the police in *Bleak House*. Though Chancery Court, to make itself tolerable, produces a desire for the detective story, as for that which will confer on it the legibility of a traditionally patterned meaning, this desire, far from issuing in an order that can be comfortably proffered and consumed as the essence of the chaos that is Chancery's appearance, threatens to reduplicate such chaos in the yet more explicit form of social disaggregation. What keeps the production of this desire from being dangerously excessive—what in fact turns the dangerous excess back into profit—is that the detective story, following the same logic whereby it was produced among the effects of Chancery, produces among *its* effects the desire for its own authoritative version and regulatory agency. Out of control to the point that, at Tulkinghorn's murder, the very principle of sense-making appears to have gone "stark mad" (665), the detective story eventually asks to be arrested by the Detective Police.

Such regulation should not be seen purely as a repressive practice, involving, for instance, the capture of a murderer like Mademoiselle Hortense or a runaway like Lady Dedlock. The police not only repress but also, profoundly, satisfy the desire to which Chancery gives rise. For in addition to doing the negative work of correcting for the socially undesirable consequences of amateur projects of detection, it performs the positive work of discharging for society as a whole the function that these amateur projects had assumed unsuccessfully: that of providing, within the elusive organization of Chancery, a simplified representation of order and power. The novel's shift in focus from Chancery Court to the Detective Police encompasses a number of concomitant shifts; which all operate in the direction of this simplification: from civil law and questions of liability to criminal law and less merely legal questions of guilt; from trivial legal hair-splitting to the urgency of the fact, beyond such disputing, of murder; from a cause with countless parties represented by countless attorneys in an anonymous system, to a case essentially reduced to two personal duels, between the criminal and his victim and between the criminal and the detective; from long, slow, to all appearances utterly inefficient procedures to swift and productive ones; and finally, from an institution which cannot justify its power to one which, for all the above reasons, quite persuasively can. It is as though every complaint that could be made about the one institution had been redressed in the organization of the other, so that one might even argue, on the basis of Dickens's notorious willingness to serve as a propagandist for the New Police, that the excruciating *longueurs* of Chancery existed mainly to create the market for Mr. Bucket's expeditious *coups*.[10] Along these lines, one might even want to read, in the police activity that develops over the dead body of the law ("or Mr Tulkinghorn, one of its trustiest representatives" [305]), Dickens's exhilarated announcement of the agencies and practices of social discipline that, claiming to be merely supplementing the law, will come in large part to supplant it.[11] Yet to the extent that we stress, in the evident archaism of Chancery, the emergence of a new kind of bureaucratic organization, and in the blatantly modern Detective Police (instituted only ten years before the novel began to appear), a harkening back to a traditional and familiar model of power, then we need to retain the possibility that Dickens's New Police still polices, substantively as well as nominally, *for* the law, for the Chancery system, and that, as a representation, it serves a particular ideological function within this system, and not against it. Made so desirable as a sort of institutional "alternative" to Chancery, the police derive their ideological efficacy from providing, within a total system of power, *a representation of the containment of power*. The shift from Chancery to the police dramatically localizes the field, exercise, and agents of power, as well as, of course, justifies such power, which, confined to a case of murder and contained in a Mr. Bucket, occupies what we can now think of as the right side. And when the novel passes from adulatory wonder at the efficiency of the police to sad, resigned acknowledgment of its limits (such as emerges in Hortense's last exchange with Bucket), the circumscription of power, reaching the end to which it always tended, has merely come full circle.

III

The police thus allow for the existence of a field outside the dynamic of power and free from its effects. Once installed in this realmless realm, one could cease to internalize—as the desperate, hopeful psychology of compulsion—the lures of the Chancery system; from within it, one could bear witness to the possibility of a genuine criticism of that system, one that would no longer be merely the sign of the impossibility of withdrawing from it. Shifting focus from Chancery Court to the Detective Police, the novel works toward the recovery of this place elsewhere, in a two-pronged strategy whose other line of attack lies in Esther's absolute refusal to be touched by the suit and in the constitution of Bleak House that her refusal enables. For in point of fact the "outside" of power is specified as a domestic space, occupied by an ideal of the family. Not the least evil of the Chancery system in this respect was that, in it, police and family blurred into one another. As an apparatus of power concerned to impose, protect, and extend itself, Chancery naturally included a policing function, but it had the aspect of a family as well, not only because the suits that came before it arose from family disputes, but also because (as when it put its wards Ada and Richard under the guardianship of John Jarndyce) it sanctioned families of its own. In effect, the emergence of Bleak House on the one hand and Mr. Bucket (who, though Mrs. Bucket is as fond of children as himself, has none) on the other achieves the extrication of the family from the police, a disarticulation into separate domains of what it was a trick of Chancery's domination to have knitted seamlessly together.

We mustn't be surprised, however, if there is a trick to this new arrangement too—and perhaps a far better one. When Mr. Bucket escorts Mr. Snagsby through Tom-all-Alone's (much as Inspector Field took Dickens with him on his tours of duty), the detective's thoroughgoing knowledge of the place as well as the extreme deference shown to him by its inhabitants (who call him "master") indicate the degree to which the police have saturated the delinquent milieu. If the saturation doesn't appear to have much curtailed delinquency, or even, strangely, to have prevented Tom-all-Alone's from continuing to serve as a refuge for those wanted by the police, these perhaps were never the ends of police penetration. What such penetration indubitably does secure is an apparent containment of crime and power together, which both become visible mainly in a peripheral place, "avoided by all decent people" (220).[12] The raison d'être of Tom-all-Alone's is that it *be* all alone, as the text is prepared to admit when it speculates "whether the traditional title is a comprehensive name for a retreat cut off from honest company" (220). Yet the marginal localization of the police thus achieved is subjected to a dramatic ambiguity as soon as, beyond ensuring the circulation of vagrants like Jo or the apprehension of murderers who, doubly exotic, come from foreign parts and the servant class both, the police pass into the fashionable upper-class world of Chesney Wold or even the just barely respectable shooting gallery of Mr. George. Though disturbed by Bucket's nighttime visit, heralded only by the glare of his bull's-eye, the denizens of Tom-all-Alone's are neither surprised nor shamed by what is evidently a very familiar occurrence. Compare their dull acceptance to Sir Leicester's appalled imagination:

> Heaven knows what he sees. The green, green woods of Chesney Wold, the noble house, the pictures of his forefathers, strangers defacing them, officers of police coarsely handling his

most precious heirlooms, thousands of fingers pointing at him,
thousands of faces sneering at him. (743–44)

Compare it even to Mr. George's sharp mortification:

'You see ... I have been handcuffed and taken into custody, and
brought here. I am a marked and disgraced man, and here I am.
My shooting-gallery is rummaged, high and low, by Bucket; such
property as I have—'tis small—is turned this way and that, till it
don't know itself...' (705)

The sense of scandal that informs both passages, even as it acknowledges that
the police can break out of their limits to become a total, all-pervasive
institution like Chancery, reinforces our perception of the boundaries that
ordinarily keep them in their place. It qualifies the police intervention in
either case as an exceptional state of affairs, warranted only by the
exceptional circumstances that call it into being.

   The representation of the police, then, is not just organized by a
comforting principle of localization; it is also organized within the fear-
inspiring prospect of *the possible suspension of this principle*. One may read the
resulting ambiguity in the very character of Mr. Bucket. The fact that the
representation of the police is virtually entirely confined to the portrayal of
this one character is already revealing of the strategy of containment
whereby the topic of the police is constituted. Chancery Court required
dozens of lawyers in the attempt to represent it, and even then the attempt
had always to remain unequal to a system whose essential anonymity resisted
being seized as character. The police, however, can be adequately rendered
in the character of a single one of its agents, and this fact, among others,
makes it a superior institution. Whereas the law is impersonal and
anonymous, the law enforcement is capable of showing a human face—if that
is the word for the mechanically recurring tics and character-traits that
caused Inspector Bucket to be received at the time of the novel's publication
as one of Dickens's most "delightful" creations.[13] Yet if police power is
contained in Bucket, Bucket himself is *not* contained in the way that
characters ordinarily are. A master of disguise, who makes himself appear in
as "ghostly" a manner as, with a touch of his stick, he makes others "instantly
evaporate" (308, 310), Bucket seems superhuman and his powers magical. To
Mr. Snagsby, confused and impressed, he appears "to possess an unlimited
number of eyes" (315); and Jo, in his ignorance and delirium, believes him
"to be everywhere, and cognizant of everything" (639). With ironic
reservations that only refine the ambiguity, the narration even offers its own

language in support of these baffled perceptions: "Time and place cannot bind Mr Bucket" (712), it tells us, and "nothing escapes him" (713).

Another way to bring out the ambiguity that invests the established limits of the police is to ask: on behalf of whom or what does the Detective Police do its policing? Answers in the text, accurately reflecting an historical ambiguity, are various. Bucket works now in the capacity of a private detective employed by individuals such as Tulkinghorn; now as the public official of a state apparatus that enjoins him, for instance, to secure Gridley for contempt of court; and now in some obscure combination of the two functions, as when, at the end, he seems to police simultaneously on behalf of society at large and at the behest of Sir Leicester Dedlock. In a sense, the progress toward the legitimacy of power that we read in the focal shift from Chancery to the Detective Police occurs within the representation of the police itself, which, at the beginning acting as the agent of an arbitrary system or an equally arbitrary individual will, acquires in the end—via murder and a missing person—the means of legitimizing the exercise of its power, even though this is still nominally in the hire of Sir Leicester. Yet this effort of the narrative sequence to legitimize the power of the police leaves looking all the more unresolved the question of their whereabouts, which are established in so many places, as so many indistinct, overlapping, competing jurisdictions, that they cease to seem established at all.

All the ambiguities about the police, of course, serve to establish a radical uncertainty in the nature of private, familial space. "As [Mr. Bucket] says himself, what is public life without private ties? He is in his humble way a public man, but it is not in that sphere that he finds happiness. No, it must be sought within the confines of domestic bliss" (675–76). But as we know, Bucket here maintains the difference between public (institutional) and private (domestic) spheres as part of a successful attempt to neutralize it. The difference on which he affably insists allows him to be welcomed into the Bagnet household, where at the proper moment—no longer as a new friend of the family, but now a public official—he can arrest their friend and guest Mr. George. Is the private sphere autonomous or not? The representation of the police in *Bleak House* permits us to answer the question either way: to insist, when this is necessary, on the elsewhere opened up by the localization of the police (who considerately police, among other things, their own limits); or to suggest, when this is desirable, the extent to which this elsewhere is constantly liable to being transgressed by the police. The police simultaneously produce and permeate (produce as permeable) the space they leave to be "free."

If, therefore, we need to say that, in its representation of bureaucracy and the police, *Bleak House* regularly produces a difference between these institutions and the domestic space outside them, we must also recognize that it no less regularly produces this difference *as a question*, in the mode of the "problematic." The bar of separation and even opposition that it draws between the two terms is now buttressed, now breached, firm and fragile by turns. On one hand, Chancery is a total system of domination, engendering resistances whose mere inversions or duplications of its injunctions only entrench its power more deeply. On the other hand, Chancery's domination seems to cease precisely at the points where one elects to erect bulwarks against it such as Esther's Bleak House. Or again: if the police represent a reduction of the domination of Chancery, and thus permit a domestic autonomy, it is also suggested that the police, as all-encompassing as Chancery, can at any moment abolish that autonomy. Or still again: the police are other, better than Chancery, but they are also the organ that polices on its behalf and thus works to preserve it. We cannot too strongly insist that these "paradoxes" are not merely confusions or historical contradictions that tug and pull at a text helpless to regulate them, but rather productive ambiguities that facilitate the disposition, functioning, and promotion of certain ideological effects, some of which we have already suggested. Neither, however, should *"Bleak House*, by Charles Dickens" be denounced—or congratulated—as the ultimate strategist of these effects, as though one could allow such effects their broad cultural resonance without also recognizing their broad cultural production and distribution. Yet if the novel no more "manipulates" the equivocations we have traced than "succumbs" to them, perhaps the most pertinent reason is that it lacks the distance from them required to do either. We shall see how, in the first place, these equivocations *are its own*, always already borne in the novel as a form; and also how, in the last instance, these equivocations *come to be its own*, as the novel reproduces in the relationship between form and content the dialectic that occurs within each of its terms.

IV

It would certainly appear as though the existence of that sheltered space which the novelistic representation labors to produce—but with, we have seen, such dubious results—is unconditionally taken for granted in the novel form, whose un folding or consumption has never ceased to occur in such a space all along. Since the novel counts among the conditions for this consumption the consumer's leisured withdrawal to the private, domestic sphere, then every novel-reading subject is constituted—willy-nilly and almost before he has read a word—within the categories of the individual, the inward, the domestic. There is no doubt that the shift in the dominant literary form from the drama to the novel at the end of the seventeenth century had to do with the latter's superior efficacy in producing and providing for privatized subjects. The only significant attempt to transcend the individualism projected by the novel took place precisely in Victorian England as the practice of the *family reading*, which may be understood as an effort to mitigate the possible excesses of the novel written for individuals by changing the locus of reading from the study—or worse, the boudoir—to the hearth, enlivened but also consolidated as a *foyer d'intrigue*. A Victorian novel such as *Bleak House* speaks not merely for the hearth, in its prudent care to avoid materials or levels of explicitness about them unsuitable for family entertainment, but from the hearth as well, implicitly grounding its critical perspective on the world within a domesticity that is more or less protected against mundane contamination.

Yet if only by virtue of the characteristic length that prevents it from being read in a single sitting, the novel inevitably enjoins not one, but several withdrawals to the private sphere. Poe, who first raised the issue of the effects of this length, considered the discontinuousness of novel-reading one of the liabilities of the form, which thereby had to forego "the immense benefit of *totality*." In the novel state, Poe thought, the autonomy of "literary concerns" was always being frustrated by the foreign intervention of "worldly interests."[14] If, however, novel-reading presupposes so many disparate withdrawals to the private sphere, by the same token it equally presupposes so many matching returns to the public, institutional one. An important dimension of what reading a novel entails, then, would lie—outside the moment and situation of actual perusal—in the times and places that interrupt this perusal and render it in the plural, as a series. Just as we read the novel in the awareness that we must put it down before finishing it, so even when we are not reading it, we continue to "live" the form in the mode of *having to get back to it*. Phenomenologically, the novel form includes the interruptions that fracture the process of reading it. And the technical equivalent of this phenomenological interpenetration of literary and worldly interests would be the practice of various realisms, which, despite their manifold differences, all ensure that the novel is always centrally about the world one has left behind to read it and that the world to which one will be recalled has been reduced to attesting the truth (or falsehood) of the novel. It is not quite true, therefore, that the novel is simply concerned to attach us to individuality and domesticity, to privacy and leisure. What the form really secures is a close *imbrication* of individual and social, domestic and institutional, private and public, leisure and work. A drill in the rhythms of bourgeois industrial culture, the novel generates a nostalgic desire to get home (where the novel can be resumed) in the same degree as it inures its readers to the necessity of periodically renouncing home (for the world where the novel finds its justification and its truth). In reading the novel, one is made to rehearse how to live a problematic—always surrendered, but then again always recovered—privacy.

V

The same opposition—or at least the question of one—between private-domestic and social-institutional domains that is produced in the representation and consumed as the form occurs again in the relationship between the representation and the form. For though the form projects itself as a kind of home, what is housed in this home, as its contents, are not merely or even mainly comfortable domestic quarters, but also the social-institutional world at large. If the novel is substantially to allege its otherness in relation to this world, and thus to vouch for its competence to survey, judge, and understand it, then far from seeking to be adequate or isomorphic to its contents (when these are carceral, disciplinary, institutional), it is instead obliged to defend itself against them by differentiating the practices of the world from the practices of representing it. The current critical fondness for assimilating form and content (via homologies, thematizations, *mises-en-abyme*) becomes no more than a facile sleight-of-hand if it does not face the complication it in fact encounters in the question of the difference between the two that the novel regularly raises.[15] Specifically, as I hope to show in a moment, *Bleak House* is involved in an effort to distinguish its own enormous length from the protractedness of the Chancery suit, and also its own closure from the closed case of the Detective Police. But even remaining at a general and fundamental level, we can see the difference imposing itself in the fact that, for instance, while the world of *Bleak House* is dreary enough, yet were the novel itself ever to become as dreary, were it ever to cease *making itself desirable*, it would also be the same token cease to be read. Pleasurably, at our leisure and in our homes, we read the novel of suffering, the serious business of life, and the world out-of-doors. Moreover, the critical and often indignant attitude that *Bleak House*, by no means untypically, takes toward its social world reinforces this "erotic" difference with a cognitive one: the novel views the world in better, more clear-sighted and disinterested ways than the world views itself.

The suit in *Bleak House* has only to be mentioned for its monstrous length to be observed and censured. "Jarndyce and Jarndyce still drags its dreary length before the Court, perennially hopeless" (4). The suit is not merely long, but—here lies the affront—excessively so, longer than it is felt it ought to be. Yet what Dickens calls the "protracted misery" of the suit

(54)—by which he means the misery of its protractedness as well as vice versa—cannot be explained merely as the consequence of gratuitous *additions* to a necessary and proper length, left intact, which they simply inordinately "pad." One of the ill effects of the length of the suit has been precisely to render unavailable the reality of a proper measure, of which the suit could be seen as an unwarranted expansion and to which it would be theoretically possible to restore it by some judicious abridgment. The further the length of the suit is elaborated, the more it abandons any responsibility to the *telos* or finality that originally called it forth, nominally continues to guide it even now, and would ultimately reabsorb it as the pathway leading to its own achievement. And along with the *formality* of an ending—the juridical act of decision—, what would constitute the *substance* of one is concomitantly put in jeopardy: namely, the establishment of the meaning of the original will. So nearly intertwined are ending and meaning that to adjourn the one seems to be to abjure the other: "This scarecrow of a suit has, in course of time, become so complicated that no man alive knows what it means" (4).

The suit's effective suspension of teleology is, of course, scandalously exemplary of a whole social sphere that seems to run on the principle of a purposiveness without purpose. The principle is enunciated and enforced not only by the bureaucratic officials who, when Jo is sick, "must have been appointed for their skill in evading their duties, instead of performing them" (432), but even by the various policemen in the novel who enjoin Jo to "move on" in his perpetually maintained, displaced itinerary to nowhere. Internalized, it emerges as character defects: the long-windedness of Chadband, the aestheticism of Skimpole (who begins sketches "he never finished"), the flightiness of Richard. Such instances, however, in which the sense of an ending seems entirely given up are no more symptomatic of the general social suspension of finality than the abstract impatience and hopeful voluntarism with which the sense of an ending is merely imposed on a state of affairs which must thereby be misunderstood. Miss Flyte is mad to expect a judgment "shortly," and Richard is certainly on the way to madness when, choplogically, he argues that "the longer [the suit] goes on, ... the nearer it must be to a settlement one way or other" (182). In the progress of Hegelian Spirit, "the length of this path has to be endured because, for one thing, each moment is necessary" to the emergence of the result;[16] whereas, in the mere ongoingness of the un-Hegelian suit, any attempt to make sense of this length as a necessity, or in terms of the end-orientation which it formally retains but from which it has substantially removed itself, brings those who make it to madness. Finally, however, to recognize that the length of the suit is devoid of necessity is true only in terms of an eventual judgment. Just as the inefficiency of power in Chancery showed up from another standpoint as the power of inefficiency, so too what are on one perspective the superfluous, self-subversive elongations of procedure become on another the necessary developments of a power that—call it the English law—has for its one great principle "to make business for itself" (548). Accordingly, the delays and remands that amount to an effective suspension of its declared end should not be seen to debilitate Chancery, but rather to allow one to take it seriously as—in Dickens's facetious phrase from *The Old Curiosity Shop* (1840–41)— "the long and strong arm of the law."[17]

In light of the fact that the novel about this long arm itself exercises a considerable reach—that the representation of length goes on at length too—, we are invited to consider the extent to which the novel runs the risk of resembling the Chancery suit that it holds in despite. Certainly, the unfolding of the novel could be thought to parallel the elaboration of the suit insofar as it threatens an analogous failure to bring its ever more abundant materials to a proper or conceivably adequate summation. We already noted how the long novel foregoes "the immense benefit of totality" because it cannot be read at a single sitting; but even if we were to export to the nineteenth century the anachronism of a "speed-reader," Victorian practices of distributing the novel-product would still render the interruptedness of reading all but inevitable. Serial publication necessarily barred the reader from ever having full physical possession of the text he was reading until he was almost done with it; and even once the novel was published in volume form as a "three-decker," the ordinary subscription to the circulating libraries (which provided the majority of readers with their access to it) allowed to a borrower only one volume at a time. These determinations are of course merely external, but they are fully matched by the compositional principles of discontinuity and delay that organize the form from within its own structure: not only in the formal breaks of chapters, installments, volumes, but also in the substantive shifts from this plot-line to that, or from one point of view or narration to another; and generally in the shrewd administration of suspense that keeps the novel always tending toward a denouement that is continually being withheld. In Dickens, of course, the fissured and diffused character of novel form is far more marked than in the work of any of his contemporaries, extending from the extraordinary multitude of memorably disjunct characters, each psychologically sealed off from understanding another, to the series of equally disparate and isolated spaces across which they collide. And, like the larger structure of suspense, even individual sentences will frequently derive their effects from the lengths to which they will go in withholding predication.[18] No doubt, both as a system of distribution and as a text, the Victorian novel establishes a little bureaucracy of its own, generating an immense amount of paperwork and both physically and mentally sending its readers here, there, backward and forward, like the circumlocutory agencies that Dickens satirizes. On this basis, it could be argued that, despite or by means of its superficially hostile attitude toward bureaucracy, a novel like *Bleak House* is profoundly concerned to train us—as, at least since the eighteenth century, play usually trains us for work—in the sensibility for inhabiting the new bureaucratic, administrative structures.

This of course would be to neglect what Roland Barthes has identified as the "readerly" orientation of the traditional novel: the tendency of its organization to knit its discontinuities together by means of codes such as those ordering our perception of plot and suspense.[19] If *Bleak House* baffles us in the first few hundred pages by featuring a profusion of characters who seem to have nothing to do with one another, a miscellany of events whose bearing on a possible plot is undecidable, and even two separate systems of narration that are unequal and unrelated, it simultaneously encourages us to anticipate the end of bafflement and the acquisition of various structures of coherence: in the revelation or development of relationships among characters; in the emergence of a plot whereby the mysteries of the text will be enlightened and its meanings fully named; and in the tendency of the two narrations to converge, as Esther's account comes to include characters and information that at first appeared exclusively in the anonymous one. In other words, the novel dramatizes the liabilities of fragmentation and postponement within the hopeful prospect that they will eventually be overcome. We consume the enormous length of a novel like *Bleak House* in the belief that it is eminently digestible—capable, that is, of being ultimately rendered in a readerly *digest*: a final abridgment of plot and character which stands for—and so dispenses with—all that came before it. From the standpoint of this promised end, the massive bulk of the novel will always have concealed the perfectly manageable and unmonstrous proportions of a much shorter, tauter form.

Yet however sustained, the mere promise of an ending, far from being sufficient to differentiate the novel from Chancery, would positively enlarge on the analogy between the novel's practices and those of the Court, which also entices its subjects by means of promises, promises. We read the novel under the same assumption as Richard makes about the suit, that "the longer it goes on, ... the nearer it must be to a settlement"; and if the assumption is to be validated in the one case as it is discredited in the other, the novel is under obligation to make good its promise by issuing in judgments and resolutions. For even if we always know about the novel (as we do not about the suit) that its length is finite, involving only so many pages or installments, the vulgar evidence of an endpoint can never amount to the assurance of an *ending*: that is, the presence of a complex of narrative summations that would match or motivate the external termination of discourse with its internal closure. The suit, which attains an endpoint but no ending, embodies the distinction that the novel, to be different, will have to obliterate. Though the suit reaches a point at which it is correctly declared "over for good" (865), this point is determined extrinsically by the lack of funds that prevents the protracted, complex cause from being pursued to a proper conclusion of its own. "Thus the suit lapses and melts away" (867), instead of coming to the judgment that would have constituted a proper internal resolution. It is never known, for instance, whether the new will is a genuine document, and the project of finding out has been "checked—brought up suddenly" upon what Conversation Kenge retains sufficient professional finesse to term the "threshold" (866).

In a pointed and self-serving contrast, the novel brings its characters to judgment, its mysteries to solution and its plots to issues that would make further narrative superfluous. Immediately following the end of the suit, as a sort of consequence and reversal of it, Richard's death illustrates the contrast. Insofar as this death is premature, of course, it may look as though Richard will merely reenact the abrupt check of the suit. Juridical discourse has ceased not because it has said what it wanted to say, but only for lack of funds to say it; and similarly, Richard's utterance is simply "stopped by his mouth being full of blood" (868). But what is staged on the scene of Richard's deathbed is in fact his full recovery. In the paradoxical logic of nineteenth-century novelistic closure, whereby one sums up by subtracting, Richard is purged of unsteadiness and suspicion and so made whole. Whereas the suit ends as up in the air as ever it was, Richard's end achieves a fundamental clarification: "the clouds have cleared away, and it is bright now" (869). His tearful recognition that John Jarndyce, whom he mistrusted, is "a good man" renders him once more a good man himself. And his desire to be removed to the new Bleak House ("I feel as if I should get well there, sooner than anywhere") announces the redemptive turn from public institutional involvements to the domestic haven. As a result, even his death—no longer premature, but occurring only after the resolution of his character has been attained—bears witness to the seriousness of his conversion by making it permanent, the last word possible about him.

Unlike Chancery, then, the novel is willing to reward the patience that, like Chancery, it has required. The destiny of the long-suffering Esther is only the most obvious figure for the link the novel everywhere secures between the practice of patience and its pay-off. In the reader's case, the link is affirmed each time he gets an answer to one of the questions or riddles he has endured; each time he enjoys the jubilation of recognizing a character who has appeared earlier; each time a new installment comes out to reward his month-long wait for it. It isn't Esther alone in *Bleak House* who is extraordinarily self-deprecating and diffident in the face of authority, be it the heavenly Father in whom "it was so gracious ... to have made my orphan way so smooth and easy," or simply John Jarndyce, to whom she declares: "I am quite sure that if there were anything I ought to know, or had any need to know, I should not have to ask you to tell it to me. If my whole reliance and confidence were not placed in you, I must have a hard heart indeed" (27, 99). The novel puts every reader in an equally subservient position of reliance upon the author, who, if one waits long enough (as, given the nature of the readerly text, one cannot but do), will delight us with the full revelation of his design, offering the supreme example of those happy surprises that Dickens's benevolent father-figures are fond of providing for those they patronize. Still less obviously, the novel develops our trust in the machinery of distribution itself, which can, for instance, be counted upon to provide the next installment at exactly the interval promised. In short, the novel encourages a series of deferential cathexes—all the more fundamental for being unconscious—onto various instances of authority. What is promoted in the process is a paternalism that, despite the dim view the novel takes of the power-structures of the British state, can only be useful in maintaining such structures. To submit to the novel's duration is already to be installed within an upbeat ethic of endurance. If, as we speculated above, the novel trains us to abide in Chancery-like structures—by getting us to wait, as it were, in its very long lines—, it does this only insofar as it is organized as a *reformed* Chancery, a Chancery that can moralize its procrastinations in a practice of delayed gratification. Recklessly, the Court demanded an attendance so futile that it inspired dangerously anarchistic fantasies of destruction. More prudently, the novel, urging us to wait, also promises (to use the very formula of prudence) that we shall wait *and see*.

VI

Though it goes to great lengths, *Bleak House* also goes to extremities to save these lengths from lapsing into the mere unproductive extensions of the Chancery suit. Or rather, it saves them from such a fate *at* the extremities, or end-parts, in the production of a closure. Even so the novel cannot yet be considered to have won free of public, institutional attachments. For the very closure that secures a formal narrative difference between the novel and bureaucracy simultaneously implicates the novel in a formal narrative resemblance to the institution that has played a sort of rival to the bureaucracy, the police. It is clear that the difference that obtains between Chancery and the novel applies equally in the relationship between Chancery and the police. In determining its own closure as revelation and fixed repose, the novel appears to have rejected the conception of termination proper to bureaucracy only to espouse that proper to the police. The closural specimen that takes place, for example, at Richard's death-bed, even if it begins as though it will merely reflect the bureaucratic logic of lapse, achieves a permanent clarification of his character that rather subsumes the scene under the police model of closure as a double (cognitive and practical) apprehension. It can be further argued that, as it arouses a desire for expeditious, conclusive solutions, but only represents a single agency capable of providing them, the novel subtly identifies the reader's demand for closure with a general social need for the police, thus continuing (with only a considerable increase of cunning) the apologetics for the new forces of order that Dickens began as an essayist in *Household Words*.

The novel, however, is just as little anxious to appear an agency of the police as it was to resemble a relay of the Chancery system. The relatively friendly treatment that *Bleak House* accords to the Detective Police is qualified by a number of reservations about the nature and effects of its power. Most of these, like the other aspects of the police, are carried in the characterization of Inspector Bucket. His black clothes, linking him sartorially with Tulkinghorn and Vholes, darken his character as well with an association to the Court; and like the undertaker to whose costume this dress also makes allusion, Bucket induces an ambivalence even in those he works for. Depending on the regularity of corruption, his profession has the doubly offensive aspect of a speculation on human weakness that happens also to be invariably justified. Yet the grief betokened by "the great mourning ring on his little finger" (310) might as well take Bucket himself for its object as any of his clients. His nature subdued to what it works in, Bucket too may be counted among the victims of crime. "Pour bien faire de la police," Napoleon is supposed to have said, "il faut être sans passion." The moral horror of crime, which Dickens preserves (among other things) in his sensationalistic treatment of it, must be irrelevant—might even be counterproductive—to the professional dispassion required for the task of apprehending the criminal. This task may no doubt be considered itself a moral one. But the game function of detection thoroughly dominates whatever ethical ends it presumably serves; and, as Bucket himself can assure Sir Leicester, his profession has placed him utterly beyond the possibility of being scandalized:

> '... I know so much about so many characters, high and low, that a piece of information more or less, don't signify a straw. I don't suppose there's a move on the board that would surprise *me*; and as to this or that move having taken place, why my knowing it is no odds at all; any possible move whatever (provided it's in a wrong direction) being a probable move according to my experience....' (726)

The ethical perspective survives only in the faint melancholy with which Bucket, truly the "modern prince" in this respect, appears to regret the necessity of his own pessimism; or in the personal askesis that, when every consequence of desire proves criminal, is perhaps the only humane response remaining. Nonetheless, the melancholy is hardly sufficient to prevent him from eliciting the very weaknesses that are the object of its contemplation. The momentary collaboration between Skimpole and Bucket revealed at the end of the novel, an alliance of two species of moral indifference, throws no more discredit on the aesthete who delivers a dangerously ill child over to the police for no better reason than a bribe, than on the officer who extends the bribe for no better reason than to cover his client's prying. Even the askesis surrenders its moral truth to the extent that it is the very evidence of Bucket's amoral professionalization. As Tulkinghorn's fate exemplifies, amateur detectives run amok because they are motivated by personal desires for possession. Renunciation is thus for the professional detective a positive qualification, much as what Bucket appears to lament as his barren marriage shows a clear profit as an amicable and highly efficient business partnership.

These reservations are most tellingly inscribed in the novel as a narrative difference, once again centering on the question of ending, between the novel and the detective story that it includes. According to what will later be codified as the "classical" model, the detective story in *Bleak House* reaches it proper end when Bucket, having provided a complete and provable account of her guilt, arrests Mademoiselle Hortense for Tulkinghorn's murder. In the classical model, one may observe, though the security of its preferred decor, the locked room, is regularly breached, it is also invariably recovered in the detective's unassailable *reconstruction* of the crime. And similarly, in this not yet quite classical example, Bucket's ironclad case against Hortense may be understood as the reparation of Tulkinghorn's tragically vulnerable chambers. Yet if one tradition, the detective story, violates its closed rooms only to produce better defended versions of them in the detective's closed cases, another tradition, let us call it the Novel, violates even these cases. In this latter tradition, to which *Bleak House* ultimately bears allegiance, there is no police case so flawless that a loophole cannot be found through which its claims to closure may be challenged. Here our vision of the loophole is supplied by Mlle. Hortense:

> 'Listen then, my angel,' says she, after several sarcastic nods. 'You are very spiritual. But can you restore him back to life?'
> Mr Bucket answers, 'Not exactly.'
> 'That is droll. Listen yet one time. You are very spiritual. Can you make an honourable lady of Her?'
> 'Don't be so malicious,' says Mr Bucket.
>
> 'Or a haughty gentleman of Him?' cries Mademoiselle, referring to Sir Leicester with ineffable disdain. 'Eh! O then regard him! The poor infant! Ha! ha! ha!'
> 'Come, come, why this is worse Parlaying than the other,' says Mr Bucket. 'Come along.' 'You cannot do these things? Then you can do as you please with me. It is but the death, it is all the same. Let us go, my angel. Adieu you old man, grey. I pity you, and I despise you!' (743)

Hortense enumerates the various existential problems that, outlasting Bucket's solution, make it seem trivial and all but inconsequential. Her purely verbal qualification is soon worked into the actual plot when Bucket sets out in search of Lady Dedlock and finds her dead body instead. However skillfully prosecuted, the work of detection appears capable only of attaining to a shell from which the vital principal has departed. Other closural moments in *Bleak House* similarly end by producing a corpse, as though the novel wanted to attest, not just the finality, but also the failure of a closure that, even as it was achieved, missed the essence of what it aspired to grasp. In its ostentatious awareness of this failure, the novel defines its relationship to the materials of police fiction that it has adopted. On one side of this relationship there would be a detective story whose shallow solution naively gratifies our appetite for closure; on the other, there would be a Novel which, insisting at the very moment of solution on the insoluble, abiding mysteriousness of human and literary experience, provides superior nourishment by keeping us hungry.[20] Not to be identified with Chancery, the novel contrasts the aimless suspension of the suit with the achievement of its own ending; but not to be confused with the police either, it counters the tidy conclusion of the case with a conspicuous recognition of all that must elude any such achievement. If in the first instance, the novel must affirm the possibility of closure, in the second it is driven to admit the *inadequacy* of this closure.

In the end, then,—precisely there—the novel's attempt to differentiate its own narrative procedures from those of the institutions it portrays falters, and the effort to disentangle itself from one institution only implicates it once again in another. So the seemingly perverse pattern continues wherein the novel is eager to produce a sheltered space whose integrity it is equally willing to endanger. We have seen how the novel establishes the opposition between the private-domestic and the social-institutional (1) within the representation, as the contrast between Esther's Bleak House and Chancery, and between the former and the police; (2) as a formal practice of consumption, in which the novel-reading subject shuttles to and fro between the home in which the novel is read and the world in which it is verified; and (3) at the intersection of the novel's own representational practice with the represented practice of institutions that it includes in its content. We have also seen how, in every instance, the opposition is accompanied by the possibility that it may be, or have been, nullified. At the same time as the existence of an "outside" to institutional power is affirmed, that very affirmation is undercut with doubt.

Yet to describe the novel's rhetorical operation in this way, as the work of destructuration and subversion, is to identify it wholly with what is in fact only its negative moment.[21] We need to envision the positivity of this operation too, for what is put in question has also by the same token been put in place, and can be put to use as well. The ideological dividends paid in the difference between the "inside" and the "outside" of power are clear. The "outside" gives the assurance of liberty that makes tolerable the increasingly total administration of the "inside" and helps avoid a politicization of society as a whole. It also provides an authentically critical space from which amendments and reforms useful to this administration can be effectively broached and imposed. As we began by observing, however, *Bleak House* troubles the straightforwardness of this difference, which it transforms into the question of a difference. What, then, are the ideological dividends paid in *bringing the difference in question*? A full answer would have to inquire into a whole range of practices whereby our culture has become increasingly adept in taking benefit of doubt.[22] But we can provide the synecdoche of an answer by turning in conclusion to the specific practice that, though we have seen it continually emerge both as an effect of various institutions and as the term of sundry oppositions, we have stopped short of considering in itself.

Yet it is the practice that *Break House* is most concerned to promote: the practice of the family.

VII

Even in what otherwise would be her triumph, when the recognition of her merit has assumed public proportions, Esther Summerson retains her modest blindfold: "The people even praise Me as the doctor's wife. The people even like Me as I go about, and make so much of me that I am quite abashed. I owe it all to him, my love, my pride! They like me for his sake, as I do everything I do in life for his sake" (880). And to Allan's affirmation that she is prettier than ever she was, she can only respond:

> I did not know that; I am not certain that I know it now. But I know that my dearest little pets are very pretty, and that my darling is very beautiful, and that my husband is very handsome, and that my guardian has the brightest and most benevolent face that ever was seen; and that they can very well do without much beauty in me—even supposing—. (880)

Just as earlier Esther could barely speak of Allan, or her desire for him, so now, at the moment this desire is returned, she can only stammer. With her unfinished sentence, *Bleak House* "ends." Though one easily supplies what Esther keeps from saying ("even supposing I have my beauty back"), the modesty that consigns this assertion to silence is, to the last, radically inconclusive. Like woman's work, which is the external means to Esther's social recognition, the labors of modesty, its inner correlative, are never done.

What might be a matter for grief or grievance, however, as Esther's "neurotic" inability to relinquish her self-doubt in the hour of success, also means that the energy that has gone into consolidating and sustaining one Bleak House after another will not be dissipated in the complacency of enjoyment or relaxation. The text has posed the origin of Esther's self-doubt in the question of her proper place in a family structure (her illegitimacy), and this origin has shaped her tacit ambition to install herself securely within such a structure. Given a twist, however, by the psychology of modesty through which it is obliged to pass, the ambition attains to a frustration that is exactly proportionate to its achievements. Esther never ceases to earn her place, as though, were she to do so, she might even at the end be displaced from it. Yet there is a twist to the frustration too, as Esther's endless modesty finds its non-neurotic social validation in the family that, no less precarious than her own sense of identity, requires precisely such anxious and unremitting devotion for its survival. Or, as these relations might be generally summarized: the insecurity of the family subject is indispensable to counter the instability of the family structure, of which it is an effect.

The instability of the family, therefore, is constitutive of its very maintenance. As Jacques Donzelot has shown, the nineteenth-century family develops within two registers, which he calls *contract* and *tutelage*. Contract indicates the free and easy family autonomy ensured through "the observance of norms that guarantee the social usefulness of [its] members"; whereas tutelage designates the system of "external penetration" of the family, transformed into an object of surveillance and discipline. The two registers are positive and negative dimensions of a single policy of incentive: if the family satisfactorily performs its social tasks, then it is granted the liberty and autonomy of contract; but should it fail to pay back the privileges thereby conferred upon it in the proper accomplishment of responsibilities, then it must fall back into the register of tutelage.[23]

With these two registers, one can correlate the two causes that Dickens's novels regularly ascribe to the faultiness of the family: on one hand, the external interference of institutions that (like the workhouse in *Oliver Twist*) dislocate and disjoin the family; and on the other, the internal dynamic that (as exemplified in *Oliver Twist* by Monks's Oedipal and sibling rivalry) determines its own divisions and displacements. If the first cause amounts to a demand for contract, the second is a concession to the necessity of tutelage. The theme of outside interference bears a message to society at large to reform its institutions in the interest of preserving the only natural and naturally free space within it. (The argument is never free from the utilitarianism that Dickens's sentimentality about the family rationalizes rather than resists. The novels continually imply the family's advantages over other agencies in producing acceptable citizens of the liberal state both in quantitative terms—as its greater economy—and in qualitative ones—as the superiority of the bonds between its members.) The theme of internal disruption, on the other hand, addresses its message to the family itself, which had better do its utmost to stay together or else face the misery of being dispersed or colonized by remedial institutions. In the first instance, Dickens advises society to police for the family, which would thereby be safeguarded as the home of freedom; in the second, he counsels the family to police itself, that it might remain free by becoming its own house of correction. The two apparently incompatible themes, informing the representation of the family throughout Dickens's work, are in fact complementary. Likewise, the "practical" recommendations attached to each find their mutual coherence precisely in the way that they cancel one another out. For if society reformed itself so that state institutions would, if not wither away, become minimal and humane, then there would no longer exist an outside threat to consolidate the family in the face of its internal dangers; and to the extent that the family could successfully repress these dangers itself, it would only reproduce such institutions in their worst aspects. With the disappearance of social discipline, the emancipated family would prove in greater need of it than ever; and in the enjoyment of its unobstructed independence, it would restore the discipline from which it was meant as an asylum, either in its own practice or in that of the institutions that would inevitably make their reappearance upon its breakdown.

Neither the social nor the familial "policing of the family," therefore, can be carried very far without giving rise to the very regimentation it was supposed to curtail. In this respect at least, Dickens's vigorous reformism makes better sense as an undeclared defense of the status quo: the social recommendations would merely be the weights (like most weights, not meant to be carried very far) to preserve the family in its present delicate balance. For the family's freedom is founded in the possibility of its discipline, and thus to enjoy the former means to have consented to the latter. Esther's insecurity, we said, works to oppose the instability of the family structure from which it results. It supplies the constant vigilance wanted to keep the contractual family from lapsing into the subjection of tutelage. It is equally true, however, that Esther's insecurity *confirms* the family in its faultiness. In the same degree as it propagates the worry and anxiety needed to maintain the family, it keeps alive the ever-present danger of its fall. The novel everywhere publishes the same fear of falling and implies the same urgency about holding one's place. The "outside" of power regularly incurs the risk that it may be annexed—or worse, may already have been annexed-by the "inside." So, for instance, the family will sometimes be shown for only a slight modulation of Chancery bureaucracy (comfortably domesticated with the Jellybys), or of the police (one of whose different voices can be heard in Mrs. Pardiggle, the "moral Policeman" who regiments her own family in the same spirit she takes others "into custody" [107]). And the risk touches us more nearly than do these unadmirable characters, for even the excellent Bagnets rely on an explicitly military order, and Esther herself may be only better directed than Mrs. Jellyby when she sits at her desk "full of business, examining trademen's books, adding up columns, paying money, filing receipts, and ... making a great bustle about it" (122). Envisioning the family now as a firm counterweight to social institutions, now as a docile function of them, here as the insuperable refuge from the carceral, there as the insufferable replica of it, the novel poses the question of the family, which it thereby designates as the object of struggle. Rather as Esther takes up this question as the necessity of founding and keeping Bleak House, so the novel extends the question to its readers, both as a principle of hope and an exhortation, as it were, to work at home. Mr. Bagnet's famous catchword formulates what is no less the objective than the condition of the family in Dickens's representation of it: "Discipline"—within the domestic circle as well as outside it—"must be maintained."

VIII

Queen Victoria confided to her diaries: "1 never feel quite at ease or at home when reading a Novel."[24] *Bleak House* makes itself as anxiogenic and incomplete as the home with which it identifies. For in an age in which productivity is valued at least as much as the product, the novel must claim no less the inadequacy than the necessity of closure. This inadequacy can now be understood—not in the old-fashioned way, as a failure of organic form, nor even in the new-fashioned way, as the success of a failure of organic form—but, in the broader context of institutional requirements and cultural needs, as the novel's own "work ethic," its imposing refusal of rest and enjoyment. Certainly, reading this novel, though in the reasons of the hearth it finds its own reason for being, one never feels quite at home; perhaps, having finished it, one knows why one never *can* feel at home. For what now is home—not securely possessed in perpetuity, but only leased from day to day on payment of continual exertions—but a House? And what is this House—neither wholly blackened by the institutions that make use of its cover, nor wholly bleached of their stain—but (in the full etymological ambiguity of the word) irresolvably Bleak? "Bleak House has an exposed sound" (68).

NOTES

1. Charles Dickens, *Oliver Twist* (Oxford: Oxford University Press, 1949), pp. 95 and 94. For a more ample account of the novel along the lines sketched out here, see D. A. Miller, "The Novel and the Police," *Glyph* 8 (Baltimore: The Johns Hopkins University Press, 1981), pp. 129–33.

2. Charles Dickens, *Bleak House* (Oxford: Oxford University Press, 1948), p. 7. For all future citations from the novel, page references to this edition will be given parenthetically in the text.

3. John Forster, in an unsigned review for the *Examiner* (October 8, 1853): 643–45; reprinted in Philip Collins, ed., *Dickens: The Critical Heritage* (New York: Barnes and Noble, 1971), p. 291.

4. George Brimley, in an unsigned review, *Spectator* (September 24, 1853), 36: 923–25; reprinted in Collins, p. 283.

5. A euphoric account of the destiny of Victorian bureaucracy may be found in David Roberts, *The Victorian Origins of the Welfare State* (New Haven: Yale University Press, 1961). For a detailed treatment of Dickens's attitude toward the Detective Police, see the relevant chapter in Philip Collins's invaluable study, *Dickens and Crime*, 2nd ed. (London: Macmillan, 1964).

6. I have in mind the tradition founded in Louis Althusser, "A Letter on Art," *Lenin and Philosophy*, translated by Ben Brewster (New York and London: Monthly Review Press, 1971), pp. 221–27, and elaborated in Pierre Macherey, A *Theory of Literary Production*, translated by Geoffrey Wall (London: Routledge & Kegan Paul, 1978). Althusser's claim that art performs an "internal distanciation" on ideology in the course of representing it ("Letter," p. 222) receives its working-through in the theory and practical criticism of Macherey, for whom "the finished literary work ... *reveals* the gaps in ideology" by "specifically literary means" (*Literary Production*, pp. 60, 238). The best example of this tradition in English (and also the most relevant to the work in progress here) is Terry Eagleton, *Criticism and Ideology* (London: New Left Books, 1976). In the chapter called "Ideology and Literary Form," which includes a discussion of Dickens and other nineteenth-century English novelists, "ideology" (*qua* "organicism") once again provides the principle of coherence that "literary form" once again brings into disarray: "In English literary culture of the past century, the ideological basis of organic form is peculiarly visible, as a progressively impoverished bourgeois liberalism attempts to integrate more ambitious and affective ideological modes. In doing so, that ideology enters into grievous conflicts which its aesthetic forms betray in the very act of attempted resolution" (p. 161). In all cases, the category of artistic form remains where bourgeois aesthetics used to situate it: beyond social tensions or, what comes to the same, invariably on the right side of the struggle.

7. A first, but decisive expression of this view is given in J. Hillis Miller's introduction to *Bleak House*, by Charles Dickens (Penguin, 1971), pp. 11–34.

8. Charles Dickens, *Little Dorrit* (Oxford: Oxford University Press, 1953), p. 104.

9. Trollope, the only other major Victorian novelist to take up the subject of bureaucracy, offers us a similar perception in *The Three Clerks* (1858), where the new system of competitive examinations introduced by the Civil Service Reform inspires one of the examiners with the definitive dream of bureaucracy: to turn the end it serves into the means of its own expansion. "Every man should, he thought, be made to pass through some 'go.' The greengrocer's boy should not carry out cabbages unless his fitness for cabbage-carrying had been ascertained, and till it had also been ascertained that no other boy, ambitious of the preferment, would carry them better." Anthony Trollope, *The Three Clerks* (Oxford: Oxford University Press, 1943), p. 128.

10. Frequently drawn from the end of the eighteenth century to our own day, the contrast between the delay of the law and the dispatch of the police typically emerges (as here in Dickens) on the side of the police. A *locus classicus*: "Entourée de formes qu'elle ne trouve jamais assez multipliées, la justice n'a jamais pardonné a la police sa rapidité. La police, affranchie de presque toutes les entraves, n'a jamais excuse dans la justice, ses lenteurs; les reproches qu'elles se font mutuellement, la Société les fait souvent à l'une ou à l'autre. On reproche à la police d'inquiéter l'innocence, à la justice de ne savoir ni prévenir, ni saisir le crime ..." Joseph Fouché, Minister of Police, in a circular addressed to the prefects of France, 30 Brumaire, Year VIII; quoted in Henry Buisson, *La Police, son histoire* (Vichy: Imprimerie Wallon, 1949), p. 167.

11. See Michel Foucault, *Discipline and Punish*, translated by Alan Sheridan (New York: Pantheon, 1977), esp. pp. 222–23.

12. In installing criminals and police in the same seat—the conspicuous and closed world of delinquency—Dickens follows what was routine practice throughout the popular literature of the nineteenth century. To quote from a single, but highly influential example: "Le quartier du Palais de Justice, très circonscrit, très surveillé, sert pourtant d'asile ou de rendez-vous aux malfaiteurs de Paris. N'est-il pas étrange, ou plutôt fatal, qu'une irrésistible attraction fasse toujours graviter ces criminals autour du formidable tribunal qui les condamne à la prison, au bagne, à l'échafaud!" Eugène Sue, *Les Mystères de Paris* [1843], 4 vols. (Paris: Editions Hallier, 1977), vol. 1, p. 15.

13. See the editor's summary of the Victorian reception of *Bleak House* in Collins, *Dickens*:

14. Edgar Allan Poe, "Tale-Writing—Nathaniel Hawthorne," in *The Complete Works of Edgar Allen Poe*, ed. James A. Harrison, 17 vols. (New York: George D. Sprout, 1902), vol. 13, p. 153.

15. Even critics who propose an immediate identification of form and content in *Bleak House* are in practice compelled to acknowledge that the novel itself resists their enterprise. J. Hillis Miller's claim that "*Bleak House* has exactly the same structure as the society it exposes" has frequent recourse to concessive clauses that make allowance for "Dickens's generous rage against injustice, selfishness and procrastination" or his "sympathy for Gridley's indignant outrage" against the Chancery system (Introduction, pp. 29, 27). And Terry Eagleton, for whom the novel is "obliged to use as aesthetically unifying images the very social contradictions ... which are the object of [Dickens's] criticism," is quite happy to register the "contradictory" nature of the unity thus established (*Criticism and Ideology*, p. 129). Yet since both critics only recognize the difference between the novel and its world in the process of annulling it, they never permit themselves to consider seriously the *question* of the difference, and each is finally willing to pass off as a weakness of the text what is only a weakness in his account of it. In Miller's argument, in the absence of further treatment, evidence of the difference goes only to show that Dickens was curiously inconsistent. And in Eagleton, such evidence would merely point to a text that is, to use his own expressive phrase about *Dombey and Son* (1846–48), "self-divided and twisted by the very contradictions it vulnerably reproduces" (*Criticism and Ideology*, p. 127). Yet when, as it begins to appear, the difference between novel and world belongs to a series of analogous differences operating in the novel at several levels, then in dismissing the difference as an inconsequence or laying it to rest as a contradiction, we neglect a crucial aspect of the novel's own program, a central feature of its self-definition.

16. G. W. F. Hegel, *Phenomenology of Spirit*, tr. A. V. Miller (Oxford: Oxford University Press, 1977), p. 17.

17. Charles Dickens, *The Old Curiosity Shop* (Oxford: Oxford University Press, 1951), p. 553.

18. For example: "Jostling against clerks going to post the day's letters, and against counsel and attorneys going home to dinner, and against plaintiffs and defendants, and suitors of all sorts, and against the general crowd, in whose way the forensic wisdom of ages has interposed a million of obstacles to the transaction of the commonest business of life—diving through law and equity, and through that kindred mystery, the street mud, which is made of nobody knows what, and collects about us nobody knows whence or how: we only knowing in general that when there is too much of it, we find it necessary to shovel it away—the lawyer and the law-stationer come to a Rag and Bottle shop ...." (135)

19. "To end, to fill, to join, to unify—one might say that this is the basic requirement of the *readerly*, as though it were prey to some obsessive fear: that of omitting a connection. Fear of forgetting engenders the appearance of a logic of actions; terms and the links between them are posited (invented) in such a way that they unite, duplicate each other, create an illusion of continuity. The plenum generates the drawing intended to 'express' it, and the drawing evokes the complement, coloring: as if the *readerly* abhors a vacuum. What would be the narrative of a journey in which it was said that one stays somewhere without having arrived, that one travels without having departed—in which it was never said that, having departed, one arrives or fails to arrive? Such a narrative would be a scandal, the extenuation, by hemorrhage, of readerliness." Roland Barthes, *S/Z*, translated by Richard Miller (New York: Hill and Wang, 1974), p. 105.

20. *Bleak House* is thus one of the first texts to adumbrate a position that with Modernism becomes commonplace: namely, that a literature worthy of the name will respect mystery by keeping it inviolate. For a canonical allusion to the position, see Kafka's remarks on the detective story in Gustav Janouch, *Conversations with Kafka*, translated by Goronwy Rees, 2nd ed. rev. (New York: New Directions, 1971), p. 133; and among recent rehearsals, see David I. Grossvogel, *Mystery and its Fictions: From Oedipus to Agatha Christie* (Baltimore: The Johns Hopkins University Press, 1979).
Yet insofar as the modernist cult of the irresolvable is perfectly consistent with the efficient workings of Chancery Court, *Bleak House* is also one of the first texts to indicate the difficulties with this position, which advancing beyond cheap consolations, may only bind us more profoundly to a society that thrives on delayed and ever-incomplete satisfactions.

21. The moment exclusively occupies those two modes of literary criticism which this essay may be thought to address itself: Marxism and Deconstructionism. Contemporary Marxist criticism would construe the ambiguities we have noticed as the contradictions that inscribe the text's inevitable failure to make its domestic ideology cohere. By virtue of "internal distanciation," the literary text finds itself compelled to betray this ideology, if only in its hesitations, silences, discrepancies. Not altogether dissimilarly, Deconstruction would take such ambiguities for the aporias in an allegory of the process and problems of signification itself. Intended meaning is always exceeded in the signifiers to which it commits its expression, since by their nature those signifiers defer meaning even as they differentiate it. The "trace" of such differentiation, furthermore, carrying over as a kind of residue from one signifier to another, undermines the integrity of each: so that, in the case of an opposition, one term will invariably prove to be contaminated with the term it is meant to oppose. Without insisting on the comparison, one might say that Marxist criticism, urgently putting under scrutiny the evidence of a text that thereby never fails to convict itself, proceeds rather like the Detective Police; whereas a Deconstructive criticism, patiently willing to remain on the threshold of interpretation in the wisdom that every reading it might offer would be a misreading, behaves somewhat like Chancery Court. If only from *Bleak House*, however, we know that a practice claiming to resemble neither the bureaucracy nor the police merely uses this pretension to camouflage its alliances with both. For us, therefore, it cannot exactly be a matter of repudiating these critical modes, but rather of writing against them, as against a background. "Against" Marxism, then, we stress the positivity of contradiction, which, far from always marking the fissure of a social formation, may rather be one of the joints whereby such a formation is articulated. Contradiction may function not to expose, but to construct the ideology that has foreseen and contained it. And "against" Deconstruction, we should urge (rather as did Hegel in confronting the nothingness of skepticism) that undecidability must always be the undecidability of *something in particular*. The trouble with the Deconstructionist

allegory of signification is not that it is untrue, but that, despite the deceptive "closeness" of the readings, it is abstract. Two things, I think ought to remove the effects of undecidability and contradiction from the void in which Deconstruction places them. For one, they have a history or genealogy that determines them and whose traces must be registered. It may be ultimately true, for instance, as J. Hillis Miller has said, that "*Bleak House* is a document about the interpretation of documents" (Introduction, p. 11), but the formulation elides the rivalrous differentiations among institutional practices through which the concern with interpretation comes to emerge (and then, not as a theme so much as the stakes in a contest). As a result, one misses seeing the extent of the novel's assumption that it is *not* a document like those it is about. For a second, these effects, once formed, are never left at large and on the loose to wreak havoc on discursive and institutional operations. On the contrary, the latter have always already drafted them into a service which takes its toll and whose toll, accordingly, needs to be assessed in turn. Thus, Miller's account keeps characteristic silence about what even *Bleak House* (for highly partisan reasons of its own, of course) is quite willing to publicize: that the hermeneutic problematic itself is an instrument in the legal establishment's will to power.

22. At the level of subjective practices, a central and quite literal example would be the continuity noted by Max Weber between the religious ethos of Protestantism and the mental disposition of capitalism. The Calvinist subject's doubt as to his salvation engages him in intense worldly activity as a means to attain self-confidence. Such self-confidence is thus made to ride on restless, continuous work in a calling—a process that may surpass the moment of possession or remain on this side of it, but in any case never coincides with it. The task of proving one's election becomes as endless as the increase of capital that is the sign of its being successfully accomplished. Dickens is far enough from—or close enough to—this psychological structure to make it a prime target of his criticism, either as the spiritual bookkeeping of a Mrs. Clennam or the entrepreneurial pieties of a Bounderby. Yet the end of such criticism is not to repudiate the nexus between personal doubt and worldly duty, but rather to free its terms from their limiting specifications. This means, in effect, re-encoding it within the organization of the family. Weber's Protestant ethic is replaced by Freud's Family Romance, as a structure linking self-doubt with worldly ambition. When the specific doctrinal source of doubt (predestination) has been familialized as a problematic of the "orphan," uncertain both of his parents' identity and hence of his place in the world; when even the "calling" has been transferred from the primary capitalist sphere (where with the advent of industrialism its integrity had been seriously compromised) to the still undisparaged domain of domestic economy, then Robinson Crusoe returns as Esther Summerson: both the doubt-ridden, self-effacing orphan, always on the verge of being overwhelmed by the question of her origin and the consequent problem of her destiny, and at the same time, the "methodical" housekeeper (92) "with a fine administrative capacity" (597), who, admonishing herself "Duty, my dear!" shakes the keys of her kingdom to ring herself "hopefully" to bed (80).

23. Jacques Donzelot, *The Policing of Families*, translated by Robert Hurley (New York: Pantheon, 1979). The discussion of contract and tutelage that is paraphrased and cited here occurs on pp. 82–95.

24. Viscount Esher, ed., *The Girlhood of Queen Victoria: A Selection from her Diaries 1832–40*, 2 vols. (London: J. Murray, 1912), vol.2, p. 83, reprinted in Collins, *Dickens: The Critical Heritage*, p. 44. The citation comes from an entry for December 23, 1838.

GEORGE LEVINE

Dickens and Darwin

DICKENS is the great novelist of entanglement, finding in the mysteries of the urban landscape those very connections of interdependence and genealogy that characterize Darwin's tangled bank. Certainly, Dickens is not self-evidently a Darwinian novelist—much of his catastrophist and apocalyptic imagination is incompatible with Darwin's gradualist world. Yet in many respects, particularly in his energetic tendencies to multitudinousness and the mysteries of imperceptible connection, he is close indeed to Darwin's "nature," far from the ordered world of natural theology. Even his "catastrophism," with its implicit recognition of progressive change rather than Lyellian stasis, belongs to Darwin's world, for, as I have suggested, Darwin's achievement was in part the absorption into uniformitarianism of catastrophist progression.

From the start Dickens's preoccupation with irrepressible multiplicity contends against an aspiration to order and meaning. When Mr. Pickwick slams the door on the suffering outside his prison room, Dickens dramatizes the loss of an unambiguous sense that the world makes sense and is ultimately ordered and just. He yearns for a "nature" that is indeed God's second book, as in the tradition of natural theology. But, like Darwin, he describes a world that resists such ordering. Unlike Darwin, he is often driven to arbitrary manipulation of plot to reinstate what his imagination has expelled.

From *Darwin and the Novelists: Patterns of Science in Victorian Fiction.* © 1988 by the Presidents and Fellows of Harvard College.

The refrain "What connexion can there be?"[1] which echoes implicitly through all of *Bleak House* is answered by genealogy, just as Darwin's question about the meaning of the "natural system" is answered: "All true classification is genealogical; ... community of descent is the hidden bond which naturalists have been unconsciously seeking, and not some unknown plan of creation" (*Origin*, p. 404). The juxtaposition of the separate worlds of Chesney Wold and Tom-All-Alone's in sequential chapters implies just such a "hidden bond," which is laden with moral implications.

Esther is the natural daughter who links the apparently unrelated city and rural life, poverty and wealth, lower class and aristocracy, and she is a figure for the moral bond that society ignores. Many in Dickens's society thought that Darwin's establishment of such natural connections of descent implied the destruction of the very moral bonds Dickens used genealogy to affirm. Both *Bleak House* and the *Origin* bespeak, in their different ways, the culture's preoccupations with "connexion" where physical juxtaposition, as in the cities, seemed to reveal startling spiritual, even biological discontinuity. What has Jo the crossing sweep got to do with Tulkinghorn the rich and powerful lawyer? Much of the battle about evolutionary theory implied the culture's deep discomfort with its new social juxtapositions, its attempt to deny the implicit religious context of the "hidden bond" as it appears in Dickens, its unwillingness to know that we are all literally one family.[2] Dickens's preoccupation with discovering connections links him in one way with a tradition of narrative that goes back to Oedipus, in another, with the Judaco-Christian insistence that we are our brothers' keepers, and in yet another, to Darwinian styles of investigation and explanation.

Dickens certainly admired Darwin's theory, as Darwin took pleasure in Dickens's novels. There is no evidence that Dickens, like the more austere and dogmatic Carlyle, found Darwinism anathema. And it has been suggested that "the organisation of *The Origin of Species* seems to owe a good deal to the example of one of Darwin's most frequently read authors, Charles Dickens."[3] No literate person living between 1836 and 1870 could have escaped knowing about Dickens. After 1859, the same would have been true about Darwin. While Darwin rewrote for nineteenth-century culture the myth of human origins, secularizing it yet giving it a comic grandeur and a tragic potential, Dickens was the great mythmaker of the new urban middle class, finding in the minutiae of the lives of the shabby genteel, the civil servants, the "ignobly decent," as Gissing's novelist Biffin called them, great comic patterns of love and community, and great tragic possibilities of dehumanization and impersonal loss.

Given the pervasiveness of their fame, Dickens and Darwin had to have known each other's myths. In the crucial period of the late 1830s, in the notebooks that show him developing his theory, Darwin recorded that reading a review of Comte "made me endeavour to remember and think deeply," an activity that gave him an "intense headache." In contrast, he noted "the immediate manner in which my head got well when reading article by Boz."[4] The pleasures of Dickens remained with Darwin permanently. Although Darwin claimed that later in life he lost the power to enjoy poetry, he was a constant reader of literature from his youth,[5] and to the end, as he indicates in his *Autobiography*, he read novels steadily—or had them read to him.[6] In a well-known passage in his letters, he returns casually to *Pickwick Papers*—one of his favorite books—for a little philosophy: "As a turnkey remarked in one of Dickens's novels, 'Life is a rum thing'" (*Life and Letters*, II, 446). He even uses a Dickens description of a snarling mob in *Oliver Twist* to support his argument that human expressions are ultimately derived from rudimentary animal behavior.

What matters far more is that Dickens's development implies a confrontation with the very kinds of problems that Darwin, in his much different way, was also addressing. Dickens would turn the preoccupation with connections into moral parables, but his major narrative and moral difficulty had to do with the problem of change, about which he was much more ambivalent than Darwin. Although he supported the developments of the new science, that greatest instrument of change, and he despised the ignorance and prejudices of the past, there remains a strain of essentialism in his writing that led to trouble when he tried to imagine change of character; and though he brilliantly satirizes those who deny change, his style itself often denies it.

Dickens greeted with eagerness the radical developments in knowledge and communications that marked the nineteenth century. It would have been impossible for anyone, no less someone as imaginatively alive as Dickens, to have written without absorbing into his language something of the way science had been changing it. But he always regarded science as means to a human end, and he characteristically used scientific fact and method for moral purposes. According to Jonathan Arac, Dickens absorbs and transmutes the development in late eighteenth-century discourse by which scientific language was transferred to social theory. Arac points out, for example, how in the description of Tom-All-Alone's, Dickens "conveys less a specific physical description of the slum ... than an attitude of scientific precision about it ... Dickens's insistence on 'truth' in his preface to *Bleak House* ... leads him to draw wherever possible on scientific authorities, for he was convinced that there was no conflict between science, rightly understood, and the imagination."[7] The megalosaurus waddling up Holborn Hill, to take an obvious but minor example, was a discovery of nineteenth-century geology and paleontology, and was named by William Buckland, apparently no earlier than 1824. Dickens's friend, the famous anatomist Richard Owen, made megalosaurs an important element in his own theorizing and regarded them as the highest forms of reptile, with real affinities to mammals. Moreover, there are signs on the very first page of *Bleak House* that Dickens was aware of and could use for his own purposes the early-century debate among geologists over the question of whether the mineral world and the fossil record are to be accounted for by flood or fire. At first Dickens seems a Neptunist, as Ann Wilkinson points out,[8] but his Neptunism is opposed by Vulcanism, as, for example, in the fires of Rouncewell's mill, Mr. Krook's spontaneous combustion, and the "transferred" spontaneous combustion of the whole Jarndyee and Jarndyee case. These more or less plausible and respectable geological positions were scientifically argued and subserved traditional religious ends. Part of Dickens's materials for imagining the world, they are evidence that he used science as much for metaphor as for the latest news about the cosmos. But he did turn to it, he would not be reckless about what science had already revealed. His Neptunism and Vulcanism are a literary convenience that required no belief, but "spontaneous combustion" did. On that, too, Dickens thought he had science on his side.[9]

He was in fact extremely alert to modern scientific and technological developments. As Alexander Welsh has noted, it would be unwise "to underestimate the degree to which Dickens was aware of the intellectual ferment of his time."[10] Harvey Sucksmith points out that Dickens was "receptive to biological ideas throughout his life."[11] Unlike Carlyle and Ruskin, with whom he is often associated, Dickens does not look back nostalgically to a golden past. There is a strain in him that does praise "merrie olde England" and revere the old-fashioned. But the old, old fashion, Paul Dombey discovers, is death. Dickens was very much a man of his time, "a pure modernist," Ruskin notoriously complained,—"a leader of the steam-whistle party *par excellence*—and he had no understanding of any power of antiquity except a sort of jackdaw sentiment for cathedral towers."[12] Despite the wonderful extravagance, Ruskin was right. The savage satire at the start of book II of *The Tale of Two Cities* is only one example of Dickens's attitude toward the past; the more complex celebration of the railroad in *Dombey and Son* is another.

The bias of Dickens's world is toward the new. His attack on modern bureaucracy is more often than not an attack on a system that madly repeats the worst of ancient practices and traditions: the circumlocution office, chancery, charity schools, and new poor law, almost invariably reenforce the values and methods of the old. Even Dickens's vendetta against utilitarianism and laissez-faire economics is directed not at the new and industrious middle class, but, rather, at the heartlessness of bureaucratic and institutional England. And these Dickens shows to be reflected and abetted by obstinate support of obsolete procedures and structures that confirm old class divisions and generate new ones. Society sets up against competent and innovative minds like Daniel Doyce and Mr. Rouncewell obstructive relies like Tite Barnacle or (with some vestiges of dignity) Sir Leicester Dedlock. Worse, it produces a new breed of villain, ostensibly "modern" but by gestures at respectability merely exploiting ancient injustices in pursuit of success for Number One: Fagin, Mr. Carker, Uriah Heep, Mr. Vholes, Mr. Bounderby, Bradley Headstone.

Science, for Dickens, was a means to help dispel superstition and ancient prejudice and habit. Ignorance is the enemy of morality. In a speech as late as 1869, at a point in his career when, if he had been as disillusioned with contemporary materialism as he is sometimes purported to have been, that disillusion would have emerged, he objects strenuously to the characterization of the age as "materialistic." Instead, he celebrates the scientific and technological discoveries that had improved the quality of life. The speech was an implicit attack on a recent speech by Francis Close, Dean of Carlisle, who had complained about the secularization of knowledge. "There were those," the dean had complained, "who would prefer any dream, however foolish or vain, to the testimony of God respecting the origin of our species."[13] Dickens argues energetically for the continuing expansion of scientific knowledge, always seeing it as a means to important human ends. "I confess," he says,

> that I do not understand this much used phrase, a "material age," I cannot comprehend—if anybody can: which I very much doubt—its logical signification. For instance: has electricity become more material in the mind of any sane, or moderately insane man, woman, or child, because of the discovery that in the good providence of God it was made available for the service and use of man to an immeasurably greater extent than for his destruction? Do I make a more material journey to the bedside of my dying parents or my dying child, when I travel at the rate of sixty miles an hour, than when I travel thither at the rate of six?[14]

Here, if anywhere, is the credo of the "steam-whistle party." But Dickens was not unambivalent, and the treatment of Dombey's ride in the train that seems hurtling toward death, if not its personification, can give some sense of why the problem of change was never a simple one for him. Nevertheless, the speech is unequivocal in embracing the new. And it is not merely an endorsement of technological application of scientific ideas. Practical as Dickens's orientation was, the speech shows that he believed that the practical grew from a willingness to entertain and seek new ideas, whatever their apparent application. Darwinism and the secular interpretation of nature are not the problem; the problem is dogmatic traditionalism. "Do not let us be discouraged or deceived by vapid empty words," he urges. "The true material age is the stupid Chinese age, in which no new grand revelation of nature is granted, because such revelations are ignorantly and insolently repelled, instead of being humbly and diligently sought."[15] Dickens, too, believed that science is compatible with religion: the true irreligion is conventional dogmatic religiosity.

That he was not an intellectual, in our usual sense of the word, is obvious enough. Although some of his more mature comments on science (particularly on "spontaneous combustion") may seem both ignorant and prejudiced, Dickens maintained a warm relation with science and scientists. He enlisted important scientists for help with his weekly journals—not only Owen, who wrote several pieces for *Household Words*, but also, for example, Michael Faraday, who sent him the notes for his famous lectures on the candle, which eventually became *The Chemical History of a Candle*. Dickens published a kind of summary of it in *Household Words*, a summary that Wilkinson has found useful in understanding the structure and significance of *Bleak House*.

The details of Dickens's novels often reveal that he had absorbed, like an intelligent layman, some of the key ideas issuing from contemporary developments in geology, astronomy, and physics. The evidence is most obvious in *Household Words* and *All the Year Round*, where scientific matters are taken as significant despite the homely and domestic emphases. Often surprisingly sophisticated despite their popularizing strategies, the scientific essays stressed the relation of science to ordinary life and made his journals important popularizers of scientific ideas.

This is not to deny the complicating antiscientific strain in his writing. Mr. Pickwick begins as a butt of satire, and one of his persistently satirized characteristics is scientific ambition. He is introduced, in a gently Swiftian way, as the author of "Speculations on the Source of the Hampstead Ponds, with some Observations on the Theory of Tittlebats." On his first adventure, a cab ride, he solemnly accepts and notes the cabman's sardonic exaggeration that his horse is forty-two years old, or that the horse stays out two or three weeks at a time and only can keep standing because the cab supports it. A bit later, he becomes deeply excited about an "archaeological" discovery, which turns out to read BILL STUMPS HIS MARK. Some of the animosity to trivial science is diverted later in the book to "the scientific gentleman" who manages to mistake Mr. Pickwick's lantern in the garden for "some extraordinary and wonderful phenomenon of nature."[16]

In 1846, Dickens published his last Christmas book, *The Haunted Man*. It gave him the opportunity to carry out further that attack on the scientific character comically announced in *Pickwick Papers*, for the central character is the chemist, Redlaw, who has bargained away his power of memory. The connection between the scientific pursuit and dehumanization that follows is implicit, but Dickens makes very little of it. Here was a subject designed to explore the anaesthetizing consequences of exclusively analytic mental activity such as we find in the actual autobiographies of Darwin and Mill. But Dickens does not seem very interested in pursuing it. The hard look at life is painful, so the moral goes; implicitly, the scientist sees the pain and, sensitive enough, feels it. For the most part in this very thin tale Redlaw is a sympathetic figure, whose decision to give up memory is treated with understanding, although, of course, implicitly criticized. A willingness to take a good look at the worst is as essential as a celebration of the virtuous. Thus, in appealing for a restoration of his memory, Redlaw cries: "In the material world, as I have long taught, nothing can be spared; no step or atom in the wondrous structure could be lost, without a blank being made in the great universe. I know, now, that it is the same with good and evil, happiness and sorrow, in the memories of men."[17] With the conventional moral application of excessive reliance on science, the speech is nevertheless couched in the terms of science itself; and it reveals Dickens's awareness of one of the fundamental principles of contemporary science, the conservation of matter, demonstrated by Lavoisier late in the eighteenth century. Lavoisier had shown that the actual amount of material in a chemical transformation remains the same before and after: "We must always suppose an exact equality between the elements of the body examined and those of the product of its analysis," Lavoisier said.[18] In Dickens, the indestructibility of the physical universe, like all other scientifically affirmed ideas, becomes moral metaphor. For Redlaw and Dickens the physical world signifies, as it did for the natural theologians. Here, at least, Dickens's ambivalence about "God" does not inhibit him from using the physical as a sanction and even a model for the moral; rather, as for the natural theologians, faith that what turned up would be meaningful encourages further scientific pursuit of knowledge.

Similarly, in the very year of the *Origin*, Dickens published in *All the Year Round* an essay called "Gamekeeper's Natural History," which mocks in a traditional way the abstractness of most scientific thought. "No one can paint a thing which is not before him as he paints," says the author, and "natural history is not to be written by professors in spectacles—timid, twittering, unsophisticated men—from stuffed animals and bleached skeletons."[19] But it *is* to be written from life, by naturalists, so the author says, like "Audubon, White of Selbourne, Gould." Sharing his culture's Baconian commitment to "experience" as the source of knowledge, Dickens implicitly sees the writer's and the scientist's task of representing the real as deriving from the same powers, leading to the same places.

The coverage of science in the journals does not suggest that scientific thought and experiment were dehumanizing. Taken together the essays show that Dickens was familiar with and sympathetic to the large ideas which, though not strictly anticipations of Darwin's theory, were conditions for it. For example, Darwin needed, above all, the large infusion of time that Lyell's *Principles of Geology* gave him; and Dickens was not retrograde in accepting it, as is manifest in the comfortable allusions in *Bleak House* to geological time. The essay "The World of Water" talks about the "thousand, thousand years ago" in which fossil creatures lived. It casually refers to man as a latecomer into the world (although this is true even in Genesis), and it accepts the position of Cuvier and Lyell that there has been large-scale extinction of species, even forecasting the ultimate extinction of man himself.[20]

In the essays Dickens seems particularly fascinated by the minutiae revealed under the microscope—the dramatic disparity between what is visible to the naked eye and what is really there. In essay drawing on Philip Gosse's *Evening with the Microscope* Dickens describes the similarity in all vertebrate blood. And he gives a series of dramatic and pleasantly horrific pictures of the natural world, as, for example: "We venture to say that the poet who spoke of butterflies kissing the sweet lips of the flower &c. never looked through a microscope at that flat coiled tongue bristling with hairs and armed with hooks, rifling and spoiling like a thing of worse fame, but of no worse life."[21] Dickensian gothic is merely an entertaining way to emphasize that the natural wonders revealed by science were evidence of its value, and, indeed, of its value as entertainment; it further expresses Dickens's instinctive view that matter of fact is really mysterious and wonderful and not fully visible to any but an intense and imaginative moral vision.

Thus, while Dickens was willing to consider the pursuit of knowledge for its own sake, there was a touch of the Gradgrind in him; he always wanted to know to what use the knowledge would be put. His dislike of Gradgrindian "science" is dislike for the privileging of the intellect, which turns human complexity into abstraction and allows brutality under the sanction of "Truth." Dickens wants science in his fictions as metaphor, and this is true even for such burning theological questions as whether man is a child, cousin, or sibling of the apes. The opening chapter of *Martin Chuzzlewit*, as Sucksmith reminds us, alludes comically to the theory that man is descended from the apes (probably drawing on Dr. Johnson's description of Lord Monboddo).[22] Concluding his genealogical chapter about the Chuzzlewits, Dickens writes: "It may be safely asserted, and yet without implying any direct participation in the Mondboddo doctrine touching the probability of the human race having once been monkeys, that men do play very strange and extraordinary tricks."[23]

A much later essay in *All the Year Round* called "Our Nearest Relation" comfortably accepts the biological closeness of gorilla to man. Even the essayist's misapprehension that the gorilla is a ferocious and aggressive animal is what most naturalists' accounts at the time would have asserted. Dickens and his journal take the facts where they find them, but convert them quickly into moral metaphor. The gorilla essay concludes with this passage:

> Again and again it strikes the fancy—strikes deeper than the fancy—that the honey-making architectural bee, low down in the scale of life with its insignificant head, its little boneless body, and gauzy wing, is our type of industry and skill: while this apex in the pyramid of the brute creation, this near approach to the human form, what can it do? The great hands have no skill but to clutch and strangle; the complex brain is kindled by no divine spark; there, amid the unwholesome luxuriance of a tropical forest, the creature can do nothing but pass its life in fierce sullen isolation—eat, drink, and die?[24]

The essay takes up the idealist anatomy or transcendental biology of Richard Owen, the view, as Peter Bowler describes it, that similarity in structure among living creatures expresses an "'archetype' or ground plan on which all forms of life ... are modeled."[25] Several essays in *Household Words* expound and argue for transcendental biology. One such concludes exuberantly in this way: "Thus, beyond and above the law of design in creation, stands the law of unity of type, and unity of structure. No function so various, no labours so rude, so elaborate, so dissimilar, but this cell can build up the instrument, and this model prescribes the limits of its shape. Through all creation the microscope detects the handwriting of power and of ordnance. It has become the instrument of a new revelation in science, and speaks clearly to the soul as to the mind of man."[26] The similarity among organisms, like the similarity between gorilla and human, does not imply consanguinity, and certainly not descent, for the essential pre-Darwinian tenet of almost all thinkers aware of the similarities was that there is, nevertheless, an absolute gap between humanity and anthropoid, a gap to be filled only by the "divine spark" so manifestly missing in the gorilla's brain (a position which, remarkably, A. R. Wallace also took up later in his career, to Darwin's deep disappointment).[27] Even the most partisan Darwinians would concede what Huxley, for example, called "the vast intellectual chasm" between Man and the ape; but Huxley was to argue that the similarity in physical structure of the brains was evidence of consanguinity. There was no need to assume that an intellectual difference would entail "an equally immense difference between their brains."[28]

Nevertheless, Dickens's enthusiasm for new "grand revelations" of nature seems to have led him to publish in *All the Year Round* a remarkably fair-minded review of the *The Origin of Species* only a few months after the book first appeared. The review congratulates Darwin for living not "in the sixteenth century" and not in "Austria, Naples, or Rome," but in "more tolerant times." It proceeds to a reasonably skeptical but very careful presentation of the theory (using, without quotation marks, much of Darwin's own language), and concludes in a splendidly Victorian way, with sentiments worthy of Dickens:

> Timid persons, who purposely cultivate a certain inertia of mind, and who love to cling to their preconceived ideas fearing to look at such a mighty subject from an unauthorized and unwonted point of view, may be reassured by the reflection that, for theories, as for organised beings, there is also a Natural Selection and a Struggle for Life. The world has seen all sorts of theories rise, have their day, and fall into neglect. Those theories only survive which are based on truth, as far as our intellectual faculties can at present ascertain; such as the Newtonian theory of universal gravitation. If Mr. Darwin's theory be true, nothing can prevent its ultimate and general reception, however much it may pain and shock those to whom it is propounded for the first time.[29]

Although Dickens tried to avoid controversy in any of the essays he published in the journals, one can only infer that he was willing to risk controversy on this issue. A month earlier he had published another essay, called "Species," which, without reference to Darwin, quotes him at length as though in the essay writer's voice. The prose is judiciously impartial, but it employs Darwin's own words as its own: "It may be just as noble a conception of the Deity to believe that he created a few original forms capable of self-development into other and needful forms, as to believe that He required a fresh act of creation to supply the voids caused by the action of His laws."[30] Two essays so generously indulgent of the development theory in a journal as tightly controlled as *All the Year Round* seem very unlikely unless Dickens were ready to endorse the idea himself. The strategy of the review, carefully considering objections, but proceeding with a long and unquestioned set of quotations from Darwin in the voice of the reviewer, and concluding with an open evocation of a Darwinian metaphor, suggests a far greater commitment to the idea of evolution by natural selection than is explicitly affirmed. Even as it questions Darwin's theory, it uses his dominant metaphor to predict its future.

The attitudes implicit in the language and structure of Dickens's books are, like the attitudes essayed in his journals and afloat in scientific thought in the 1830s and 1840s, premonitory of the argument Darwin was constructing; they are also often in tension with it.

Dickens's openness to science is reflected in the qualities that characterize his fiction. His novels, in their way, work with the materials that Darwin transformed in another. What Dickens could not have accepted— and *Hard Times*, for example, is in part a tract against it—is the "scientific" treatment of the human subject, although in Bucket, an ultimately sympathetic character, Dickens prepares the way even for this; and the satirical strain of the third person narrator in *Bleak House*, like the sardonic voice at the opening of *Oliver Twist*, provides rhetorical form for such detached treatment. The human in Dickens largely escapes the reduction Darwin's theory implies, but the bleaker his vision the more ready Dickens is to regard the human as scientific (that is, merely material) subject. To avoid such a fate, he leaves open rationally inexplicable avenues of plotting and characterization. Nevertheless, many of the major characteristics of Dickens's way of seeing and writing about the world are reflected in major elements of Darwin's theory. The cultural theme of connection, with its implication in genealogy, is a major concern of both writers, for example, and suggests again that the possibilities of imagination in science and literature are mutually bounded, mutually derived. Science and literature help create the conditions necessary for each other's development.

The differences between Dickens and Austen are not merely the differences of individual genius. Both may have used contrivances necessary to resolve narrative problems; but Austen's self-consciousness allows her to affirm the intelligible design of the world. Parody is possible for her because she is easy with what is parodied. Dickens, by contrast, thinks less about the contrivance of the coincidences that drive so much of his plotting because they are essential to him if he is to find any shape for a world of profusion, multiplicity, and apparent disorder, a world in which, despite his celebrations of order, he is at home. The landscapes and the architecture of these worlds are far from those ordered eighteenth-century houses and gardens that define and place the characters in *Mansfield Park*. They are the view from Todgers, the chaos of Barnaby's London, Tom-All-Alone's, the dust heaps of *Our Mutual Friend*. Dickens is closer to Darwin than Austen, and not merely chronologically.

Some of the elements of Darwin's vision that I isolated in the first chapter have their counterparts in Dickensian narrative, and for the rest of this chapter I want to consider the parallels and the points of divergence. What is true for Dickens, a writer brilliantly outside the main stream of Victorian realism, is true more emphatically for the realists. Discussion of the Darwinian elements in Dickens, even of the ways he averts Darwinian treatment, should throw light on the other novelists, as well.

First, Dickens the "catastrophist" has much of the Darwinian uniformitarian in his vision. Like the great domestic novelists of the century, Dickens is fascinated by the most trivial domestic and social details—food, furnishings, manners, and all the particularities of ordinary life. The whole movement of narrative toward these details is very much part of the movement that led to evolutionary theory, and it is evident in the rhetoric of Darwin's own argument. Second, the emphasis on the ordinary is often accompanied by a preoccupation with mystery. Somehow, the familiar resonates through all of Dickens with tones of the unfamiliar; things are and are not what they seem. As Dickens himself says (in the Preface of *Bleak House*), he is concerned with "the romantic side of familiar things." To this I juxtapose Darwin's program of defamiliarization, discussed in detail in the preceding chapter, the attempt to discover new principles of order in the midst of what we have long taken for granted. Third, the mystery of the familiar seems to generate complicated plots, full of coincidence, as amidst the multitudinous populations of each novel jostling against each other, new relationships are perceived. The whole seems to move toward catastrophe and a reversal when everything is explained; yet, on the whole, everything *is* explained and what has seemed like chance at the level of story acquires a meaning in an overall plot or design. Dickens does not quite accept the Darwinian rejection of teleology and the need for chance as explanation; chance is there, to be sure, but Dickens makes it work for teleology, even if under strain. Fourth, Dickens struggles with the cultural and Darwinian tendency to blur boundaries. The familiar Dickensian "character" has a sharply defined nature, a singular essence normally conveyed in a few tricks of manner: Pecksniff is invariably a hypocrite, although his hypocritical invention is wonderfully various; Mr. Dombey is invariably proud, Amy Dorrit invariably angelic. The reading of the essential nature of characters seems related by contrast to Darwin's nominalism, and here the question of "change," raised at the start of this chapter becomes prominent. Fifth, the question of connection is critical in both writers: things hang together in Dickens's world, stories converge, unlikely connections are made, entanglements and dependencies are inevitable. In modern jargon, Dickens has an ecological vision; and so, of course, has Darwin. Finally, sixth, all of the elements I have been noting become part of a world overwhelmingly vital because abundant, multitudinous, diverse, full of aberration, distortions, irrationality, which may or may not be ultimately reducible to the large patterns.

The importance of uniformitarianism to the Darwinian argument should by now be clear; it is worth emphasizing, however, that preoccupation with the ordinary is the very heart of romanticism, Wordsworth's responsibility in the division of labor in the *Lyrical Ballads*. Wordsworth's songs and ballads began to emerge only a few years after James Hutton's paper, in 1785, giving the gist of his position in *The Theory of the Earth* (1795). Dickens begins his career as a reporter whose skills are based on his powers of observation, with an uncanny eye for the ordinary. In his eyes the ordinary is transformed, not by miraculous or catastrophic intrusions, but by intense and minute perception. So in his sketches he examines door knobs and reports on the behavior of cabbies, shopkeepers, marginal gentlemen. Wherever he looks, even in the Vauxhall Gardens by daylight, when the ordinariness leads to pervasive disenchantment, the ordinary carries its own enchantment. Describing "early coaches," for example, he notes that "the passengers change as often in the course of one journey as the figures in a kaleidoscope, and though not so glittering, are far more amusing."[31]

The extraordinary popularity of such trivia presupposes a shift to an audience concerned with middle-class domesticity and to the recognition from that perspective of how completely the largest events of our lives evolve from the accumulation of precisely such minutiae. The essay from *Household Words* already alluded to, "Nature's Greatness in Small Things," explores the similarity between the minutest microscopic organism and the largest. "Not unfrequently," says the author, "it is seen that forms the most minute are most essential," capable of working "immeasurable changes."[32] The popular fascination with books about what the microscope revealed is also related to the preoccupation with the domestic and the ordinary. All of these phenomena are part of the same movement that made concern for the domestic the dominant motif of the self-consciously "realist" fiction of the high Victorian period.

Aesthetically, the fulfillment of the uniformitarian vision was articulated in the Victorian novel's constant reversion to the ordinary, and to its treatment of it as normative. We find it most completely formulated in George Eliot's celebration of the art of the Dutch realist school of painting as a kind of model for her fiction. The antirevolutionary implications of this aesthetic are worked out in Eliot (see her handling of politics in *Felix Holt* as the most obvious example). Later, when Razumov of Conrad's *Under Western Eyes* scrawls "Evolution not Revolution," Conrad is affirming both a political and an aesthetic tradition that, by late in the century, was breaking down. I will be taking Razumov's attempt to affirm evolution against the revolutionary substance and style of the novel he occupies as a convenient marking point for a shift from Darwinian thinking in fiction. Evolutionary theory, Victorian realism, and antirevolutionary ideology go together very tightly through the century. Ironically, the materialist and secularizing implications of the revolutionary views that Jane Austen was resisting, when embodied in evolutionary theory, become conservative.

While it is common to see realist and Dickensian art in opposition, Dickens, with what Arac describes as a "scientific" attitude, seems even more concerned to insist on the literal truth of his writings than the more conventionally realistic writers.[33] For however much Dickens is to be regarded as a great entertainer or as metaphysical novelist, he *claimed* that he was a realist. Perhaps the earliest claim is in the preface to *Oliver Twist*, in which he attacks those who cannot stand the unhappy truths he has revealed. "There are people of so refined and delicate a nature, that they cannot bear the contemplations of such horrors," he says contemptuously. But he would not for those readers "abate one hole in the Dodger's coat, or one scrap of curl-paper in the girl's dishevelled hair." And as for the character of Nancy, "it is useless to discuss whether the conduct and character of the girl seems natural or unnatural, probable or improbable, right or wrong. IT IS TRUE." He bases this claim on his own experience of watching "these melancholy shades of life." Notice that here, in the defense of the reality of his fiction, Dickens rejects romance literature, which ignores surface details, and that this rejection entails mimetic particularity, attention to the minutiae of ordinary life. Have these sordid facts he has revealed "no lesson," Dickens asks, "do they not whisper something beyond the little-regarded warning of an abstract moral precept?"[34] The ordinary—the hole in the Dodger's coat, Nancy's disheveled hair—is given in Dickens some of the quality of allegory.

In the preface to *Martin Chuzzlewit* Dickens makes a similar point, emphaizing how perspective determines what is to be considered "realistic."

"What is exaggeration to one class of minds and perceptions, is plain truth to another ... I sometimes ask myself whether it is *always* the writer who colours highly, or whether it is now and then the reader whose eye for colour is a little dull." This eagerness to assert the literal truth of his fictions continued to the end of Dickens's career. In the postscript to *Our Mutual Friend* he talks of the "odd disposition in this country to dispute as improbable in fiction, what are the commonest experiences in fact," and he proceeds to defend as realistic old Harmon's will and his treatment of the Poor Law with evidence from *The Lancet*.[35]

Perhaps the most famous and egregious instance of Dickens's defense of the literal reality of his stories comes in the preface to *Bleak House*, where he defends the scientific validity of spontaneous combustion. "Before I wrote that description," he says, "I took pains to investigate the subject" (p. 4). It is particularly strange that an episode that has such coherent symbolic significances should seem to require from Dickens a defense of its literal truth. The spontaneous combustion of Krook is formally like the shooting of the albatross, and in the novel it is self-evidently the physical equivalent of the consumption in "costs" of the case of Jarndyce and Jarndyce, and the externalization of the moral nature of "justice" in Chancery. But again it suggests that while a "Coleridgean" novelist, showing himself most advantageously in extreme and quasi-supernatural situations, Dickens always saw himself as a realist, committed to the truthful representation of commonly experienced particulars. Thematically, his enterprise *was* very similar to that of the realists.

But Dickens had the confidence of natural theology, in which material reality corresponds meaningfully to a moral reality. The great analogy of natural theology, between physical and spiritual nature, is embedded in his imagination; the Darwinian disanalogy is the threat. If it is not quite the designed world of the natural theologians, it is nevertheless a world in which the fall into secularity is not inevitably a fall from grace. Allegory is not so much an invention as a representation, a mirror as much as a lamp.

In realist fiction of the kind Eliot wrote, "Nature has her language, and she is not unveracious; but we don't know all the intricacies of her syntax just yet."[36] In Darwin's writing nature is not illegible, but its syntax is difficult, and its meaning does not imply a moral reality inherent in the material, only its own nature. Eliot, through her conception of nemesis, often tries to infuse nature with moral meaning. But equally often she can sound like Darwin reminding us of the difference between "the face of nature bright with gladness"—the face that the natural theologian tends to see—and the destruction and devouring that accompany that "gladness." So she tells also of "what a glad world this looks like," but how "hidden behind the apple blossoms, or among the golden corn, or under the shrouding boughs of the wood, there might be a human heart beating with anguish."[37] In the wooden roadside cross Eliot finds a fit "image of agony" for the representation of what lies beneath the visible loveliness. It is a human symbol for a nonhuman nature. That is, the realist can find symbolic representations of the moral implication, but the symbol and the moral reality are human inventions. Nature is Darwinian. For Eliot, as for Dickens, the novelist was to make the ordinary resonant with myth, to show that the dream of romance is an absurd distortion and inferior to the romance of the ordinary, which contains within it forms of myth. But the romance of the ordinary is never inherent in nature. Nature's language is neutral.

The romantic-uniformitarian leaning of Dickens is partly undercut in the longer novels in which the traditions of stage melodrama are used to allow for quite literal catastrophe. Yet the distance between the uniformitarian and catastrophist position is much less absolute than it may at first seem. Both are romantic positions—the Wordsworth and Coleridge of science, as it were. In Dickens, the "catastrophe" of the murder of Tulkinghorn, for example, or the literal collapse of the Clennam house, can be seen as a metaphor for the consequences of the tedious daily accumulation of depressing facts—the slow grinding of Chancery, the moral bankruptcy of the deadening, static, circumlocutory world of bureaucracy and business. Dickens saw that the ordinary world was full of the extraordinary; he saw, too, that the extraordinary was the inevitable consequence of what seemed merely trivial, as an earthquake is caused by minute, almost undetectable movements over long periods of time. The argument between uniformitarians and catastrophists was, thus, double-edged, and we can feel analogous ambivalence in Dickens. If all extremes are merely accumulations of the ordinary, all the ordinary is potentially extreme.

The ordinary, then, is latent with possibilities of the extraordinary. It is a trick of contemporary horror movies, whose fundamental strategy is to focus on recognizable people in recognizable situations and then intrude something monstrous upon them. In Dickens, it is not only such gothic strategies (the talking chair in the *Pickwick Papers*, for example). But it is also Mrs. Copperfield bringing home a second husband who becomes, in his Puritanical austerity, a monster to the child. It is Boffin's dust heap, the dreary refuse of a recognizably ugly city, which becomes a mysterious treasure to Wegg; it is the clock greeting young Paul Dombey with "How-is-my-little-friend?"; it is Boz's superb account of the clothing in the window of the "emporium for second hand wearing apparel," which suddenly enact their melodramatic and yet commonplace histories. Like Darwin, who said, we must "no longer look at an organic being as a savage looks at a ship, as at something wholly beyond his comprehension," and must learn "to regard every production of nature as one which has had a history" (*Origin*, p. 456), Dickens makes us see the history—and the melodrama—in the commonplace object. He often affirms a world beyond the secular, but his works for the most part lose their touch with that world beyond, and with any authority except time, chance, and personal avarice. The world he creates—even Amy Dorrit's—is, like Darwin's, time-bound. Truth is not on the surface, after all, except as the surface offers to the keen observer clues to its history. All things imply histories but hide their pasts. By the time of *Bleak House*, only the professionally trained—police inspectors, like Bucket—can pierce through appearances with any confidence.

As he puts it at the start of his sketch "A Visit to Newgate," "force of habit" exercises great power "over the minds of men" and prohibits them from "reflection" on "subjects with which every day's experience has rendered them familiar." The essay "Character" is almost archaeological in that it infers whole lives from mere surfaces: "There was something in the man's manner and appearance which told us, we fancied, his whole life, or rather his whole day."[38] These attitudes and strategies are characteristic of Dickens's method throughout his career.

Such strategies parallel the views of the most advanced thinkers about science at the time. Herschel does sound occasionally like a romantic poet, or, perhaps more precisely, he formulates in the language of science ideas that were powerful in both poetry and fiction. If undisciplined experience leaves us open to our prejudices of opinion and of sense, a close look at nature—the glitter of a soap bubble, the fall of an apple—under the restraint of rational discipline, transforms it into a wonderland. "To the natural philosopher there is no natural object unimportant or trifling. From the least of nature's work he may learn the greatest lessons."[39] But the mysteries of the ordinary are only there for those who, like the readers of Dickens's novels, have been taught to look for clues.

As I pointed out in the last chapter, Darwin learned from Herschel and tried to emulate him. And although Herschel was not entirely pleased with Darwin's theory, he would have found in Darwin's work the same fascination with details, the same recognition of the miraculous nature of the ordinary, that he had tried to imbue in his readers. Darwin not only investigated the most ordinary phenomena—seeds in his garden, worm castings, bird excrement, bees' nests, pigeon breeding—but as a consequence discovered and persistently revealed that the details are not what they seem: plants travel; and organisms are frequently maladapted to their environment, or have organs irrelevant to adaptation. The strategy of defamiliarization so central to the *Origin* in its reeducating of natural philosophers and weaning them from creationism and natural theology, is akin to the strategies of domestic novels—as in Eliot's reminder in "Amos Barton" to learn to see some of "the poetry and the pathos ... lying in the experience of a human soul that looks out through dull grey eyes."[40] The poetry and the pathos of natural history are evident in this piece of domesticated science, in which Darwin builds his argument about the way seeds can be transported: "I took in February three tablespoonfuls of mud from three different points, beneath water, on the edge of a little pond; this mud when dry weighed 6 3/4 ounces; I kept it covered up in my study for six months, pulling up and counting each plant as it grew; the plants were of many kinds, and were altogether 537 in number; and yet the viscid mud was all contained in a breakfast cup!" (*Origin*, p. 377). Such defamiliarization, characteristic of Darwin as well as of Dickens, makes it impossible to tuck nature into the neat formulas of natural theology. It is not only that the distribution of vegetation all over the world can be accounted for by natural means, but that nature is extravagant, wasteful, busy in activities not perceptible to the casual observer. Domestic detail changes under rigorous scrutiny. And such a passage is part of an overall strategy that suggests once more that there is nothing stable in the world around us. Species are not fixed but endlessly varying. All the stable elements of our gardens, our domestic animals, our own bodies are mysteriously active, aberrant, plastic.

On the issue of teleology Dickens tried not to be Darwinian. In novels so chance-ridden as his, one would expect to find real compatibility with Darwin, whose theory posited a world without design, generated out of chance variations. But since Darwinian variation occurs without reference to need, environment, or end, Darwin's chance is antiteleological. Contrarily, in traditional narrative of the sort Dickens wrote, chance serves the purpose not of disorder, but of meaning—from Oedipus slaying his father to the catastrophic flood at the end of *The Mill on the Floss*. The order "inside" the fiction might be disrupted—Oedipus's reign, or the life of Maggie—but the larger order of the narrative depends on such disruptions.

The difference might best be indicated by the fact that while both Dickens and Darwin describe worlds in which chance encounters among the myriad beings who populate them are characteristic, for Dickens chance is a dramatic expression of the value and ultimate order in nature, and it belongs recognizably to a tradition that goes back to Oedipus. Each coincidence leads characters appropriately to catastrophe or triumph and suggests a designing hand that sets things right in the course of nature. The "contrivances" in Darwin, however, though they tend to move the species toward its current state of adaptation or extinction, appear to be undesigned. Chance in nature drains it of meaning and value. The variations even in domestic animals, carefully bred, are inexplicable. Only close attention of a breeder, who discards variations he doesn't want, leads to the appearance of design. But the breeder is entirely dependent on the accidents of variation. Darwin and Dickens in a way tell the same story, yet the implications are reversed.

Working in a theatrical and literary tradition, Dickens must use apparent chance to create a story with a beginning, a middle, and an end. And it is a story much like that told by natural theologians, which makes "chance" part of a larger moral design, thus effectively denying its chanciness by making it rationally explicable in terms of a larger structure. The feeling of coincidence is merely local. Such manipulation is a condition of storytelling, where "chance" must always contradict the implications of the medium itself. Even in narratives that seem to emphasize the power of chance over human design, narrative makes chance impossible. Design is intrinsic to the language of storytelling, with its use of a narrative past tense. "Once upon a time" already implies design. Moreover, the focus of narrative attention on particular characters makes everything that happens in the narrative relate to them. It may be that the relation is a negative one: the character, like Micawber, waits for something to turn up, and it never does; but in the end, of course, Micawber has been in the right place at the right time, and while the narrator might applaud Micawber's sudden energy, what happened is not because he chose it. At the same time, the narrative certainly did choose it, both because it in fact helps Micawber achieve the condition to which he has always aspired, and because it allows the exposure of Uriah Heep and the righting of all the wrongs with which that part of the story has been concerned. Ultimately, it is all for the sake of David Copperfield as the happy resolutions of *Mansfield Park* are for Fanny.

Chance in narrative has at least two contradictory aspects. When Eliot's narrator condemns "Favourable Chance" in *Silas Marner*, she is among other things suggesting (what Darwin would have agreed to) that the world is not designed for any individual's interest. What Godfrey or Dunstan wants has no more to do with the way the world operates than what the giraffe wants. The giraffe's long neck does not develop because he wants it, but because longer-necked giraffes had on the whole survived better than shorter-necked ones. Nothing is going to shorten the trees for any given giraffe; nothing, presumably, will put gold in Dunstan's hands or rid Godfrey of his wife. Dickens, I believe, would subscribe to this way of seeing, although his attacks on chance are less obvious and direct. Yet in *Silas Marner* all the major events are the result of "chance."[41] The narrative does not make credible a necessary connection between the events and the behavior of the characters, nor does it try. The fabular structure of the story is outside the realistic mode that the expressed sentiments of the narrator affirm. In being much more self-consciously a "tale," and less a "realistic" representation of the world in all its complexity, *Silas Marner* exposes boldly what is usually more disguised in realistic fiction, where the necessary "coincidences" are normally made to appear natural and causally related.

The "chance" events in *Silas Marner* self-consciously work out a parable (complex as it becomes), in which they all reflect moral conditions and shadow forth a world in which the principle of nemesis, works, in which we bear moral responsibility for what we do; and that moral responsibility is worked out in nature and society. The effect of the narrative is to convey the sense that the "chance" events were determined by a designing power, intrinsic to nature itself, that used to be called God.

Narrative, it is assumed, is different from life, however, and presumably "real" coincidences would not imply the design of some "author." But any language used to describe events will turn into narrative and import design once more. Sudden catastrophes invariably evoke the question, "Why?" "Why did he have to die?" The question implies that there are "reasons" beyond the physiological and that the explanation, he was hit by a car, or his heart stopped, is not satisfactory or complete. What moral end was served? Where is the justice in the death? Or, if catastrophe is avoided, the language is full of "luck," the remarkable luck that we canceled off the plane that crashed, and the accompanying sense that we weren't "meant" to die yet. Often, others' catastrophes inspire guilt, as though the survivors are responsible, or could have managed to swap positions had they the courage. Even in trivial affairs, this tendency of ordinary language is powerful. We talk about bad weather as though it were designed to ruin our one day off, or we carry umbrellas and half believe that this will trick the rain away.

Such anthropocentric language is characteristic of natural theology, and Dickens does not resist it. But Dickens still uses chance to project a world governed by a great designer, even if he often has difficulty doing so. Putting aside the random abundance of the earlier works, we find that the self-consciously less episodic and more thematically coherent later novels use mysterious and apparently inexplicable details for the sake of human significance. Inevitably, Dickens does produce a Darwinian excess, which he needs to ignore or compress into order to achieve the comfort of significance; but his plotting is determined by the illumination and intelligible explanation of *apparently* random detail. The collapse of Mrs. Clennam's house is both literal and figurative, of course. Oliver's innocence is preserved and triumphant. Carker is crushed by the new railway, which we earlier learned opens for all to see the ugliness and misery of London.

Dickensian narrative derives much of its energy from the gradual revelation of the design that incorporates all accidents, just as Herschelian science derives its energy from the attempt to explain all of the minutest natural phenomena in terms of general law. Characters struggle to discover its existence, and to work out its particular meaning, while the reader is always several steps ahead of the characters and several behind the author. We know that there is meant to be nothing chancy about Dickensian chance.[42]

Whereas Dickens, then, could exploit the metaphorical implications of language with confidence in its power to reveal design, Darwin had to resist language's intentionality and implications of design in order to describe a world merely there—without design or meaning. We have seen how in the very act of developing his theory and rejecting arguments from design he fell into the metaphorical and storytelling structures of the language to talk about "Natural Selection" as a "being." But the development of genetic variations, as Waddington points out, is not causally connected with the selective process that will determine whether the variations survive. In narrative terms this suggests that there can be no moral explanation, no superphysical "justification" of the development. The gene and its phenotype develop regardless of their narrative context. Such a separation drains nature of its moral significance and links Darwinism with the realist project that Dickens resisted even as he more than half participated in it. The matter of chance and teleology constituted the core of Dickens's defense, his attempt to keep nature from being merely neutral.

But Dickens did not reject science in order to resist that cold neutrality. It was Darwin, most effectively, who split scientific from theological discourse on this issue: science would not allow any "explanation" that depended on unknown principles that might be invoked, erratically, whenever empirical investigation failed. Scientific faith in law need not extend to scientific belief in the good intentions of the natural world. Dickens, like Darwin, would exclude mere caprice from the universe, but Darwinian "law" might well be regarded as capricious from the human point of view.

Yet another essay in *All the Year Round* provides a typical Victorian affirmation of the value of science, which grows from "Patience," while "Magic," its ancient forebear in the quest for meaning and control, is based on "Credulity." For science to emerge, the essay argues, "the phenomena of Nature, at least all the most ordinary phenomena, must have been disengaged from this conception of an arbitrary and *capricious* power, similar to human will, and must have been recognized as *constant*, always succeeding each other with fatal regularity."[43] These are certainly principles to which Darwin, like Lyell and Herschel before him, would have subscribed. The writer here, in eagerness to dispel "caprice," is not considering the full human implications of this apparently unimpeachable, modern, scientific position. In narrative, ironically, the ultimate effect of the "scientific" view of order and regularity is that the world begins to feel humanly erratic. That is, it becomes a fatalistic or deterministic world, like Hardy's, in which events do indeed develop inexorably from the slow accumulation of causes; yet they are, from the human perspective, entirely a matter of chance, because they are not subject to the control either of will or consciousness. Such a world is not, strictly, disordered, but it is, as Mayr has argued, probabilistic: "No one will ever understand natural selection until he realizes that it is a statistical phenomenon."[44] Not only does it work regardless of the interests of individual members of the population, but its working can only be described statistically, without explanation of why in any case or in the majority of cases, things develop as they do. Natural selection is humanly meaningless. Narrative forces what abstract discourse can avoid, a recognition of the difficulty and potential self-contradictoriness of the very ideas of chance and order.

The radical difference between Darwin and Dickens, despite Dickens's predisposition both to science and to the overall Darwinian vision, is simply in that Darwin's "laws" have no moral significance. Although they can be adapted for moral purposes (and were, immediately and continuingly), they do not answer questions like "Why?" except in physical or probabilistic terms. Birds can carry seeds in their talons, or deposit them thousands of miles away in their excrement. But what design is there in these particular seeds, these particular species making the trip? Why did the bird eat this plant rather than that, travel to this island rather than that? Survival in Darwin's nature is not *morally* significant. Adaptiveness is not designed, being the mere adjustment of the organism to its particular environment, and it has no direction. There is no perfection in Darwin's world, no intelligent design, no purpose. Fact may not be converted to meaning.[45]

This is a very tough sort of "chance," and its toughness evoked resistance from scientists as well as writers and theologians. In Dickens, while Darwinian chance threatens almost instinctively to overwhelm order, chance largely derives from another tradition, the one, in fact, that Darwin was self-consciously combatting. His novels tend to act out the arbitrariness of the connections they want to suggest are natural (and in that unintended sense, even here they are Darwinian). Dickens tries to tie event to meaning in a way that removes from chance its edge of inhumanity. This is the very tradition that Darwin identifies when, in *The Descent of Man*, he explains why he had perhaps overestimated the power of natural selection in the early editions of the *Origin*: "I was not able to annul the influence of my former belief, then widely prevalent, that each species had been purposely created; and this led to my tacitly assuming that every detail of structure, excepting rudiments, was of some special, though unrecognised, service" (I, 15). Every detail, on that earlier model, means something. Insofar as Dickens's later novels begin to suggest a chasm between event and meaning (delicately intimated in the "usual uproar" that concludes *Little Dorrit*), Dickens moves, like the later Darwin, away from the natural-theological tradition that had dominated his imaginative vision.

It is perhaps a measure of how far Dickens has traveled from Austen's way of seeing, however, that even where he persists in the contrivances of coincidence, their discontinuity with the worlds he is creating is disturbing. Such discontinuity is particularly striking in *Little Dorrit* and *Our Mutual Friend*. In most cases, while there are no naturalistic laws by which to account for the "chances" in Dickens's novels, coincidence feels too often like a matter of the conventions of narrative. Of course, Lady Dedlock *must* die at the gate of the wretched source of all plagues, where Jo had given off one ray of light in his gratitude to the now dead Nemo. The characters cannot perceive the design, but it is really there. Still, though there are scientific laws that make the development of organisms intelligible, the comfort of intelligibility does not lead to the comfort of meaning and purpose: in Darwin's world, it is random.

Darwin could get nowhere with his theory as long as language was taken to imply an essential reality it merely named. As Gillian Beer points out, in this respect, as with the question of chance, Darwin was forced to use a language that resisted the implications of his argument. Language, she says, "always includes agency, and agency and intention are frequently impossible to distinguish in language."[46] Yet more generally, to borrow a page from Derrida, language implies "presence." It assumes an originary reality ultimately accessible. Here as elsewhere, Darwin avoided epistemology to stick to his biological business, and here again he was forced to resist the implications of the language with which he made his arguments.

I have shown how at the center of his theory is a redefinition of the word "species," by which he almost undefined it. Species can have no Platonic essence, and Darwin was content to use the word as others used it, while demonstrating that species could be nothing but time-bound and perpetually transforming aggregations of organisms, all of which are individually different. For the most part, Darwin tried to do without a definition of species at all, for a definition would have got him into the kinds of serious difficulties already discussed, leading to the view that his book, as Louis Agassiz claimed, was about nothing: if "species" is merely an arbitrary term not corresponding to anything in nature, then *The Origin of Species* is about nothing.

Definition would have implied an essentialist view of the world, one entirely compatible with natural theology, and incompatible with evolution by natural selection. Essentialism, as Mayr has noted, implies a "belief in discontinuous, immutable essences,"[47] and this belief is reenforced by the reifying nouns characteristic of our language. John Beatty, in a revision of his argument that Darwin in fact was denying the existence of species, points out that Darwin could "use the term 'species' in a way that agreed with the use of the term by his contemporaries, but not in a way that agreed with his contemporaries' *definitions* of the term."[48] Darwin was not a poststructuralist and would not have argued that there is nothing out there to correspond to his language. But he knew he would have been paralyzed by accepting the definitions of "species" current among fellow naturalists. Recall that when Darwin talks of the "something more" naturalists think is implied by the natural system, he is working with their general nonevolutionary understanding of "natural system" and classifications within it; what he does, to follow Beatty's point, is accept their usage but not their definition so that he can replace the essentialist "something more" with the "hidden bond" of "propinquity of descent."

Essentialism was the enemy of evolutionary thinking, creating the greatest obstacle to conceptions of change. Mayr singles out Platonic essentialism, "the belief in constant *eide*, fixed ideas, separate from and independent of the phenomena of appearance," as having had "a particularly deleterious impact on biology through the ensuing two thousand years." Essentialism made it almost impossible to name a *kind* of animal—say, horse—without implying both its permanence and the "real" nature of its identity in all important qualities with all other horses, regardless of its merely accidental, that is, its particular physical and living characteristics. "Genuine change, according to essentialism" notes Mayr, "is possible only through the saltational origin of new essences,"[49] and clearly Darwin, for whom nature made no leaps, found essentialism a large obstruction.[50]

In plotting and characterization, change (as I have earlier said) was Dickens's greatest difficulty. His narratives and his characters seem to belong to a saltational world. For the narratives do make leaps, and when characters change they often do so (particularly in the earlier work) through abrupt conversion, as, for example, Scrooge. As opposed to a realist like Eliot, who writes from within a tradition much more clearly related to Darwinian thought and to the advanced science and psychology of the time, and whose narrator claims that "character is not cut in marble," Dickens writes out of an essentialist tradition. Barbara Hardy has pointed out that his novels rarely escape some tinge of the tradition of the *Bildungsroman*, but Dickens's use of that tradition of character development and change rarely explores the slow processes by which characters in that tradition learn and grow.[51]

Typically, Dickensian characters behave as though they had single, discoverable selves that constitute their essence. Mr. Jarndyce is a good and generous man, all of whose strategies in the world are designed to reaffirm that goodness. To be sure, this also entails a certain deviousness, for if he is to accept congratulations on his goodness, he can no longer regard himself as disinterested. But this ambivalence is built into his essence, and one of his most characteristic self-expressions is his complaint about the wind being in the East, which signals either bad news or the self-division that comes when he is about to receive praise or gratitude. So it is, in other ways, with most of Dickens's characters, who have been criticized through the years by critics seeking more fluid, complex, unstable, and I would say Darwinian, "selves."

The essentialist nature of Dickens's imagination is perhaps most evident in the clarity with which he usually distinguishes goodness and badness. Dickens's tendency is to read character into these categories, even when by virtue of his extraordinary sympathetic imagination he creates sequences like that of Sikes on the run or Fagin in prison, which shift our perspective on the melodramatic narrative. But the moral borders are firmly drawn. As Leo Bersani has observed, "In Dickens, the mental faculties dramatized in allegory are concealed behind behavior which *represents* those faculties. And the critical method appropriate to this literary strategy is one which treats the words and acts of literary characters as signs of the allegorical entities which make up these characters."[52] In this respect Dickens is most distant from Darwin and realism. Eliot's emphasis on mixed conditions, mixed natures, and her virtual incapacity (until Grandcourt in *Daniel Deronda*) to create a figure of unequivocal evil, fairly represents the difference. Dickens, writing within the "metaphysical mode" as Edward Eigner defines it, is heavily dependent on plot and emphasizes the external rather than the internal, but only because he counts on the adequacy of the natural to express meaning. In keeping with the natural-theological tradition, the emphasis on the external itself depends on strong confidence in the legibility of the material world, its expression of spiritual and moral realities comprehensible to those who choose to see. Ironically, when the world is secularized, as in the Darwinian scheme, narrative must turn inward because the material world becomes increasingly unintelligible. In Dickens, whom I have been characterizing as essentialist, there is visible a growing inability to be satisfied with the essentialist imagination.

The process of making narrative more literal by turning from allegorical representation to psychological mimesis under the pressures of secularization parallels the strategies Darwin uses in breaking with essentialism. One of the great Christian metaphors, and one of the central concerns of Victorian writers, becomes in Darwin a literal fact: we are all one family. Not the idea, but physical inheritance connects all living organisms. The move severed event from meaning (in a way contrary to Dickens's largely allegorical use of event) and destabilized all apparently permanent values by thrusting them into nature and time. Essentialism and nominalism were, therefore, no merely abstract metaphysical problems. On the whole, common sense and tradition required a world in which the ultimate realities remained outside time, and in which an ideal essence (as opposed to biological inheritance) defined the self. The concept of "character" itself implies such an essence.

The implications of this distinction extend into every aspect of narrative art. The essentialist mode is, for the most part, metaphorical. On the one hand, it depends on the likeness between physical and moral states, and the Dickensian emphasis on the physical peculiarities belongs to such a metaphorical tradition. On the other hand, the nominalist position, like Darwin's, severs the physical from the moral, and Darwin begins to make the connection metonymically. That is, in *The Expression of the Emotions in Man and Animals*, Darwin tries to read feeling from expression. But his reading is predominantly physiological. For example:

> Although ... we must look at weeping as an incidental result, as purposely as the secretion of tears from a blow outside the eye, or as a sneeze from the retina being affected by a bright light, yet this does not present any difficulty in our understanding how the secretion of tears serves as a relief of suffering. And by as much as the weeping is more violent or hysterical, by so much will the relief be greater—on the same principle that the writhing of the whole body, the grinding of the teeth, and the uttering of piercing shrieks, all give relief under an agony of pain.[53]

Just as, for Darwin, organisms are connected by physical inheritance, so moral and emotional states are expressed by physiological activity directed at physical defense and relief. All those aspects of human identity and experience that are traditionally regarded as uniquely human, connected with spiritual states unavailable to lower organisms, are in fact physical conditions shared by other organisms. Darwin had observed monkeys in zoos, for example, to discover whether "the contraction of the orbicular muscles" was similarly connected with "violent expiration and the secretion of tears." He notes that elephants sometimes weep and contract their orbicular muscles! Of course, novelists in the realist tradition did not need to accept Darwin's extension of the "uniquely" human to the rest of the natural world, but their emphasis on close analysis of character, increasingly from the inside, corresponded to a decreasing (but never extinguished) reliance on the conformity of physical and moral states, of the sort so characteristic of Dickens.

Nevertheless, Dickens's fiction does participate in the move toward a Darwinian imagination of the world, a growing uncertainty about the notion of an "essential" self or about the possibility of detecting the moral through the physical (a quest that is increasingly professionalized, requiring a Bucket to do the work); and he is thematically urgent about the need for change. Abruptness remains characteristic, yet his preoccupation with the slow but inevitable movements in nature toward change, and with the consequences of refusing it is something more than a throwback to old comic literary traditions. It is as though he accepts uniformitarianism but rejects the gradualism that Lyell imposed upon it; like Darwin he seems to be reconciling the progressivism of catastrophism with the naturalism of uniformitarianism. Several of his most wonderful narratives focus on this problem: Mrs. Skewton in *Dombey and Son*, Miss Havisham in *Great Expectations*, and Mrs. Clennam all succumb to the forces of change their whole lives would have denied. And yet the very figures Dickens uses to thematize change are static (essentialist in conception) and require extravagances of plot to force them into time. They dwell in worlds not where change evolves slowly through time, but where it comes catastrophically, through melodrama, revelation, conversion. In a world of Bagstock and Barnacle, Captain Cuttle and Flora Finching, Mr. Toots and Mr. Merdle, it is hard to imagine that each of us does not have some essential, inescapable selfhood. But Clennam, Sidney Carton, and John Harmon, not to speak of Pip and Eugene Wrayburn, all flirt with doubts about the self so profound that they verge on self-annihilation. Each of them either literally or metaphorically dies, almost as though it were suicide. The question of change, even of the reality of the self, moves from the periphery to the center of Dickens's art and brings him to the edge of the Darwinian world, which feels like a threat, but can also, as for Clennam, be a liberation.

In other respects Dickens's worlds often seem to be narrative enactments of Darwin's theory. Beer makes the connection by pointing to the "apparently unruly superfluity of material" in Dickens's novels, "gradually and retrospectively revealing itself as order, its superfecundity of instances serving an argument which can reveal itself only through instance and relations."[54] *Bleak House* is only Dickens's most elaborate working out of the way all things are connected, and connected by virtue of mutual dependence and relationship. The answer to the question, "What connexion can there be?" we have noted, is a genealogical one, that Esther is Lady Dedlock's daughter. Mr. Guppy and Mr. Tulkinghorn detect it immediately. But all characters eventually connect, in other literal ways, from the brickmakers, who deceive Bucket in his pursuit, to Jo, the literal bearer of the plague, to the lawyers who drain the life from Richard, to Mr. Jarndyce, Skimpole, Boythorn, and Sir Leicester himself.

Bleak House embodies in every aspect of its plots and themes the preoccupation with connections, across place, class, and institutions. But almost all of Dickens's novels from *Dombey and Son* to *Our Mutual Friend* are novels of crossing and interconnection and responsibility. And throughout these works Dickens employs devices beyond the plot to enforce an overwhelming sense of hidden bonds, dependencies that have about them the quality of mystery appropriate to both religious intensity and gothic narratives.

The great dramatic moments in Dickens are often framed by apparently irrelevant natural scenes. Among the most vivid is the passage in *Bleak House* that precedes the ominous image of Allegory pointing above Mr. Tulkinghorn's heads on the evening of the murder. It wanders, by way of the moon, far from Mr. Tulkinghorn: He looks up casually, thinking "what a fine night, what a bright large moon, what multitudes of stars! A quiet night, too." And the passage moves across the whole of the English landscape, hill summits, water meadows, gardens, woods, island, weirs, shore, the steeples of London. The universal silence is violated by the shot, and when the dogs stop barking, "the fine night, the bright large moon, and multitudes of stars, are left at peace again" (pp. 584–585).

The passage effectively intensifies the event, implying merely by description some larger significance, but it does not express in its physical nature the moral condition at the center of the narrative. The vast silent panorama, disrupted only by the barking of the dogs, is antithetical to the murder going on. And surely it is not mere ornamentation. Passages such as this (there are equivalent ones in *Little Dorrit*) are the scenic counterpart of Dickens's commitment to multiple plots. The natural world, for Dickens, contains and limits human action. Often, as in the passage just quoted, it comments ironically on the action. But the effect is always larger than irony. The world is larger than anyone's imagination of it; connections extend out endlessly. In its vast and serene movement, it seems indifferent to human ambition. Regardless of the arbitrariness and violence of human action, nature continues its regular movement, has its own plot, as it were, which inevitably crosses with and absorbs the human plot.

The novels from Dickens's great middle period forward, with one or two possible exceptions, build thematically on the conception of society as integrally unified, with the revelation of that unification a central element of plot as well as theme. It is clear in the relation between the Toodles and the Dombeys, as in that between Esther and the Dedlocks. Even in *Hard Times* the circus and Mr. Bounderby's past confirm connections among classes and types denied by social convention. *Little Dorrit* explores in William Dorrit's genteel ambitions and in the fate of the Marshalsea and Bleeding Heart Yard the inevitability of connections. *The Tale of Two Cities* acts out melodramatically and in the context of revolutionary action the undeniable mutual dependence of class on class. And *Our Mutual Friend*, in its river and dust heaps, in its tale of the crossing of classes, makes the theme of "connections" both symbolic and literal. The mutual dependencies on which organic life depends in Darwin are dramatized socially in Dickens through his elaborate and multiple plotting and through his gradual revelations, often through the structure of a mystery plot, of the intricacy of relations disguised by sharp demarcations and definitions of classes.

Dickens's world, then, is as much a tangled bank as that evoked by Darwin at the end of the *Origin*. Of course, Dickens takes the metaphorical, Christian view, that Darwin was to make literal, that we are all one and deny our brotherhood at our peril. And he strains his plotlines to do it. Darwin tells us that seeing all organisms as "lineal descendants of some few beings which lived long before the first bed of Cambrian system was deposited," makes them seem to him "ennobled" (*Origin*, p. 458). The world is a tangled bank on which "elaborately constructed forms, so different from each other, and dependent upon each other in so complex a manner," struggle and evolve yet further into the "most beautiful and wonderful of forms" (p. 460). Had Darwin not written this passage in almost the same form ten years before *Bleak House*, one might have thought he was trying to sum up that great novel.

It is not, however, simply in the fact of complex interrelationship and interdependence that Dickens's and Darwin's worlds seem akin. In both there is an almost uncontrollable energy for life. Dickens's novels are densely populated, full of eccentrics, variations from the norm, and, as in the case of Jo or the retarded Maggie of *Little Dorrit*, or Barnaby Rudge, or Smike of *Nicholas Nickleby*, marginal figures who test the validity of the whole society. Darwin, for his part, needs to locate the unaccountable variation, the deviant figure or organ that will not be accommodated in an ideal and essentialist taxonomy, like woodpeckers who do not peck wood, vestigial organs that serve no adaptive function. Relentless in the pursuit of detail, he qualifies almost all generalization, even his own charting of the descent of species, with the muted and powerful "nature is never that simple."

Victorian clutter and Dickensian grotesque are akin to Darwin's encyclopedic urge to move beyond the typical. In this quality Darwin transcends again the kind of rationalist law-bound science that he inherited from Herschel. Darwin is not very interested in types. I would argue that although Dickens's characters seem to be "types," they are atypical in their excesses. Old Jocy B, Josh Bagstock, is not so much a type as a grotesque— an aberration from the norm whose fictional strength lies in the way the excesses echo recognizable and more apparently normal human behavior. That sort of grotesque, in its multiple manifestations, is very much in the Darwinian mode. As Michael Ghiselin has suggested, the Darwinian revolution, in its overthrow of essentialism, lays "great emphasis on the 'atypical' variants which the older taxonomy ignored."[55] Distortion, excess, and clutter are the marks of Victorian design, of Dickens's novels, and of Darwin's world.

For both Dickens and Darwin, knowledge (and humanity) are not attainable unless one learns to see the multiplicity of variants that lie beyond the merely typical. Biology revolutionized nineteenth-century science because it displaced mathematical models (however briefly) as an ultimate resting place for belief. Darwin's book insisted that one could not understand the development of species unless one recognized that individual variations were always occurring, and that the world is filled with developments from variations which might once have been considered aberrant.

Thus, for Darwin—and the pressure for this is evident in the sheer abundance of Dickens's novels as well—variety is not aberration but the condition for life. Dombey attempts to limit the Dombey blood, and in rejecting the fresh blood and milk of Mrs. Toodles causes his son's death. *Our Mutual Friend* concludes with one of the most remarkable moments in Dickens: Wrayburn is redeemed and brought back to life by crossing the class boundary to marry Lizzie Hexam. In the final scene Twemlow is forced to redefine language in a Darwinian way, moving the idea of "gentleman" from a fixed and permanent class definition to a vital (and indeed sexual) one that becomes so wide-ranging as to lose its exclusivity. "Sir," returns Twemlow to the permanently Podsnapian Podsnap, "if this gentleman's feelings of gratitude, of respect, of admiration, and affection, induced him (as I presume they did) to marry this lady ... I think he is the greater gentleman for the action, and makes the greater lady. I beg to say, that when I use the word, gentleman, I use it in the sense in which the degree may be attained by any man" (p. 891).

Mixing and denial of absolute boundaries become the conditions of life in Dickens's novels as they will be in Darwin's biology. In Darwin, the unaccountable variation, the crossing—of sexes and varieties, if not of species—increases vitality. On the old model life was determined by separate creation and eternal separation into ideal and timeless orders. On the Darwinian model life is enhanced by slight disturbances of equilibrium, by change.

Learning to confront change and to make it a principle of life was Dickens's great trial as a novelist. It is a long way from Pickwick to the timid Twemlow, who affirms the value of mixing in a society constructed to deny it. Twemlow is, moreover, one of the very few minor characters in Dickens who actually change, and whose change is not abrupt reversal, but the quiet consequence of a long accumulation of frustrations. While Pickwick's novel happens episodically and manages to return to the moral condition of innocence by slamming the door, the later Dickens moves increasingly to the structure of Paradise Lost—you can't go home again; change is irrevocable. The Darwinian revolution entailed the rejection of cyclical history, or ideal history: time moved in one direction only (and in this respect, it made a powerful companion to the otherwise initially hostile science of thermodynamics, which introduced the irreversible "arrow of time" into physics—a development I will discuss in the next chapter, on *Little Dorrit*). And yet Dickens goes on, as in the Christian dispensation, to make the change he can no longer avoid facing, the loss of stasis and ideal innocence, into the condition of a greater redemption.

The resistance of Victorian intellectuals to Dickens as a truly serious novelist might be attributed, partially, to two different emphases that can be traced conveniently in the reading of Darwin. The one, the more strictly intellectual, exemplified by G. H. Lewes and George Eliot, absorbed Darwin into the uniformitarian-scientific mode and, as it were, domesticated him and the chancy dysteleological world he offered. The other reads Darwin within a fully comic vision, lights instinctively on the aberrant and extreme cases of the sort that Darwin had to emphasize to disrupt contemporary religious and scientific thought and to reveal a world prolific and dynamic in the production of endless and sometimes grotesque varieties of life. Yet Dickens always struggled back toward the possibilities of essentialist thought and morality. The aberrant comes round to the ideal, at last.

While Dickens often strains toward the comfort of design, he has an astonishing eye for the aberrant and energy for abundance and for life. Perhaps equally remarkable, like Darwin, he managed to use inherited idealist and design-permeated conventions to build almost mythic structures of crossing and recrossing appropriate to the sense of modern urban life (Ruskin deplores this in his "Fiction, Fair and Foul," where he totes up the number of deaths and diseases in *Bleak House*) Dickens's capacity to imagine himself beyond the conventions of order that dominated Victorian social and political life allowed him to write in a way that helped open the culture for the Darwinian vision toward which, in his increasingly courageous confrontation with change, he himself was moving. Podsnap's relation to Twemlow parallels society's first response to Darwin. We should not be surprised that Dickens did not play Podsnap himself.

NOTES

1. Charles Dickens, *Bleak House*, ed. George Ford and Sylvere Monod (New York: W. W. Norton, 1977), p. 197. Page numbers in text refer to this edition.
2. Stephen Jay Gould, in "Flaws in a Victorian Veil" (in *The Panda's Thumb*), discusses Louis Agassiz's resistance to Darwin's theory in this context. Agassiz was appalled that blacks might be related to whites and as a consequence he turned unscientifically to the idea of polygeny (we cannot *all* be descended from the same original sources). Gould quotes Agassiz:
I shudder from the consequences. We have already to struggle, in our progress, against the influence of universal equality, in consequence of the difficulty of preserving the acquisitions of individual eminence, the wealth of refinement and culture growing out of select association. What would be our condition if to these difficulties were added the far more tenacious influences of physical disability. Improvements in our system of education ... may sooner or later counterbalance the effects of the apathy of the uncultivated and of the rudeness of the lower classes and raise them to a higher standard. But how shall we eradicate the stigma of a lower race when its blood has once been allowed to flow freely into that of our children. (pp. 174–175)
3. Beer, *Darwin's Plots*, p. 8.
4. Charles Darwin, *Metaphysics, Materialism, and the Evolution of Mind: Early Writings of Charles Darwin*, ed. Paul H. Barrett (Chicago: University of Chicago Press, 1974), p. 20.
5. See Gillian Beer, "Darwin's Reading and the Fictions of Development," in *The Darwinian Heritage*, pp. 543–588.
6. Nora Barlow, ed., *The Autobiography of Charles Darwin* (New York: W. W. Norton, 1958), pp. 138–139.
7. See Jonathan Arac, *Commissioned Spirits: The Shaping of Social Motion in Dickens, Carlyle, Melville, and Hawthorne* (New Brunswick, N.J.: Rutgers University Press, 1979), pp. 126, 131. Arac offers an interesting discussion of how scientific language pervades the novel.
8. Ann Wilkinson, "*Bleak House*: From Faraday to Judgment Day," *ELH*, 34 (1967): 225–247. I draw on this excellent essay frequently in my discussion of *Bleak House*.
9. See E. Gaskell, "More about Spontaneous Combustion," *Dickensian*, 69 (1973): 23–35.
10. Alexander Welsh, *The City of Dickens* (Oxford: Oxford University Press, 1971), p. 117.
11. Harvey Sucksmith, *The Narrative Art of Charles Dickens* (Oxford: Oxford University Press, 1970), p. 171.
12. E. T. Cook and Alexander Wedderburn, eds., *The Library Edition of the Works of John Ruskin*, 39 vols. (London: George Allen, 1905), VII, 7.

13. K. J. Fielding, ed., *The Speeches of Charles Dickens* (Oxford: Oxford University Press, 1960), p. 403.

14. Ibid., p. 404.

15. Ibid.

16. Charles Dickens, *The Posthumous Papers of the Pickwick Club*, ed. Robert L. Patten (Harmondsworth: Penguin Books, 1972), pp. 73–74, 647.

17. Charles Dickens, *The Haunted Man*, in *The Christmas Books*, 2 vols. (Harmondsworth: Penguin Books, 1971) II, 322.

18. Lavoisier quoted in Gerald Holton, *Introduction to Concepts and Theories in Physical Science* (Princeton: Princeton University Press, 1985), p. 231.

19. Charles Dickens, "Gamekeeper's Natural History," *All the Year Round* (September 10, 1859): 474.

20. Charles Dickens, "The World of Water," reprinted from *Household Words*, in *Home and Social Philosophy; or, Chapters on Everyday Topics* (New York: G. P. Putnam, 1852), p. 245.

21. See *All the Year Round* (September 17, 1859): 490.

22. Stephen Toulmin and June Goodfield (in *The Discovery of Time*) cite Boswell quoting Johnson: "But, sir, it is as possible that the Ourang-Outang does not speak, as that he speaks. However, I shall not dispute the point. I should have thought it not possible to find a Monboddo; yet he exists" (p. 98).

23. Charles Dickens, *The Life and Adventures of Martin Chuzzlewit* (London: Thomas Nelson, n.d.), p. 7.

24. Charles Dickens, "Our Nearest Relation," *All the year Round* (May 28, 1859): 114–115.

25. Bowler, *Evolution*, pp. 123–124.

26. Charles Dickens, "Nature's Greatness in Small Things," *Household Words* (November 28, 1857): 513.

27. Cf. Bowler, *Evolution*, p. 222.

28. T. H. Huxley, *Man's Place in Nature* (1863; repr., Ann Arbor: University of Michigan Press, 1959), p. 122.

29. Review of *The Origin of Species*, *All the Year Round* (July 7, 1860): 293, 299.

30. "Species," *All the Year Round* (June 2, 1860): 176.

31. Charles Dickens, *Sketches by "Boz"* (London: Macmillan and Co., 1958), p. 128.

32. Dickens, "Nature's Greatness," p. 511.

33. Cf. John Romano, *Dickens and Reality* (New York: Columbia University Press, 1978): "A single-minded stress on the separation of Dickens' fictive world from our own slights the realistic or representational elements in the novels and their persistent claim, like the claim in Tolstoy, that they are set in the real world" (p. 3). Romano's important claims for Dickens as realist locate a crucial distinction of the realist's enterprise: "The realist puts in doubt the very enterprise of art. As a corollary of the affirmation of the real, realism discredits the precondition of its own existence, that form which confines, distorts, de-actualizes reality in the process of assimilating it" (p. 84). But it is precisely here where the claims for Dickens as a realist might be most usefully assimilated to my argument about natural theology and uniformitarianism. Dickens's commitment to realism is combined with something like a natural-theological faith in the order of experience itself; hence, there is no real sign in Dickens of that characteristic Thackerayan irony at the expense of art itself.

34. Charles Dickens, *Oliver Twist* (Harmondsworth: Penguin Books, 1966), pp. 36, 35.

35. Charles Dickens, *Our Mutual Friend* (Harmondsworth: Penguin Books, 1971), p. 893. Page numbers in the text refer to this edition.

36. George Eliot, *Adam Bede* (Harmondsworth: Penguin Books, 1980), p. 198.

37. Ibid., p. 410.

38. Dickens, *Sketches*, pp. 185, 199.

39. Herschel, *Preliminary Discourse*, p. 14.

40. George Eliot, "The Sad Fortunes of the Reverend Amos Barton," in *Scenes of Clerical Life* (Harmondsworth: Penguin Books, 1973), p. 81.

41. Two recent essays discuss this contradiction in the novel. The form of the novel itself seems to run counter to expressed narrative intent. This problem deserves yet fuller treatment. See Susan R. Cohen, "A History and a Metamorphosis: Continuity and Discontinuity in *Silas Marner*," *Texas Studies in Literature and Language*, 25 (Fall 1983): 410–446; Donald Hawes, "Chance in *Silas Marner*," *English*, 31 (1982): 213–218.

42. "The effect of Dickens's characteristic method," says Harland Nelson, "is an impression of an all-pervading design in human affairs, unexpectedly encompassing and harmonizing the profusely various elements of the story; not (as in a novel by Collins) an impression of an unbroken chain of events, unobtrusively laid down and given a final shake to bring the whole linked series at once into view" ("Dickens's Plots: 'The Ways of Providence' or the Influence of Collins?" *Victorian Newsletter*, 19, 1961: 11). But the strain to make the harmony is evident in the great novels, and the ways of providence or of natural theology are often challenged by the methods designed to affirm them.

43. Charles Dickens, "Magic and Science," *All the Year Round* (March 23, 1861): 562.

44. Mayr, *The Diversity of Life*, p. 37.

45. Manier's summary of Darwin's views on the wars of nature that help further natural selection demonstrates how inappropriate moral and generalizing application of Darwinian theory was:
Success in these wars of organic being could *not* be traced to variations which were *favorable* in some *absolute* sense; on the contrary, a variation must be understood to be *successful in relation* to some particular segment of the range of alternative variations, and in the context of the chances of life which happened to be available in the given physical circumstances or conditions. Such expression as "chance offspring" or "round of chances" alluded to the complexity of the predictions used in Darwin's hypothesis, and implied that this complexity could not be reduced in the way that Newton had reduced the complexity of planetary motion by formulating a few generally applicable laws. (*The Young Darwin*, pp. 121–122)

46. Beer, *Darwin's Plots*, p. 53.

47. Mayr, *The Diversity of Life*, p. 283.

48. Beatty, "Speaking of Species," p. 265.

49. Mayr, *The Growth of Biological Thought*, pp. 304–305, 38.

50. Darwin was not totally consistent in his rejection of essentialism. Not only is such consistency impossible given the nature of our language, but Darwin could himself employ arguments that imply an essentialist reality. This is particularly so when, under the pressure of antievolutionary arguments, he revises the *Origin* in later editions and makes many more concessions on the inheritance of acquired characteristics. Daniel Simberloff emphasizes the importance of the rejection of essentialist typology in the Darwinian revolution and points to various Darwinian ideas that nevertheless revert to essentialism. See "A Succession of Paradigms in Ecology: Essentialism to Materialism and Probabilism," *Synthese*, 43 (1980): 3–29, where he cites Richard Lewontin in arguing that Darwin's belief in the blending (not particularistic) theory of inheritance is "readily traced to [his] attachment to essentialist, typological thought." Darwin was hampered by his lack of knowledge of genetics and of Mendelian theory, which made evident that inheritance

was not a blending but a 1:2:1 distribution of genetic materials, some of which would not be visible in the parent. Simberloff also notes Lewontin's description of Darwin's "retreat to idealism or essentialism" in his theory of "pangenesis," for the hypothetical "gemmules" are "egregiously ideal essence-conferring entities" (pp. 6–7). See also R. D. Lewontin, "Darwin and Mendel—the Materialist Revolution," in *The Heritage of Copernicus: Theories "More Pleasing to the Mind,"* ed. J. Neyman (Cambridge, Mass.: MIT Press, 1974), pp. 166–183.

51. Barbara Hardy, *"Martin Chuzzlewit,"* in *Dickens and the Twentieth Century*, ed. John Gross and Gabriel Pearson (Toronto: University of Toronto Press, 1962), pp. 107–120. Hardy points out that the abruptness of Martin's conversion is typical of Dickens: "There is no point in comparing Dickens's conversions here with the slow and often eddying movement traced in George Eliot or Henry James. But I think this change is even more abrupt in exposition, relying heavily on compressed rhetoric, than the fairly abrupt conversions of David Copperfield or Bella Wilfer, though the important difference lies in the context of dramatized moral action. Dombey, Steerforth, Gradgrind, Pip, and other major and minor examples of flawed character—not necessarily changing—are demonstrated in appropriate action, large and small" (p. 114). Hardy is criticizing not the abruptness but the way the abrupt change is dramatized and contextualized. The Dickensian mode of change, belonging to a very different tradition, has its own constraints.

52. Bersani, *A Future for Astyanax*, p. 18.

53. Charles Darwin, *The Expression of the Emotions in Man and Animals* (1872; repr., Chicago: University of Chicago Press, 1965), p. 175.

54. Beer, *Darwin's Plots*, p. 8.

55. Ghiselin, *The Triumph of the Darwinian Method*, p. 61.

PAM MORRIS

Our Mutual Friend:
The Taught Self

Somewhere around 1863–4 a moment of hesitation, or of discontent, made itself felt in dominant discourse. As if, after a decade's consolidation of prosperity and hegemonic consensus, there came a doubt as to what actually had been achieved, an intimation of sterility, and a stirring of desire for some new direction, some revitalizing vision beyond the endless pursuit of wealth and self-interest. This ambivalence is articulated frequently in a recurrent trope of the river, in association with a proliferating play upon oppositions of surface and depth, corruption and regeneration, almost as rich in their ramifications as the identical imagery in *Our Mutual Friend*.

There is nothing mysterious about this common choice of language. Not only Darwin's *Origin of Species* (1859), but a continuous stream of archaeological and geological claims, discoveries, books, and lectures created a public consciousness of the evolutionary processes of change, and of the degeneration and regeneration, the 'decline and fall', of civilizations and species. Many of the geological explorations were sited in the mud and dust deposits of river beds and lake shores. In addition to this, public imagination was stirred by the discovery of the source of the Nile in 1862 and by the Suez Canal Project, not completed until 1867. For most Victorians, too, the religious association of Egypt brought readily to mind ideas of bondage, promises of renewal, and birth. The *Methodist Magazine* attacked 'miserable

From *Dickens's Class Consciousness: A Marginal View*. © 1991 Pam Morris.

[evolutionary] theories' which would 'lay man lower than the dust' and asked bitterly, 'Are we to be dragged through the slime of Egypt?' (1863, p. 816). In an article celebrating the discovery of the Nile source, *The Times* stressed its revitalizing function as a fountain of life' to Egypt (29 November 1862). It needed no great leap of association to link this interest in the Nile to public concern with the Thames, the scandalously polluted state of whose waters and tendency to dangerous flooding were at last being tackled by very extensive embankment and drainage projects. Throughout 1862–3 *The Times* carried frequent editorial articles upon this work, asserting its necessity, since the poorer population clustering its banks were 'exposed to the evils not only of tide-locked sewers, but of destructive floods. The waters of the Thames burst upon them periodically with the most calamitous effect' (18 January 1862).

The embankment project made the neglected state of the 'teeming populations which lie along the waterside', like those represented in *Our Mutual Friend*, topical during the early 1860s. Unlike the revitalizing mud of the Nile, the polluted flooding of the Thames brought death and endemic disease to these districts. They were focussed upon in the controversial report of the Committee on Education (1861–2)[1] as illustrating the danger of neglecting the education of the poorest sections of the working class: 'the festering soil of these congregated masses *must* be tilled ... if we would not see it covered with such rank growths of vice and crime as would, ere long ... bring us swift and irremediable ruin' (*Christian Observer* (1862), pp. 894–5). This lurid identification of the riverside population with the excremental mud they lived beside, expressed the fears of 'civilized' sections of society that these riverside areas would prove a source of national degeneration and corruption rather than any source of new life. Education was seen as the main evolutionary means of 'cultivating' the 'savagery' of the working-class poor, and the evangelicals were prominent in providing ragged schooling for these poverty-stricken districts. However, the kind of education offered was not intended to stimulate new ideas, let alone generate social change or revitalization. The *Methodist Magazine* declared that education was undertaken 'for the purpose of putting down social disorder and confusion' (1863, p. 256). The evangelicals warned that any attempt to teach the working class the new scientific Darwinian ideas would undermine the authority of religion, that 'only sure bulwark against disaffection and political chaos' (*Methodist Magazine*, 1863, p. 817).

Fears of the degeneration and corruption of national culture also coloured another topical issue of the early 1860s: a concern with what the *Edinburgh Review* called a 'Darwinian competition of languages' (120 (1864), p. 162). There was anxiety that the vulgar speech of the 'uncivilized' and uneducated would defile and overwhelm the purity of 'cultivated' English. Gladstone's abolition of tax on paper in 1861 provoked a noisy public debate. The measure was seen as likely to increase yet further the 'flood' of cheap periodicals and popular newspapers. The evangelicals, in particular were hostile to these as encouraging frivolous and worldly attitudes.[2] In 1863, the *Methodist Magazine* printed a long article on the dangers of the 'streams of journalism' winding through every street, village, and city 'sometimes sparkling with truth and purity, but more frequently muddy and pestiferous' (1863, p. 1127). Like the analogy of the Harmon murder story ebbing and flowing with the tide, the *Methodist Magazine* saw these journalistic streams as carrying 'gossip to the idle', and spreading a 'banquet of burglaries, suicides and murder before the morbid'—just as the Veneerings and their friends are represented as dining greedily upon their own sensation story. The *Christian Observer* took up the same theme, blaming the 'unhealthy appetite' for sensational stories from the lowest levels of social life for the corruption and degeneration of the English language (1864, p. 614).

These comments formed part of its discussion of Henry Alford's *The Queen's English* which was being extensively reviewed and debated at the time. The *Edinburgh Review* gave extensive coverage to Alford's fears that the 'well of pure sound English' was in 'peril of permanent defilement', setting out his views of a continuous struggle for survival between the purity of the written language of the 'cultivated few' and the spoken language of the 'uncivilized' mass, now being reproduced to provide 'colour' in cheap periodicals (120 (1864), p. 40). However, a reverse form of Darwinian conflict in language had been asserted in a series of popular lectures given by Max Muller at the Royal Institution in 1861, and also discussed at length in the *Edinburgh Review*. For Muller, spoken dialects were 'streams of living speech' flowing beneath and around the 'crystal surface' of literary and cultivated language. This latter had been taken out of 'the living stream of spoken words', lost its 'unbounded capability of change' and become 'artificial'. Muller contended that at times when the higher classes were crushed by social struggles or forced to mix with the lower classes, the 'undercurrent' of vulgar dialect would rise up 'like the waters in spring' to revitalize language and culture (*Edinburgh Review*, 115 (1862), p. 79). Despite the opposite intent of Alford's argument, his conclusions were not so different. A nation whose speech had become 'high-flown and bombastic' must be 'not far from rapid decline, and from being degraded from its former glory' (*Edinburgh Review*, 120 (1864), p. 42).

On the surface of political, social, and religious life in the early 1860s there seemed nothing to indicate any decline from glory. Dominant discourse elaborated a chauvinistic rhetoric of national greatness in which scientific, material, and moral 'progress' were acclaimed as triumphant indications of Britain's evolution into an ever higher scale of civilization. All voices within dominant discourse were united in recognizing the imposing stability and wealth of the nation. The *Methodist Magazine* expressed the consensus view that 'at home there is general prosperity ... Never, perhaps, throughout the country was there more of political quiet and popular content' (1863, p. 1028). The evangelicals had good cause for self-congratulation; their moral sobriety and cult of respectability dominated national culture and professed public values.

Yet despite this, a loss of confidence creeps into their discourse; an anxiety that religious conformism can co-exist comfortably with material corruption and even provide a convenient cover for its existence. The *Christian Observer* admitted, 'The surface of society has of late years been more decent than was perhaps ever known. But the current has been running dark and foul underneath' (1863, p. 801). This article was attacking public complicity with 'vice', especially prostitution, but a frivolous and worldly materialism evinced in obsession with 'amusement' and in increased crime also seemed a symptom of moral degeneration. Thus the journal spoke out against 'expensive habits' of consumption in all classes resulting in increased want of money, so that 'in every walk of life ... malversation, embezzlement, breach of trust, purloining, and even forgery, are becoming matters of everyday occurrence' (1864, p. 242). Such descriptions bring us close to the dishonest pursuit of wealth represented at all social levels in the text of *Our Mutual Friend*.[3] The *Methodist Magazine* wrote in similar vein, acknowledging the 'wide overspreading religiousness of our time', but hinting that this surface veneer cloaked a frivolous materialism and spiritual desuetude (1862, p. 317). In its anxiety over this dislocation of surface profession from inner conviction, the *Methodist Magazine* turned critically upon the hegemonic myths it had fostered and sustained throughout earlier decades of political crisis. The continual lauding of 'self-help', 'self-made men', and 'competition', it complained, fostered hardness of heart in the prosperous. By affirming 'that "if a man does not succeed it is his own fault" ... poverty becomes a species of sin; and it is no great step in advance to treat it as a crime' (1863, pp. 885). Nothing could more surely mark the lessening importance of religion as an ideological apparatus than the willingness to make this admission.

Liberals and Utilitarians also had good reason for contentment. The hegemonic consensus was theirs, with self-interest and the pursuit of wealth everywhere accepted as legitimate motives of desire, and national 'progress' measured solely in terms of these individualistic aspirations. In effect, throughout the early 1860s there was no political opposition. The *Christian*

Observer wrote that all the 'great political questions are well-nigh adjusted' (1863, p. 479), while *The Times*, never a friend of Liberalism, admitted that there was not one Conservative politician who could 'pretend that his party has any other policy than to do what the present Ministry has done' (4 February 1862). The Liberal *Edinburgh Review* expressed anxiety lest this 'unanimity' be condemned as 'stagnation', whereas, it asserted, political contentment was a sure sign of an advanced evolutionary state of civilization (117 (1862), pp. 269–271). *The Times*, however, dismissed the early Parliamentary session of 1863 as 'barren' (28 July 1863), and the *Westminster Review* echoed this growing sense of sterility, of Parliament as a political and moral Sahara. 'So barren and wearying a Parliament has not been seen for generations', it wrote, '... a placid, sleek, stultifying kind of self-content [has begun] to steal over the nation'. This 'barrenness' had been brought about by the failure or exhaustion of vision. The Tory party, wrote the reviewer, were without a political creed, whilst Liberalism was the victim of its own success—'a respectable mediocrity has done it to death' (81 (1864), pp. 124–187).

Below this surface of complacent mediocrity, motivated by money, corruption was rife. 'The plain truth is that any pushing, clever man who has a private interest to serve by entering Parliament ... can always obtain money', wrote the *Westminster Review* (78 (1862), p. 70), and this resort to bribery and corruption was admitted in all sections of dominant discourse. The *Christian Observer* hoped that Parliament would take steps to purify the Thames, but warned of greater difficulty in cleaning its own House, 'if the waters are foul, the mere turning on of more foul water will not purify the stream' (1862, p. 239). However, as with religion, there was a sharp dislocation between surface profession and underlying intent. Verbally, political corruption, no less than commercial corruption, was condemned on all sides as an intolerable disgrace to national pride, whilst, on all sides, both forms were widespread and intricately interrelated. Veneering was undoubtedly a 'representative man'. Foreigners, wrote *The Times* sarcastically, would think corruption the next worst crime to parricide according to the rhetoric of the House, only to discover outside the House that it was not a crime at all (4 March 1863).

Discontent with the hypocrisy and sterility of dominant culture, with its underside of corruption and greed, articulated within public discourse a current of desire for a regenerating vision. And what that impulse for renewal moved towards, with varying degrees of conscious recognition, was a concept of mutuality, founded in working-class culture. Again the reason for this is not wholly mysterious. 1864 marked the twentieth anniversary of the Rochdale Pioneers and produced a flurry of books on the Co-operative

Movement. In reviewing some of these, the *Edinburgh Review* commented upon the increased appreciation the societies had enjoyed of late, with even the ultra-Conservative *Quarterly Review* noticing them favourably. What they have shown, wrote the reviewer, is that 'co-operation may be as productive as competition, whilst ... as to the moral superiority of the brotherly principle to that of rivalry, there can, we suppose, be no question' (120 (1864), p. 431). Trade unionism was also the subject of several publications and public lectures. In 1861, the *Westminster Review* printed a remarkable essay in which unions were justified as the expression of working-class idealism of which other sections of society now stood in great need. It would be difficult, declared the writer, 'to exaggerate the importance of keeping alive and cultivating that profound social and moral instinct which still exists among the working classes, in spite of all the selfish individualism so sedulously inculcated in them from above' (76 (1861), p. 526). Only among the poor, the article claimed, is the sentiment of fraternity 'not quite extinct', for 'there is in them a deep flow of generous sympathy for their fellow man, which in these latter times is not easily found elsewhere' (76 (1861), p. 542).

The third great force of mutuality constructed out of the privations of working-class life were the friendly societies, which, wrote *The Times*, 'spread underneath the surface of our working-class life like a network of nerves' (5 November 1863). These societies were brought to public attention by the report into their affairs conducted by Mr Tidd Pratt in 1863. *The Times* devoted several lengthy leading articles to them, its tone a comical mixture of admiration and exasperation. 'They have names expressing all imaginable ideas of fellowship and sympathy, but the titles that look like business are relatively rare,' it wrote. The following day it concluded, 'The mischief that is done in commercial companies by dishonesty, is done in these societies by a misconception of their duties and objects'. The mistaken duties were later named as 'pity, kind feelings and generosity. We are far from undervaluing these principles ... but they ought to be kept in their right place' (5, 6, 9 November 1863). Despite which, *The Times* had used its Christmas issue in 1862 to argue that genuine acts of kindness and charity only grew from 'humblest means and opportunities, out of hunger, thirst, nakedness and dear life itself. That, and not the charity of the guinea list, is the only bond to tie the hearts and hands of three million next-door-neighbours' (25 December 1862).[4]

Clearly, the text of *Our Mutual Friend* is intersecting dialogically with dominant 'evolutionary' discourse in its articulation of these issues within public concern. Just as *Bleak House* parodies and unveils the mystifications of a hegemonic discourse upon Providence, so *Our Mutual Friend* constructs a parodic mockery of rhetoric of national progress evinced in a search for origins in dust and mud, and the siting of patriotic pride in the desert of cultural and political life. The nullity of such enterprises is condensed into the imagery of sifting dust heaps; 'There's some things that I never found among the dust' says Boffin (91).[5] The language of the novel plays upon current interest in evolutionary change with characters named as 'brutes' and showing visible signs of degeneration (528, 157, 800). Gaffer and Riderhood barely emerge from the primal slime of the river bed, while Wegg is in mid-process of evolving into insensate woodenness. The final stage of 'civilized' evolution into artificial items of consumption is achieved only in Society; by Twemlow as an 'innocent piece of dinner-furniture', Mrs Podsnap as a magnificent rocking-horse; and the Veneerings smelling 'a little too much of the workshop'—not even, honest wood! (6)

As in *Bleak House*, parody in *Our Mutual Friend* is accompanied by anger, but unlike the felt indignation expressed at the plight of Jo the crossing-sweeper, the positive anger articulated around the character of Betty Higden seems somewhat perfunctory.[6] The deeper pulse of anger within the narrative discourse of *Our Mutual Friend* is almost wholly negative; a surge of physical disgust and hatred for the characters represented. This is expressed most clearly in the brutality and violation of the language used: 'you might scalp her, and peel her, and scrape her ... and yet not penetrate to the genuine article' (119). In a novel about degenerating into savagery, narrative (literary?) language is characterized by a compulsion to slide across boundaries of 'civilized' control.

However, alongside this negative discourse of parody and anger there is articulated an opposing current of positive desire for transformation and resurrection. The picture of the Canterbury pilgrims referred to casually in Chapter Three in fact offers a *mise en abyme* of this central preoccupation of the text. The allusion holds together a fusion of physical and spiritual desire for regeneration which impelled the pilgrims to seek apotheosis after the stagnation and sterility of winter months. This desire is sustained in the references which follow to the Raising of Lazarus and the Deliverance from Egypt (19). These belong to the character discourse of Charley Hexam, who is represented as an evolutionary mixture of 'uncompleted savagery and uncompleted civilization' (18). His desire for individualistic transformation, to 'raise himself in the scale', pressing through into his use of those two biblical illustrations, is echoed in the discourse of many other characters, especially those from the poorer sections of society.[7] Contrary to the views of those like Alford, the impulse for regeneration is represented in the text as at its strongest in those who are culturally and materially most deprived. This desire for some vision beyond the 'one dull enclosure' of poverty is consistently registered and validated in the text (466). It is only the means of escape sought which is subjected to question.

However, narrative discourse, too, is threaded with allusions to the sacraments of burial and baptism, both of which express regeneration of life out of death. Nevertheless, the most persistent marker of desire within narrative language is a recurrent use of 'as if' or 'as though' kinds of formulation. Within narrative discourse, metaphorical descriptions of social conditions in London are closed off as fact by an unqualified use of the verb 'to be'. Thus the Holloway region 'was a tract of suburban Sahara' and 'every street was a sawpit' (33, 144); no linguistic space is allowed for any contention of this grim urban evolution. In contrast to this closed form, the frequent 'as if' formulations connect things as they are to an imaginative openness of possibility. When Jenny Wren wants to 'change Is into Was and Was into Is, and keep them so' (435), Riah points out that this change would seal off the possibility of further change, perpetuate her present suffering, and deny the liberating power of 'If' with which they have been comforting themselves. When the meek guest contests Mr Podsnap's denial of starvation, his speech is structured around four emphatic repetitions of 'as if' clauses, used ironically to challenge the closure of Podsnappian certainty with the possibility of a different reality: 'as if starvation had been forced upon the culprits' (140). Within narrative discourse the recurrent use of these formulations is immensely varied.[8] They range from the psychological insight that Jenny Wren's sharp manner 'seemed unavoidable. As if, being turned out in that mould, it must be sharp', to more whimsical descriptions like that of chimney pots fluttering their smoke 'as if they were bridling and fanning themselves' (222, 279). However, the generalized effect of this language pattern is to insinuate into narrative discourse an ever-present possibility of imaginative opening out from the closure of actuality. This transformative impulse is most explicitly articulated in the use of the phrase 'as if' at the end of the passage describing workers leaving the paper mill. In its details, the passage itself seems almost a prevision of William Morris's industrial utopianism. The concluding images are of release and expansion, from the 'rippling circles' in the river to the 'ever-widening beauty of the landscape ... where the sky appeared to meet the earth, as if there were no immensity of space between mankind and Heaven' (689). It is the conjunction of those two small words 'as if' which bridges that space, preventing desire for transformation from floating off into the total escape of a heavenly utopianism. Visionary hopes are retained in a connecting recognition of necessity—of things *as* they are.

John Harmon's discourse also asserts this need to connect imaginative impulses with actuality. Having thought of himself as if he were a ghost among the living, he is represented as saying, 'But this is the fanciful side of the situation. It has a real side ... Don't evade it John Harmon, don't evade it' (366). Undoubtedly, evasion is the defining quality of most character discourse imaged in the text, and almost invariably this involves a corruption or abuse of the inventive play of signifiers: the 'as if' capacity of language. Fictionalization is represented as the prevailing tendency of social discourse. Incidents of human misfortune are dislocated in the sensation press from the actuality of suffering, becoming forms of frivolous entertainment to dispel the prevailing boredom of dinner guests. On the other hand there is a busy fabrication of stories whose function is to gloss over inconvenient facts of poverty and social distress. Such is Fledgeby's 'very convenient fiction' of Riah's secret wealth, and a similar fable about Betty Higden constructs 'a comfortable provision for its subject which costs nobody anything, [thus] this class of fable has long been popular' (278, 504). Literature itself is appropriated in this dislocation of words from actuality. Georgiana Podsnap is shown as persuaded to suspend disbelief in Fledgeby as a suitor by the fairytale invocation of 'once upon a time' (259). Wegg's character discourse exploits the 'sincerity' capital of poetry as a false signifier of friendship. Fiction is shown to be further corrupted in its use as ideological myth. Pupils attending ragged schools are taught the hegemonic tale of moral and material progress in the 'Adventures of Little Margery' and 'Thomas Twopence', whilst cultural mediocrity is glorified in the arts as regulated by Podsnap (214, 128).

However, the most corrupting dislocation of discourse from things as they are is represented in the text as the appropriation of the language of imaginative aspiration into the inflated artificiality of oratorical profession. If Alford was correct in diagnosing a nation whose speech had become bombastic and high-flown as not far from rapid decline, then society, as represented in the character discourse of *Our Mutual Friend*, must be in a state of almost terminal degeneration. The speech images constructed from character discourses of all sections of society reproduce the clichéd ideals of their class. On all sides, the high-flown rhetoric of hypocrisy is shown to construct a 'filmy surface' over corrupt practice, mercenary self-seeking, and predatory intent. The hollow professions of timeless friendships and intimate confidences in society compete for self-righteous honour against Riderhood's pious incantation that he gets his living by the sweat of his brow: a formula to transform the worst of treachery into proletarian virtue. Meanwhile Wegg's character discourse indulges a riot of cliché to construct a sense of high moral outrage against Boffin 'that minion of fortune and worm of the hour' (306). Mr Boffin, himself, is represented as saying, 'You have my word; and how you can have that, without my honour too, I don't know' (577), but the assertion only serves to underline the general dislocation of the two.

The effect of all the falsifying rhetorical forms imaged in character discourse is to separate words from intent, signifiers from signifieds, so that characters are depicted in a state of constant chronic suspicion as to meaning. Social language, as represented in *Our Mutual Friend*, has degenerated into a competitive power game in which high ideals and moral sentiment are the circulating currency of cynical self-interest. 'Trust' is a gambit of business bluff, 'fellow-feeling' a stratagem of politics, and 'friendship' a move in the stakes of ambition or spite. Given this corruption of the language of mutuality into a dangerous game of hostility, it is not surprising that the one speech act the text represents persistently as a genuine fusion of form and intent is that of casting people off. Old Harmon's will cuts off his family without a penny, Gaffer disowns his son, Abbey Potterson enacts the social ostracization of Gaffer and Riderhood from the Fellowship, and Charley disowns Lizzie and then Headstone. When Lizzie is represented as begging him to 'unsay those words', he reaffirms their inseparability from his intent: 'I'll not unsay them. I'll say them again ... I have done with you. For ever, I have done with you!' (403).

The degenerative state of public discourse represented in *Our Mutual Friend* is an index of moral and cultural decline. Instead of forming the currency of communication, words enact the isolation of a competitive individualism. Within such an atomistic culture mutual friends do not exist.[9] Yet, within the textual representation of dislocated social discourse an intermittent impulse of desire for transformation is articulated. Matching the recurrence of 'as if' formulations in narrative discourse, the word 'fancy' is repeated within character discourse like a persistent return of what is repressed or denied. The word is associated most frequently with Mrs Boffin and Lizzie Hexam, but it figures even in the discourse of such cynical characters as Wrayburn and Fledgeby (236, 427). Most usually, it is involved in the articulation of an impulse of communality. Mrs Boffin 'takes a fancy' to secure the future of some orphan as a memorial of John Harmon; Lizzie Hexam's friendship with Jenny Wren is described by Charley as 'a ridiculous fancy of giving herself up to another' (100, 392). The ideological 'solution' constructed by the plot as a means of meeting this desire and of reversing cultural decline is the regenerating marriage between classes represented in the union of Lizzie Hexam and Eugene Wrayburn. It suggests the kind of revitalization of culture envisaged by Max Muller when the higher classes are forced to mix again with the lower so that the 'undercurrent' of vulgar dialects rises up 'like the waters in spring'. Sadly, although Lizzie's origin is among 'the accumulated scum' of the poorest waterside district (21), her speech image in the text is closer to Muller's 'crystal surface' of cultivated language than the recreative vigour of dialect. Her fanciful visions in the fire raise no imaginative spark in the language on the page.

It is the character discourse of Wrayburn which is proffered as the site of oppositional hegemonic values to those of the greed, self-interest, and duplicity imaged in the social discourse. Indeed, Wrayburn has been 'called' for a biblical seven years, only needing to discover 'something really worth being energetic about' (20). Wrayburn's discourse is far from representing a vulgar dialect, yet analysis of its qualities reveals promising similarities to the speech of Sam Weller. Wrayburn's character discourse articulates a persistent parodic cynicism as to the discourse of others, functioning throughout the text as an oppositional language image to the hypocritical bombast of prevailing social discourse. Moreover, the ironic protestation against the 'tyrannical humbug of your friend the bee' contains an alienated perspective rejecting the hegemonic glorification of industriousness and material accumulation (94). Like Sam Weller, Wrayburn is represented as far too quick-witted to allow himself to be interpellated into the meaning system of others. Charley Hexam is forced to address himself to Mortimer Lightwood, so totally does Wrayburn refuse to recognize his discourse. Yet, unlike the Podsnappian speech image, Wrayburn's discourse constructs no egoistic individualistic view of himself as Absolute Subject, aimed at imposing upon others an inhibiting sense of lack. Wrayburn's discourse openly recognizes a decentred self, identity an unfathomable riddle: 'I mean so much that I—that I don't mean' (283). This lack of any stable or coherent meaning to 'I' puts the self in process, enabling a continuous, contingent invention of identity as performance.

However, it is at this point that doubt arises. Wrayburn's performances of self, as represented in the text, share nothing of the inclusive, celebratory nature of the performances of the street characters depicted in the earlier fiction. Wrayburn's theatricality exhibits no impulse to irradiate any spectators in a communal sense of comedy and glamour. On the contrary, it is characterized by a streak of sadistic disdain, materialized, most unpleasantly, in the class-based elaboration of a hunting discourse which finds enjoyment in structuring Headstone as prey. A similar tendency is evident in the inventiveness of naming. Sam Weller's use of nicknames is represented as deflating pomposity; in Wrayburn's discourse the appellations 'Mr Aaron', 'Mr Dolls', and 'Schoolmaster' have become sneeringly demeaning. The fanciful side of Wrayburn's character discourse—the references to riddles and fairytales—stays at the level of whimsy, unconnected to any real side of things as they are. Unlike Sam's tales, which mock the causal plot of moral progress with incongruity and superfluity, or

Sairey's celebratory saga of the Harris family, Wrayburn's playfulness constructs no transforming comic vision of alternative values.

In the end, all the strengths of Wrayburn's discourse are negative. Even the friendship with Mortimer Lightwood, undoubtedly part of the oppositional image Wrayburn is intended to represent, is articulated more fully in Mortimer's discourse. Its effect is weakened, too, by a strain of adolescent hero-worship, suggestive of the ideology of the public school culture in which it has its origins. Indeed, despite its alienation from the hegemonic culture of Podsnap, the speech image constructed by Wrayburn's character discourse remains trapped in upper class origins, and thus is denied a material base from which to construct an alternative point of view. At its worst, this gives rise to a dehumanizing discourse which demeans women as 'dolls' and men as 'schoolmasters', and even at its baptized and regenerated best can materialize no transforming fictions of mutuality and gregariousness.

The position of Headstone as failed suitor in the plot positions him also as failed possibility within the ideological solution it constructs. In this, the text would seem more reactionary than those voices within dominant discourse which began to recognize positive qualities inhering in working-class culture. However, there is more to the representation of Bradley Headstone in the text than this. The characterization of Headstone presents, at its most intense, that desire for social transformation, shown to be engendered by poverty. Furthermore, the text hints at the potential within those of working-class origin, like Bradley Headstone, for offering new vitality to a declining culture: 'Yet there was enough of what was animal, and of what was fiery (though smouldering), still visible in him, to suggest that if young Bradley Headstone, when a pauper lad, had chanced to be told off for sea, he would not have been the last man in a ship's crew' (218). However, Headstone's desire for a life beyond the enclosing poverty of waterside streets seeks escape, not at sea, but through the education provided for poor boys in the national schools. The text of *Great Expectations* offers a previsionary exploration of the containment of social discontent in the dreams of consumer plenitude. In *Our Mutual Friend*, the story of the Boffins, as part of the 'solution' offered, recognizes this function of consumerism, but without the critical focus of *Great Expectations*."[10] In *Our Mutual Friend* it is the mediation of desire into educational aspiration which is brought under scrutiny. Again this is previsionary. The education reforms begun in the early 1860s, leading to improved standards in public schools and to compulsory primary education for the working class in 1872, reflected a shift of attitude among the well-to-do. Increasingly, as religion lost its influence, education was turned to as the main means of sustaining the existing social order, becoming the most effective of all ideological apparatuses. The character discourses of Wrayburn and Headstone in the text provide speech images of the two education systems: the one inculcating a disdainful superiority, the other an inarticulate self-doubt. These two voices were to continue unchanged through into this present century.

Towards the end of the novel, Headstone is represented as saying: 'I am a man who has lived a retired life. I have no resources beyond myself. I have absolutely no friends' (799). The speech image constructed by his discourse conveys this impoverished perspective. Wrayburn designates Headstone's speech 'a catechizing infection' and the text provides an image of this approved regimented discourse performed by rote in the national schools. Miss Peacher uses the question and answer routine to seal off in its closed form any dangerous reality beyond established fact (220–1). No 'as if' formulations are allowed into this discourse to open out a space for the inventiveness of desire. Bradley Headstone is the last representation in Dickens's completed fiction of a boy reared in the city streets, and what a painful sense of diminishment there is in this characterization when it is compared to that of Sam Weller. Headstone's rejection of shameful origins is represented as a loss also of the class vitality they produce. Absent from his discourse are the street wit, the spontaneous theatricality, and the conviviality of the earlier street characters. Headstone's cumbrous 'educated' language falls easily into the traps set by the aggressive word games of Wrayburn and Riderhood. His discourse is bereft of the comic and fanciful inventiveness by means of which Wrayburn is able to create an imaginative spaciousness in the midst of Lizzie Hexam's straitened life. Neither is it shown to have the capacity to articulate a language of desire. Sexual love is expressed without joy, wholly as a threat to social identity. Frequently his discourse confesses bitterly to its own impotence and lack: 'Whatever I say to you seems, even in my ears, below what I want to say, and different from what I want to say' (395). Rote education has dislocated Headstone's words from his own passion and desire.

What is most noticeably lost, also, is any capacity for playful self-invention. Desire for transformation of a pauper identity has been mediated wholly into the ego-ideal of respectability. His discourse elaborates no image of self beyond the closure of this rigid social model. His 'decent' clothes and his subdued habit signify equally with his guarded speech a total conformity to the social ideal. Even the need to present himself in persuasive terms to Lizzie Hexam falls back upon reiteration of professional competence and status: 'If you saw me at my work, able to do it well and respected in it, you might even come to take a sort of pride in me' (397). The proliferation of modifiers, 'If', 'might', 'even', 'sort', denies even the meagre confidence of this impoverished assertion of self. It represents a conception of identity reduced to the fixed term 'schoolmaster', with the possibility of playful elaboration 'subdued to the performance of his routine of educational tricks' (546). Bradley Headstone is a representation of the totally taught and regimented self.

His character discourse returns obsessively to the hegemonic lesson of moral progress expounded assiduously in schools for the working class. Self-discipline and repression earn the right to respectable status, 'the right to be considered a better man ... with better reasons for being proud' (293). However, the compulsive repetition of this claim is a register of insecurity. Status based upon denial of origins is inevitably an implicit confession of lack. In the indolent class gaze of Wrayburn, with 'its cold disdain of him as a creature of no worth', the sense of distance from the desired self is mirrored back (288). The more the assured image is confronted, the more intensely the unsure, taught self is registered as bereft of social esteem, and as cheated and deluded by the hegemonic myth. All interpellations of margin to centre, subject to Absolute Subject contain this socially dangerous potential for alienation. Desire for identification with an Absolute Ego-Ideal inevitable involves a simultaneous registering of self as lacking; this can effect a slippage of desire into a libidinous impulse to violate and destroy the image which was first sought. Headstone's murderous attempt to smash the image which mirrors his lack thus represents a simultaneous act of self-destruction, and wiping his name from the school blackboard fittingly acknowledges the erasure of his taught and only identity. The passion of anger in Headstone is represented as wholly negative, constructing no alternative perspective, and the despairing return to origins in the slime and mud of the riverbed is devoid of regenerative impulse. The complex psychological characterization of Headstone thus represents a dialogic challenge to those ideas of 'civilized' evolution current in dominant discourse. The struggling aspiring energies of the working class in the poorest waterside districts are presented in the text as a potential source of regenerative vigour to national culture, rather than as the feared source of degeneration. However, the education provided for the poor is not shown, in *Our Mutual Friend*, as a bulwark against descent into 'savagery'. On the contrary, savagery is presented as the underside of 'civilized' evolution—the effect of the repressions it exerts.

Jenny Wren's visionary promise 'Come up and be dead' chimes dialogically against Headstone's insisted 'Come down' (282, 802). This is not the only oppositional interaction of their discourses. Jenny Wren's speech image is characterized by an alert readiness to anger. Unlike that of Headstone, her anger is presented as a strategy of survival in a tough predatory world in which 'they don't care for you, those fellows, if you're not hard upon 'em', and where mutual friendship more usually masks hostile intent. As such, her sharpness of speech, like that of Sairey Gamp, articulates a positive assertion of self-worth; that she is the 'person of the house' and not to be deceived or set at naught. This is in total contrast to Headstone's destructive rage, depicted as the effect of self-negation and loss. Her anger is represented as a regenerating response to the material conditions of a childhood, 'chilled, anxious, ragged, beaten, ... [and] in pain'—as if 'the sharpness of the manner seemed unavoidable' (239). This origin of anger in hardship and oppression spreads outward from self-assertion to an indignant fellow-feeling for others experiencing privation or injustice. In the text, it is only Jenny Wren's discourse of friendship which fuses profession with an aggressive intent to act on behalf of those, like Lizzie and Riah, for whom she is concerned. The positive strength of her anger is presented as stemming from its roots in the material conditions of poverty; the negativity of Headstone's in the loss of self-esteem through rejection of those regenerative origins.

Jenny Wren's discourse also images the sharp wisdom of street culture. The 'tricks and manners' of 'all those fellows', including those of Wrayburn who is able to play such games upon Headstone's dullness, are always counterpointed and mocked in her speech. In any language game, as in the encounter with Fledgeby, she is depicted as always several moves ahead. Her parody of submissive response. 'Can't undertake to say, sir', checkmates Fledgeby's questioning at every turn, whilst she shrewdly interrogates his language for the intent it unwittingly reveals (716). Her discourse is characterized also by a 'catechizing' habit, a parody of the schoolteacher routine, but unlike Miss Peacher's evasive formulations, Jenny Wren's sharp little questions always move towards an ironic probing of intent underlying surface profession, as in the representation of her quizzing Headstone on his 'disinterested' motives in coming to see Lizzie (342). In its multiple resourcefulness, its hard-bitten cynicism as to intentions behind rhetoric, and its positive impulse of anger—all qualities originating in a material class point of view—the speech image constructed by Jenny Wren's character discourse achieves a more powerful and convincing counterforce than that of Wrayburn's to the social chorus of bombast and deceit.

As this suggests, it is the 'vulgar' discourse of Jenny Wren's speech image which is the locus of a positive, non-hegemonic, perspective based upon material cultural practice and which engages in a sustained dialogic critique of the imaginary solutions offered by the plot structure. Along with sharpness, Jenny Wren's character discourse articulates a pervasive impulse for inventive transformation. Her language constantly inscribes what is ordinary, shabby or even pathetic with a playful glamour. Thus her crutch becomes a 'carriage', Riah a 'fairy godmother', and scrambling amidst the traffic of the street for a glimpse of fashionable ladies is named 'trying on'. This is an imaginative remaking of necessity, not the escape from it represented in the consumer stylishness of the Boffin/Bells mansion. Moreover, unlike Wrayburn's naming and whimsy, Jenny Wren's transformative discourse is always inclusive, inviting others into the playful arena of the imagination. The most sustained act of naming is self-naming. As 'Jenny Wren' her 'character' discourse remakes and performs self with a creative energy which holds defiantly at bay any perception of a piteous actuality. In this performance of self even 'queer legs' and 'bad back' are brought into the control of the speaking subject's own ironic self-representation, and thus withheld from the mockery or pity of the discourse of others. The 'person of the house' so interpellates herself that she can never be constructed (taught) by anyone as a doll in a doll's house. However, despite this fictionalization of self, her discourse, like Sairey Gamp's, is marked by an insistent return to the material necessity of working for a living. 'You may take it for granted' she is represented as telling Fledgeby, 'that it's always worth my while to make money' (717).

The same binding connection between imaginative transformation and 'things as they are' structures the fiction of her drunken father as bad child. In this, the text constructs a shaming contrast between the greedy appetite of the wealthy for sensational stories of human distress as source of frivolous entertainment, and the desperate inventive strategies of the poor for securing a perception of affection and self-respect in the face of degenerative degradation. Jenny Wren's discourse of scolding and threat constructs a fable of youthful misbehaviour enacted against the persistent presence of an angry but anxious and caring parent; a transformation of sordid actuality into its reverse. However, this does not involve evasion of reality; indeed her words generalize the dangers and pain inherent in the working-class culture of the streets, now as then: 'You see it is so hard to bring up a child well, when you work, work, work, all day. When he was out of employment, I couldn't always keep him near me. He got fractious and nervous, and I was obliged to let him go into the streets. And he never did well in the streets, he never did well out of sight' (732). This insisted reality inscribed in Jenny Wren's character discourse undermines those consoling gestures of the ideological plot—the patronage of Betty Higden and Sloppy. In the words of *The Times*, these latter are shown to partake of 'the charity of the guinea list' rather than growing out of the actualities 'of dear life itself'.

Furthermore, the play upon the word 'doll' in association with the characterization of Jenny Wren produces an effect of condensation upon that image which points to hidden ideological ambiguities linking together the

Lizzie/Wrayburn and the Bella/Harmon plot 'solutions'. Jenny Wren's work in the streets is part of the impulse for playful transformation. In opposition to the 'national dread of colour' (393) under the moral regime of Podsnappian conformity, Jenny's dolls present a 'dazzling semi-circle ... in all the colours of the rainbow', that symbol of a promised renewal reconnecting earth to heaven (435). However, the worker, the producer of the dolls, which are dressed up 'for all the gay events of life' (435), has never played and her body is deformed as a degenerating effect of poverty. From this ironic perspective the dolls must be recognized as parodies not only of Lady Tippens (made and unmade night and morning), but also of Bella's love of dressing up and of Mrs Boffin's consumer dream of being 'a highflyer at Fashion' (55). It was notorious that the ostentatious display of fashionable dresses at 'gay events', like those catalogued and priced by Lady Tippens at the Lammles' wedding, were produced by dressmakers whose health was crippled by their conditions of work and by the privations imposed by starvation wages. These wages made dressmakers and seamstresses, like Lizzie Hexam, a well-known source of purchasable sex for cynical men about town.[11] During the 1860s, the controversy over the Contagious Diseases Act, which instituted compulsory medical examination of prostitutes, constructed another strand to that public discourse upon national decline and corruption. In this context, 'setting up a doll' has only one meaning; prostitutes dressed in the trashy finery of cheap consumer taste, like one of Jenny Wren's 'flaunting dolls' (731), offered an easily purchased escape from the hypocritical social regimen of the Podsnappian 'young person'. The showy surface of conspicuous consumer display was linked to its undercurrent of defilement by harsh bonds of economic necessity. In this way, the ambiguous image of Jenny's dolls contains the promise of a visionary transforming energy of productivity and playfulness, which is, at the same time, represented as abused and defiled by the class which exploits and breaks it.

This radical hidden class-consciousness is recontained by the absorption of Jenny Wren into the elect circle of wealthy patronage: those who 'have great power of doing good to others' (680). The plot attempts to cage Jenny Wren like one of the 'cultivated' birds in the expensive aviary in the Boffin mansion, the description of which reads like an inventory of luxurious consumer display (767). Throughout the text of *Our Mutual Friend*, discontent (even hatred) with things as they are is registered in a desire for transformation, split between imaginative remaking and a tired escape from the need to struggle. This latter retreat from reality is materialized in the ascent to privileged consumer contentment away from all 'girding' voices at the novel's conclusion. The split is reproduced also in the characterization of Jenny Wren: in the falsifying sentimentality of her religious rhapsodies and her siren song 'Come up and be dead'. Although from the dislocating perspective of the rooftops, Jenny only pities the 'people who are alive, crying and working and calling to one another down in the close dark streets' (281), the language of that statement undercuts its apparent assertion of disconnection from that world. As always, her character discourse testifies to the vitality and mutuality of working-class origins. Only the culture of 'common' streets and work creates that transforming vision of new life which yet retains living contact with material reality—the interconnection of 'as' with 'if'.

Early in the novel, Silas Wegg, setting out to exploit language, imaginative aspiration, friendship, and gregariousness for fraudulent gain, encounters 'Eddard' the donkey and his owner, the hoarse gentleman. By them he is engaged as participant in a spontaneous performance of comic and radiant superfluity. '"Keep yer hi on his ears," says the hoarse gentleman, and he, the hind hoofs, the truck, and Edward, all seemed to fly into the air together, in a kind of apotheosis' (55). This snatch of 'vulgar dialect' offers a theatrical image of transformation and communality, which, despite decades of inculcation of individualistic competitiveness and educational conformism, has its origins in a resilient oppositional working-class point of view. It is a voice possibly speaking still and laughing in our common streets, and offering the option of a radically regenerating mutuality.

NOTES

1. This led to the Revised Code of Education which came into operation in June 1863, establishing the principle of 'payment by results' for teachers and thus increasing the pressure on them to teach by rote. Philip Collins in *Dickens and Education* (1963), although rather unsympathetic to the presentation of Headstone, gives helpful information on the social status of national school teachers, pp. 159–71.

2. The *Christian Observer* expressed this unease in the prevailing discourse of evolution: 'A people bent on amusement is either emerging from a savage, or declining into an exhausted state ... when the populace demanded nothing but feasts and spectacles, Rome was hastening to decay ... we see many painful symptoms of this degeneracy in the present state of England' (1864, p. 408).

3. In an account of the prevalence of fraud, *The Times* (25 April 1863) referred to the representation of commercial dishonesty in Dickens's early fiction. In fact, the confidence trickster described in the *Times* article as imposing on friends by telling them that his house in Belgrave Square was in the hands of upholsterers and that 'there was no telling when those decorators would have done with so magnificent a mansion' seems very close indeed to the depiction of Alfred Lammle in *Our Mutual Friend*.

4. It is impossible here to give an accurate impression of the dispersed and varied nature of this turning towards forms of mutuality within dominant discourse; it ranges from widespread praise for the mutual help among the Lancashire cotton workers during the disastrous effects on the industry of the American Civil War, to a letter in the *Spectator*

asserting the higher obligation of social principle after fifty years experience of self-interest (17 August 1861), to a speaker at the Social Science Congress of 1863 advocating more amusement for the working class, since 'laughter is essentially a social, a sympathetic, and a contagious power' (*The Times*, 14 October 1863).

5. Reading the many reviews of the continuous stream of archeological and geological books being published in the 1860s helps to make this parodic intent more obvious. For example, a typical review in the *Westminster Review* described a geological finding thus: 'Among these cinders ... [and] among the ashes ... were a great variety of bones and implements' (79 (1863), p. 543). Contemptuous references to 'raking in the dust' were commonplace at the time among those who opposed evolutionary theories. In the contentious atmosphere aroused by Darwin's claims, his 'scientific' supporters were vociferous in depicting themselves as proponents of 'progress' and 'reason'—active in forwarding national evolution onto an even higher scale, as opposed to the entrenched 'superstition' of religious conservatism. Undoubtedly, Veneering's gloomy analytical chemist would place himself among the adherents of 'progress'.

6. In fact, *The Times* was more eloquent and less sentimental than Dickens in depicting the plight of the poor. For example, in its number for 14 November 1863, it printed a long editorial describing a pitiful scene outside the workhouse of St Martin's-in-the-Fields, where about forty people 'huddled together for mutual warmth and the consoling touch of fellow-suffering'. Most were turned away into a bitter night, submitting to their fate 'in passive despair'. *The Times* concluded 'such a scene as we have just described ought to be impossible in this rich and luxurious city ... it is plain inhumanity to let a human creature starve with cold and hunger'.

7. See, for example, pp. 29–30, 41, 53, 99–100, 406.

8. Of course, I am not suggesting that Dickens does not use such formulations (which include a repeated use of the verb 'to seem' as well as 'as if' and 'as though') in other texts, simply that in *Our Mutual Friend* these usages are foregrounded by their frequency.

9. Perhaps Dickens knew that Henry Alford had declared that grammatically there was no such person as 'a mutual friend'! (*Christian Observer*, 1864, p. 620).

10. In fact, Mr and Mrs Boffin's consumer delight (pp. 100, 466) shown as an imaginative expansive reaction to their earlier life of unremitting drudgery, is part of the text's positive underwriting of desire for transformation in the poor. Only as the novel progresses does escape into consumer luxury become a substitute for genuine transformative energy.

11. One of the most remarkable examples of the changed attitude to mutuality, referred to earlier in the chapter, was an article in *The Times* supporting an attempt to unionize dressmakers and milliners, so that 'the workwomen can combine to demand what is right for themselves'. Only by thus improving their conditions, it was argued, would they be protected 'against temptations of a certain kind' (3 September 1863).

GARRETT STEWART

Dickens and Language

Dickens and language: one of the great love-matches of literary history, with a bottomless dowry to boot. It often seems as if the untapped reserves of the English vernacular were simply lying waiting for Dickens to inherit them—by marrying their riches to his story-teller's instinct. No one ever wrote prose that way before. And at the same time few writers have ever sprung their manner from such outright imitation. The style of Dickens's novelistic career begins in pure derivation, a sustained send-up not only of the Johnsonian high style of journalistic and parliamentary claptrap in the eighteenth-century Age of Rhetoric but of Sir Walter Scott's editorial aliases and their prefatory paraphernalia—and then finds its true quasi-oratorical tone amid the cleared debris of tradition. Here is the launching sentence of his debut novel:

> The first ray of light which illumines the gloom, and converts into a dazzling brilliancy that obscurity in which the earlier history of the public career of the immortal Pickwick would appear to be involved, is derived from the perusal of the following entry in the Transactions of the Pickwick Club, which the editor of these papers feels the highest pleasure in laying before his readers as a proof of the careful attention, indefatigable assiduity,

From *The Cambridge Companion to Charles Dickens*, John O. Jordan, ed. © 2001 Cambridge University Press.

and nice discrimination with which his search among the multifarious documents confided to him has been conducted.

After Dickens, no one could write that way again and be taken seriously.

By the last paragraph of *Pickwick Papers*, months of serialized success later, the vestiges of the orotund high style, more relaxed and buoyant now, feel less like overkill than like understatement, as Pickwick enlivens his leisure "in hearing Sam Weller read aloud, with such remarks as suggested themselves to his mind, which never failed to afford Mr. Pickwick the greatest amusement." The moderated wordiness of an idiomatic litotes (or double negative) and the light trappings of alliteration in the "never *f*ailed to a*ff*ord" have by this point an almost vernacular lilt rather than a pedantic thud, and the narrative wording of "such remarks as suggested themselves to his mind" is less an evasive circumlocution than a personification allegory of comic asides, where even the language of parenthetical suggestion does indeed have a life of its own. The novel thus closes in the envisioned recurrent scene of its own reception: the oral recitation of popular prose, jauntily glossed at the domestic hearth.

In like fashion, mock-heaviness dissipates into its own levity from here on out in Dickens's career. In the opening of *Oliver Twist*, the labors of bureaucratic circumlocution—the pompous exertions of adult discourse—counterpoint a birth scene to suggest the human struggle which the newborn hero is slow to accept, for there was "considerable difficulty in inducing Oliver to take upon himself the office of respiration,—a troublesome practice, but one which custom has rendered necessary to our easy existence" (1). But it is not just archly elevated diction and swollen syntax that must submit to Dickens's tongue-in-cheek verbal lampoons. Even the purer literary mode of metaphor can be warped into the strained and mechanical, tactically so. When more than one metaphor is tried out at the same time, they can seem overdone and undersold. Examples again from *Pickwick* and *Oliver Twist*, in the move from comic picaresque to the more abiding forms of Dickensian melodrama: though the seething genius of Pickwick has just solved a major scientific mystery by tracing the origin of tittlebats to the local ponds of Hampstead, there sat the man "as calm and unmoved as the deep waters of the one on a frosty day or as a solitary specimen of the other in the inmost recesses of an earthen jar" (1). By contrast, such metaphoric overkill, when stripped of farce, can become genuinely incremental in *Oliver Twist*, a shift in the registers of simile so rapid as to communicate the fleeting events of Bill Sikes's accidental death by hanging: "The noose was on his neck. It ran up with his weight, tight as a bow-string, and swift as the arrow it speeds" (50). Taut cause and lethal effect snap shut upon each other in the figurative "transfer" (the etymological sense of *meta-forein*) from the living to the dead.

Pickwickian bombast marks one fork in Dickens's multiple paths as a stylist, Twistian melodrama another. And as his verbal irony gains confidence, even his stylistic comedy becomes both darker and more targeted. Gradgrind in *Hard Times* is so full of pedagogic emphasis that the rigidity of his own person seems a *pointed* affront, including the spiked bristles of his hair: "a plantation of firs to keep the wind from its bald head," where the sound-play on "firs" (with its anagrammatic twist in "*surf*acc") seems at once to summon and rule out the softness and comforting animality of "fur." In making his points, Gradgrind is insistence personified: "The speaker's obstinate carriage, square coat, square legs, square shoulders—nay, his very neckcloth, trained to take him by the throat with an unaccommodating grasp, like a stubborn fact, as it was—all helped the emphasis" (1). In such a grinding-in of the point about Gradgrind, we have moved well beyond the habitual Dickensian way in which language asserts the vitality of character from within the name itself, from Weller and Swiveller through Dedlock to Headstone, including, most unmistakably of all, Mr. Gradgrind's own associate, the schoolmaster M'Choakumchild. Names aside, Gradgrind's epitome of the utilitarian bureaucrat requires that his very necktie be "trained" rather than "tied," the constrictive revenge of his whole system. Best of all, there is the dodging of the expected formulaic apology for a simile in "as it were," ordinarily indicating a flight of fancy as contrary-to-fact. Not here. The tie may well seem ("as [indeed] it was") only one more among many facts or itemized data, any of which, when given the upper hand, may carry the threat of strangulation to the living organism. Not all characters in Dickens are embodied rhetorical strategies—or at least not in this overt way. But all of them tap for their essence the contours of the language that generates them.

Heavy-handed comparison, strident parallelism, deliberate contortions of idiom, rampant neologism, extended metaphor, phantom puns and phonetic undertones, these effects and countless others—including all the manipulated tics of dialogue, from Cockney slang to the stuffy argot of the shabby genteel—work to turn the Dickensian sentence into a histrionic scenario all its own, with grammatical subjects battling with objects for priority, adjectives choking the life out of nouns before they can manifest a verb, adverbs riding on the coattails of remorseless verb chains, and, everywhere in dialogue, slips of the tongue hitting home. "Joe, how are you, Joe?" (27) splutters Pip the former blacksmith in *Great Expectations*, now idle gentleman, when surprised by his servant with the introduction of his old friend from the forge. As so often in this novel of ironically echoing dialogue, the words are thrown back in his face with a difference—here by the broken parallelism of Joe's lower-class pronunciation: "Pip, and how AIR you, Pip?"[1] Joe puts into accidental circulation the high-toned "air" that Pip usually puts on.

Language, then, isn't just something Dickens mobilized or remodelled. Language *per se* is a way of reading him, a way of staying with him through the farthest stretches of invention—and of confronting there his unique place in Victorian letters. Consider, for comparison, two pieces of novelistic travel writing powerfully subordinated to drama and psychology from the two greatest writers of Victorian prose fiction. In each case a young woman is displaced from the native domestic life she has known and plunged into the luxuriant decay of fabled Italy. The first gives us Dorothea Brooke in Rome, a single sentence from the famous wedding journey of George Eliot's *Middlemarch*. The second concerns Amy Dorrit on the way south to Venice, from the Grand Tour of *Little Dorrit*. Each is a complex example of what narrative theory would call "focalization," where external description is filtered through the singular consciousness of a character.

Eliot first, sampled by one calculatedly overwhelming sentence:

> Ruins and basilicas, palaces and colossi, set in the midst of a sordid present, where all that was living and warm-blooded seemed sunk in the deep degeneracy of a superstition divorced from reverence; the dimmer but yet eager Titanic life gazing and struggling on walls and ceilings; the long vistas of white forms whose marble eyes seemed to hold the monotonous light of an alien world: all this vast wreck of ambitious ideals, sensuous and spiritual, mixed confusedly with the signs of breathing forgetfulness and degradation, at first jarred her as with an electric shock, and then urged themselves on her with that ache belonging to a glut of confused ideas which check the flow of emotion.[2]

The cadence and the burden are deliberate, along with the delayed syntactic detonation. In a distended grammatical mimesis, the whole numbing weight of splendid, empty impressions comes pressing down on the consciousness of the heroine, the novel's ethical lightning rod. Amid the sensory overload, the discriminating mind is still sorting, weighing the antitheses, even if coming up short.

By contrast, the kaleidoscopic barrage of the Dickens passage is more unreflective and nightmarish, a dizzy unfurling of contradictory impressions without any of the perspective tacitly achieved by rhetorical balance in Eliot. The whole headlong tourist trek seems, from Amy Dorrit's assaulted perspective, like a delirious dream in its senseless, expensive repetitions, so that the subjunctive verb form "would" that governs the passage is not wishful or "contrary-to-fact" but rather the sign of a willfully "iterative" or "frequentive" tense. This is what they *would* do, day in and day out: "Among the day's unrealities would be roads" leading on to "vast piles of building mouldering to dust; hanging gardens where the weeds had grown so strong that their stems, like wedges driven home, had split the arch and rent the wall" (2.3). Compared to Eliot's almost clichéd "like an electric shock," here is a subsidiary metaphor that arrests us with a violence inherent in the scene: untended nature's revenge against the neglected remnants of culture. And note the minuscule but devastating effect of the singular "building" rather than "buildings," as if it named the undifferentiated labor and waste of the whole ancient mass, thus serving to reduce "piles" from the idiomatic term for mansions to mere mountains of stone.

Onward: "Again there would be places where they stayed the week together, in splendid rooms, had banquets every day, rode out among heaps of wonders, walked through miles of palaces, and rested in dark corners of great churches" (2.3)—so that "places" seems to dilate into "palaces" (with their own "miles" of internal tramping) under the repetitive pressure of the interchangeable. The principle of aimless iteration seems to invade even the phonetic texture of the prose as well, in a jangling association of unwanted stimuli. No sooner has Dickens's ear picked out a shadowy cause-and-effect nexus in the "mist and *scent* of in*cense*" in deserted churches (2.3) than, a clause later, his description latches onto the entwined aural knotting of "by the roads of vines and o*li*ves, through squa*li*d villages." These are sites where idle luxury has reversed its terms to impoverished ennui and where, in the numbing counterplay of transitive and intransitive verbs, there "seemed to be nothing to support life, nothing to eat, nothing to make, nothing to grow, nothing to hope, nothing to do but die" (2.3).

Unlike Eliot's passage, Dickens's nauseating panorama is all drive and thrust and mounting critique: rhetorical through and through rather than weightily meditative, and honed to the straightforward vocabulary of the mind's eye. So with his famous set pieces in novel after novel, where some oddity of grammar or diction regularly offers the key to an overarching effect. There is the famous second paragraph of *Bleak House* beginning with "Fog everywhere" (1), followed by eight more freestanding verbless phrases headed by "Fog" ("Fog up the river ... Fog creeping ...") and mired in the continuous present of this same grammatical impasse—all prepared for by the layerings or "deposits" of mud in the opening paragraph, whose seemingly neutral choice of diction triggers the caustic metaphor (and fiscal send-up), "accumulating at compound interest." Strung out over a comparable parallelism early in *Our Mutual Friend*, and again in a perpetual present tense of inalterable routine, there are the eleven nounless verb phrases depending from the main clause: "The great looking-glass above the sideboard, reflects the table and the company" (1.2). This is the company gathered at one of the endless *nouveau riche* banquets given by the aptly named Veneerings, whose polish is only a thin layer of applied substance, not even skin deep, and so who seem to deserve no company but superficial reflections.

Sampling this syntactic format directs us as well to a related—and characteristic—adjectival device of Dickensian prose: "Reflects Veneering; forty, wavy-haired, dark, tending to corpulence, sly, mysterious, filmy." Three flatly descriptive adjectives pile up, followed by a participial (-ing) phrase that turns out to be a momentary stopgap against another threesome of denigrating attributes, the last of them, "filmy," aptly suggesting that an imperfect reflection in the glass would in fact best seize upon the shadowy essence of the man. The subject of all these reflections, the mirror, has long ago dropped away (into the freestanding verb "Reflects") so as to offer up the existence of the invited nonentities in a hovering limbo of their own artifice: "Reflects Twemlow; grey, dry, polite, susceptible to east wind" (1.2), and so forth. Again the discrete, stiffening trio of adjectives setting his attributes off from each other in their frailty and desiccation, and then another stunning run of adjectives, this time elongated and unpunctuated in imitation of all manner of optical and spiritual distortion: "Reflects charming old Lady Tippins on Veneering's right; with an immense obtuse drab oblong face, like a face in a tablespoon" (1.2). An anamorphic warping or merely the accurate, unflattering image of misshapen age? Superbly, there is no way to tell. By this point in the passage, reflection and reality have disappeared into each other, and only the glimpsed attribute haunts (via the disembodied hovering of modification) the place of a withdrawn reality.

I will be coming back to the enchainment and bunching of adjectives in Dickens, as this "minor" descriptive device can end up inflecting our sense of an entire novel. For now, the dismantling phrase about the aged coquette in *Our Mutual Friend* perfectly exemplifies, and twice over (as inanimate reflection and as dehumanizing simile), a longstanding truism of Dickensian stylistics: the collapsing of boundaries between people and things. Besides all the metaphors that bestow animation (often hostile) on houses and boots and neckties, or steal it from suddenly spoon-like human visages, there is, however, another stylistic habit, more specifically indebted to Dickens's literary precursors, that perhaps best captures—or further erodes—the blurred border between personality and objecthood. It is worth dwelling over this most narrowly delimited of rhetorical (or figurative) effects—usually revolving around the witty discrepancy between literal and metaphoric senses—as it can offer a test case for the reading of Dickensian narrative from the stylistic ground up.

As Dickens would have practiced it if not recognized its name, syllepsis (or zeugma—there is considerable terminological debate) is a device that, in its most recognized form, predicates in two different senses of its main verb. Take Pope's textbook example from *The Rape of the Lock*: "to stain her honour, or her new brocade." It isn't that "stain" *might* be figurative as well as literal when it is collocated at one and the same time with spirit and facade, honor and costume. It must be. The incompatibles are copresent at the same level of grammatical realization. At one point, for instance, the prose of *Pickwick Papers* forces upon the idiom "fell asleep" a recognition of its latent dead metaphor. Literalizing the verb in one of its paired usages and heightening the semantic fissure with a comma, Dickens calls attention to the way Mr. Pickwick "fell into the barrow, and fast asleep, simultaneously" (19), so that corporeality and consciousness, objectivity and subjectivity, are fused in the same plunge. When a related comic device is delegated to a character's own wit later in the novel, we get Sam Weller satirizing legal proclamations by noting, "There ain't a magistrate goin' as don't commit himself, twice as often as he commits other people" (25). Or there is the forlorn mastiff in *Bleak House*, discontent with his melancholy solitude and, in another gnawing confusion of materiality and spirit, "very much wanting something to worry, besides himself and his chain" (7).

Physical and emotional conditions turn in *Little Dorrit* on the merest flick of a prepositional shift, as when Amy finds a milliner "in tears and in bed" (1.7); or when in the same novel, across an internal/external (physiological/fiscal) divide, Tite Barnacle is said to be "more flush of blood than money" (1.10). The effects can be more prolonged and baroque, too. Quintessence of a reductive doubling between the external and internal—across the collapsed distinction between an integral self and its public reputation—is the image of the swindling financier spaced out across a looser but related grammatical format: "Mr. Merdle's right hand was filled with the evening paper, and the evening paper was full of Mr. Merdle" (2.12). The less showy versions of such sylleptic clefts in reference, however, remain the more unsettling—grammatically and conceptually. Confronted in later years with the file that had been associated with the convict on the marshes in the opening sequence of *Great Expectations*, Pip is "stupefied by this turning up of my old misdeed and old acquaintance" (10). The old acquaintance is only there by proxy, in the man presenting the file, and the former misdeed (in aiding the criminal) has been turned up not in the sense of uncovered at last. Rather, the act returns only in the mode of a repressed memory teased to the surface of consciousness. That the same verb could navigate these discordant zones of association seems, in effect, to miniaturize the psychological allegory of the novel as a whole, with its obsessive shadowing of present by past. At the opposite pole from traumatic memory is the eroticized nostalgia of a character in no way given to witty contradictions. Thus the softened sylleptic shift of Little Dorrit's letter, with its conflation of self and other in a displaced amorous testament to her eventual husband: "So dearly do I love the scene of my poverty and your kindness" (2.11). Again the sylleptic turn of phrase offers a microcosm of the novel's whole psychological structure— and moral: the self's past always intimately entwined with the action upon it of remembered others.

The laminated grammar of syllepsis goes even more to the heart of *Dombey and Son*. The device is repeatedly a manner of yoking unlike things together by a logic somewhere between metonymy (association) and metaphor (equivalence). Once the spiritual collapse of outer world upon inner life in the throes of a consuming ego has been diagnosed in an alliterative skewed parallelism like "the beadle of our business and our bosoms" (5) to describe Mr. Dombey, the syndrome can be read in the least insignia of Dombey's costume or demeanor, as in "stiff with starch and arrogance" (8). This is the depersonalizing flip-side of the Dickensian animism that bestows sentient energy upon lifeless objects, so that a human attitude is reduced to the rigidities of costume. The sylleptic phrasings continue apace in this novel. In Dombey's first separation from his son after the mother's inconvenient death in childbirth, the boy is given out to wet-nursing "borne by Fate and Richards" (6), where a laboring woman's embrace is ominously linked to the failed self-sufficiency of Dombey's bourgeois world. As with the forking between "starch" and "arrogance," the corporeal (bodily removal) again emblemizes the spiritual (human destiny) across a single grammatical frame.

This shifting between literal and figurative is the deepest common denominator of the sylleptic trope, in *Dombey and Son* and elsewhere. In another sartorial metonymy just barely avoiding the repressed cliché of "stout-hearted," Captain Cuttle is put before us as "one of those timber-looking men, suits of oak as well as hearts" (9). Enough tiny syntactic wrinkles of this sort accrue to a pleated pattern. Once the sylleptic paradigm—call it divided consciousness grammatically instantiated—has been established in the early chapters, across the "high" and "low" strands of the plot, it can be proliferated at will. There is the exit of Major Bagstock, who "took his lobster-eyes and his apoplexy to the club" (40) as if such eyes were a synecdoche as well as a medical symptom of his bulging and convulsive self-importance. Later, when Mr. Toots laments Florence's announced marriage, he bemoans the "banns which consign her to Lieutenant Walters, and me to—to Gloom, you know" (56). Revealed here again, in a comic key, is the cleaving between novelistic fate and its embodied nemesis in character. Or in a typifying implosion of outer reality upon inner ego so extreme as to question any grounding for that ego except the contingencies of fame or shame, there is Mr. Dombey confronting his wife-to-be "with a lofty gallantry adapted to his dignity and the occasion" (30). In yet another sylleptic microcosm of a novel's whole design, even marital encounter is here referred back to a shift in perspective within the devouring self-absorption of the central subject.

As already noticed, the two-ply phrasings that accumulate around a world-swallowing pride in *Dombey and Son* return in *Little Dorrit* as well, where they cooperate in their effects with the novel's habit of threefold modification. Dickens's fondness for adjectival triads sometimes sends the modifiers off in such different directions that they end up satirizing the very notion of a center, subjective or otherwise, in what amounts to a variant of sylleptic forking. Take Flora Finching, always at loose ends with herself, punished by description in the same key: "Flora, always tall, had grown to be very broad too, and short of breath" (1.13). The two initial axes of extremity, vertical and horizontal, yield to an inner dimension of breathless giddiness—and panting babble—whose way of being "short" is not a matter of spatial measure at all. In keeping with the novel's prison motif, the rhetorically adept villain Rigaud mocks the defiant Clennam, during his detention in the Marshalsea, with being "more free of speech than body" (2.18). And the ailing, jail-bound Frederick Dorrit admits his own exhaustion in an unravelling grammar of a related sort: "Late hours, and a heated atmosphere, and years, I suppose," said Frederick, "weaken me" (1.19), where time and place get counterpoised to that inward belatedness that comes with wasted age. There, of course, we get three (rather than two) explanatory nouns, jarring with and overdetermining the admission of intractable debility.

Beyond the paradigm of sylleptic splintering, human constriction is a curse usually borne in *Little Dorrit* on the backs of its congested adjectives, stalled in incremental reiteration upon a physical or psychic impasse. That such language should stutter—or gasp for air—under the onus of an asphyxiating society and its literal imprisonments is to be expected in a novel whose chief symbol of political stultification is named for a notorious figure of speech. This is the "Circumlocution" Office, denominating not only the civil bureaucracy by that name but a degenerate habit of language as well.

Wordiness is an epidemic bias of mind whose virus can attack anywhere. Though long a mainstay of Dickens's comic resources (since *Pickwick* on, as we know), the roundabout phrase has in *Little Dorrit* been rigorously assimilated to thematic purpose. At times, what is leaden and misleading about such turns of phrase is made to confront its antithesis in the deflected pithy saying or the wordy unpacking of a maxim or two. The loathsome slumlord Casby, not content with wringing blood from the proverbial single stone, is known "to get a good quantity of blood out of the stones of several unpromising courts and alleys" (1.13). It is in this capacity that he is familiar to many "in whom familiarity had bred its proverbial result perhaps" (1.13)—the last clause ladling on over twice as many words as occasion demands. An even more laughably oblique dodge of the forthright, again swamping a proverb at its core, comes with the introduction of the rakish Henry Gowan, "whose genius, during his earlier manhood, was of that exclusively agricultural character which applies itself to the cultivation of wild oats" (1.17).

A squandering of words in evasion, chicanery, or self-promotion: these are the hallmarks of Circumlocution, both as institution and as a social discourse. Even an innocent euphemism can take the taint of the procedures its user despises, for just after Arthur leaves the Circumlocution Office for the first time, he meets Mr. Meagles, hot under the collar from his own rage at the office's red tape, who says "I only wish you had come upon me in a more prepossessing condition as to coolness" (1.10). The tendency to expatiate needlessly, to make oratorical mountains out of clerical molehills, is perhaps best distilled in the habit of the chief bureaucrat, that inextricable Barnacle on the ship of state, to bestow prolongation even on a single noun, giving the very word circumlocution "the air of a word of about five-and-twenty [not even twenty-five!] syllables" (1.10). But it is Dickens's further ingenuity with the name "Circumlocution" that turns wordiness per se into something like a mock-epic conceit. So tortuous is the labyrinthine gobbledegook of the Office that it becomes torturing. In the process, Dickensian prose reactivates, through etymological wordplay and pun, the ubiquitous prison motif in the novel, a prison sequestered this time at the heart of legalism itself. This is because applicants to the Circumlocution Office's patent department, in their inventive *conviction*, are immobilized as "troublesome Convicts who were under sentence to be broken alive on that wheel" (2.10), a wheel whose *circum*ference is that of punitive circularity itself. Varying the metaphor with a trivializing allusion to *Don Quixote*, another Barnacle later explains that Circumlocution is "not a Wicked Giant to be charged at full tilt; but, only a windmill showing you, as it grinds huge quantities of chaff, which way the country wind blows" (2.28). Spewing out "chaff," that reanimated dead metaphor in British English for useless verbiage or humbug, the grinding nonsense of the Office serves merely as a weather vane for the clichéd winds of change.

From the vortex of an officiating circumlocution in *Little Dorrit*, words in search of any meaning whatever must sometimes struggle free of their own ordained syntax, edging over into separate emphases, isolated into authenticity. Adjectives always come fast and furious in Dickens, but in Little Dorrit they come consistently bunched in threes, compressed, oppressive, bereft. The syntax of constraint sets in early. "It was a Sunday evening in London, gloomy, close, and stale" (1.3) when the hero comes home to his unloving mother's house after twenty years. The adjectives crowd tight upon each other, airless and constrained. This is often the effect of these tripled clusters: no breathing-room. So with the Clennam house itself, which is later thought by him to be, as always, "wrathful, mysterious, and sad" (2.10). So with its immediate environs on a deserted Sunday: "Nothing to see but streets, streets, streets. Nothing to breathe but streets, streets, streets" (1.3). The double assonance of the long *e*'s in these fragmentary glimpses (like cinematic quick-cuts) serves to bond constricted organic functions like "s*ee*ing" and "br*ea*thing" to their unwanted objects in those numberless disjoint "str*ee*ts." In turn, this labyrinth of aimless crisscrosses and blind alleys is further captured by that interlocking nexus of *s* sounds in the multiplied "street(s), street(s), streets," where singular and plural fuse into a shapeless disjunct totality of street, street, and nothing but street. No surprise that the motto for rent-collecting deployed by the hypocritical slumlord Casby, who patrols the network of thoroughfares and blind alleys in Bleeding Heart Yard, is "squeeze, squeeze, squeeze" (2.32), a clenched obsession crushing the life out of his tenants.

Some tenancy, however, collapses under its own weight. When the Clennam house comes crashing down from dry rot in the end, past participles take up the familiar threefold burden of a fatal refrain, with the onlookers "stifled, choked, and blinded by the dust" (2.31). Sometimes the adjectives in *Little Dorrit* are welded together so tightly that they seem to shear off from adjacent grammar altogether, as in the description of the implacable Miss Wade's uninviting anteroom, such as is "always to be found in such a house. Cool, dull, and dark" (2.20). At other times the swell of modification may in itself offer a pantomime of puffed-up self-importance. The petticoated Mrs. General expands in pomposity across her very description as "ample, rustling, gravely voluminous" (2.2). Elsewhere the adjectival triad can infect the surrounding grammar, so that "a moist, hot, misty" day—where the consonant bracket may seem to put the "*mist*" back in "*moist*" as cause to effect—can then go on to contaminate in its threefold clamminess the noun series of the next sentence: "It seemed as though the prison's poverty, and shabbiness, and dirt, were growing in the sultry atmosphere" (2.29). That's the Marshalsea, the debtors' prison in London, and its pounding description feels anticipated by the threefold similes that caught the unrelenting essence of the opening prison at Marseilles: "Like a well, like a vault, like a tomb, the prison had no knowledge of the brightness outside ..." (1.1). Unlike the twofold similes in *Pickwick* or *Oliver*, here the figurative effort at variation seems locked into the inescapable despite itself. The metaphors alone incarcerate. This effect is close kin to the adjectival entrapments of the novel. Right through to the end, the threefold downbeat of delayed epithets (arriving after the name or noun) registers as emotional or environmental deadlock. Among other effects, this triadic modification is used to usher out, in adjacent sentences from the penultimate chapter, two of the least heroic characters of the book, Amy's sister and brother: "Here was Fanny, proud, fitful, whimsical ... Here was her brother, a weak, proud, tipsy, young old man" (2.33). As always, the very form of the modifiers is symptomatic. It is Fanny's fitfulness, the intermittence of her motives, that fractures her attributes into a jagged taxonomy rather than consolidating, them into a focused personality, just as her brother's character is disintegrated from within by the idle clash of his waistrel traits: three failings in adhesive contamination, then the paradoxical implosion of the last pair ("young old"), the whole lifeline in collapse.

Given the recurrent triadic device of adjectival pile-up in *Little Dorrit*, with its choke hold on both human identity and its smothering urban ambience, the recuperative finale of the novel would be well advised to moderate and rectify rather than simply to escape such a pattern. So it does. The grooves of threefold formulation seem relaxed at last to various triplings less rigid, more emotionally capacious. When Amy puts from her own mind, and keeps from Arthur's knowledge, her having been financially cheated by his mother, indirect discourse inhabits her gentle intent in triplicate. But it does so in such a way that for once we get a falling rhythm of release rather than the grip of insistence: "That was all passed, all forgiven, all forgotten" (2.33). Nearing their marriage, indirect discourse again projects the heroine's own emotional tonality, for she "never came to the Marshalsea now and went away without seeing him. No, no, no" (2.34). What in another context might come off as a forced, meretricious affirmation reads here as a curative tripling, like the magic words of an exorcism.

Within a few pages, just as Amy and Arthur have signed the wedding register in the church next-door to the prison, the last sentence of the novel's second-to-last paragraph sets up the fragmentary grammar of the closing one: "They paused for a moment on the steps of the portico, looking at the fresh perspective of the street ..." (2.34). Though there is the sense of "new prospects" as well as of mere "view" in the pictorial metaphor of "fresh perspective," the underlying connotation of draftsmanship in the phrase picks up on a more extended earlier figure. I have in mind one of Dickens's few grammatical lapses (a dangling participle with no proper antecedent), yet one that seems turned to canny advantage. "Looking back upon his own poor story, she was its vanishing-point. Everything in its perspective led to her innocent figure" (2.27). It is as if the sentence had meant to say in indirect discourse: "Looking back upon his own poor story, he realizes [as we do] that she has always been its vanishing-point." Instead, the grammar has undergone its own foreshortening, bringing forward the object of desire in the very effacement of an anchoring subject other than our own free-floating identification with his (and so her) "story." Even in a laxity of grammar, that is, Dickens can rescue—and resecure—the very nature of readerly identification as the true cornerstone of his narrative aesthetic.

At the novel's close, the cadenced fall of the prose has the new married couple hovering momentarily "in the autumn morning sun's bright rays" (2.34) before they "went down." As if building on, or lifting off from, all the compartmentalized adjectival modules of the novel, this run-up of evocation transfigures three nouns in a row into adjectival modifiers on the way to the fourth and finally descriptive "bright." The process is soon to be reversed in the nominalization of three adjectives. As the next paragraph opens upon its parallel syntactic fragments, three more predicates, punctuated as whole sentences, take up the dying fall of "Went down" as they sketch out the future lives of the couple: varied from "went down into" the modesty of their life together to "went down to" (2.34) their various earthly service.

After which the grammar collects itself for what is perhaps the most "stylish" (and stylized) sentence Dickens ever wrote: "They went quietly down into the roaring streets, inseparable and blessed; and as they passed along in sunshine and in shade, the noisy and the eager, and the arrogant and the froward and the vain, fretted, and chafed, and made their usual uproar" (2.34). After all the novel's impacted triadic adjectives, "inseparable and blessed," in its lattice-work of internal chiming, is the hard-won phrasing of parity and union, of reciprocated and interknit mutuality. With the loosening prepositional cadence of "in sunshine and in shade" recalling (and appeasing) the Marseilles prison setting of the novel's first chapter, with its starkly dichotomized title, "Sun and Shadow," the couple now accepts the world's duality in the again duplex form of "the noisy and the eager," to which is appended the last threefold modification in the book. Amid a frictional jostling of assonance and alliteration (including the "fricative" f–v; sounds capped off in "*fretted and chafed*"), the married pair must now enter among "the *arrogant* and the *froward* and the *vain*," including that final if neutralized hint of circumlocution—last vestige of the world's nonsense—in the faint semantic twinning of the near synonyms "arrogant" and "vain." In any case, threefold adjectives have by now hardened to substantives, attitudes grown personified, though somewhat shadowy and insubstantial for all that. Then at last, after five clauses depending from "went down," like a precinematic "loop" effect (one of the countless anticipations of cinematic editing in the very syntax of Dickensian prose), we come upon the tacit antithesis of the last word, "*up*roar" (my emphasis on Dickens's harbored syllabic twist), which meets the descending couple halfway—and on the world's terms. But on language's own terms as well. The least word in Dickens can have a directionality, a dynamism, a suppressed etymology all its own.

Endings often call upon unprecedented reserves of Dickensian ingenuity in this way. *David Copperfield* winds down with a simplicity of diction so extreme as to be flamboyant in its own right, when the autobiographical narrator, playing on the double meaning of "life" as both biographical and biological, closes off the former with "O Agnes, *O my soul, so may* thy face be by me when I *clo*se my life indeed" (64). Despite the clipped and simple diction, its segregated forms begin to suffuse each other under the pressure not only of feeling but of sheer phonetic proximity. Among the echoes sent rippling across the ridged surface of these decisive single words is precisely the pivotal linkage that seems to generate alike the "so" of both mortal analogy and its redemptive final prospect, with "soul" taken up in "*clo*se."

There is an even more famous and debated closural passage in Dickens, of course, having also to do with a first-person narrator's conjugal prospects. It occasions, in fact, one of Dickens's rare comments on the quality of his own language. Notoriously ceding to the suggestions of his friend Bulwer-Lytton to soften the ending of *Great Expectations* by reuniting Pip and Estella, Dickens wrote in a letter to his friend Forster, about a coda both tempered and embellished at once, that "I have put in as pretty a little piece of writing as I could."[3] But how might this self-styled prettiness connive to qualify reunion by keeping before us the unhealed scars of the past, as many have suspected about the passage from less stylistic evidence? The interpolated material begins with Pip's lingering approach to the demolished Satis house, a place yet again of pure projection, but this time the projection (at least at first) of memory rather than fantasy. "There was no house now, no brewery, no building whatever left, but the wall of the old garden" (59). Grammar negates the tripled shapes of the past even before the incremental syntax attaches "whatever left" as a kind of afterthought. The approached "place" is all "clear space" now, walled and evacuated. Again a loosened, bidirectional syntax adjusts the ensuing "passage" of Pip into his own decimated past: "A gate in the fence standing ajar, I pushed it open, and went in." As the freestanding clausal grammar (a rare format for Dickens) half insinuates by ghostly apposition, Pip alone can offer his own and only access to a past scene on which he has always kept, as it were, a door open.

This same stress on nostalgic subjectivity, with the "I" still "ajar" to desire, is carried through to the end of the novel by the complicities of diction and syntax. A metaphor of writing or drawing ("trace out") is immediately called upon to suggest the etching of memory, all while an emphatic parallel syntax seems fading away into the deletions of ellipsis: "I could trace out where every part of the old house had been, and where the brewery had been, and where the gates, and where the casks." Dickensian sentence structure has never been (and this is saying something) more sure of itself. So long gone, these last features of desolation have been deprived of all being (and its predicative grammar of "had been") save that of the mind's phantom tracery. Into this tenuous delineation of the passed and the absent, a "solitary figure" shows itself. Or not quite. Rather than "revealed itself," the "figure showed itself aware of me," checked in full disclosure by the predicate adjective ("aware") of the sentence's reflexive construction. Across seven more repetitions of the neuter pronoun ("it" for "figure" rather than person), Pip's language must slowly and tentatively retrieve the eroticized body of Estella: a figment of residual desire before it is an incarnate intention. "As I drew nearer it," for example, "it was about to turn away, when it stopped, and let me come up with it"—both catch up to it, of course, and also "come up with it" in the other sense by virtually engendering its manifestation: surfacing it from repressed desire, conjuring its renewed promise.

Such is the doubleness, slippage, and reversion that layers this closing scene even before arriving at the novel's voluminously debated last sentence, where if is grammar once more, every bit as much as the semantic evasion discussed by critics, that continues to equivocate the straightforwardness of romantic uplift—and again by pivoting around the shifting valence of the verb "show," hovering still in a syntactic limbo between self-revelation and external disclosure. This whole ameliorative finale is conditioned, of course, by the novel's recurrent symbolic "mists," rising momentarily now, lifting their ban on vision, so that "in all the broad expanse of tranquil light they showed to me" (59) we might well expect "showed" as a verb of disclosure or prophecy—awaiting its object rather than already closed round on it. Not so. What we are likely to have read as an adverbial phrase ("in all the ... light," taking "they" as subject) is unfolded instead as the beginning of a fuller subordinate clause, awaiting the subsequent main syntax of the sentence. The passage has immediately moved, that is, to activate its inversion of subject/object relations across the delayed logic of its transitive grammar, laying further stress on the continuing subjectivity of desire's double negation. Yet again Dickensian sentence structure has turned upon its heels, so that: "in all the ... light [which] they showed to me, I saw no shadow of another parting from her."

In this self-displacing grammar across the phonetic dilation of "show" into "*shadow*," the dissipated mists show forth nothing but the light they otherwise occlude, from within whose ambient gleam the squint of prediction reveals no silhouette of loss. The eighteenth-century inflections of *Pickwick Papers* are now decades behind us. The litotes ("not un-") of Dickensian comic style has been mellowed—and complicated—to the suspended disbelief of hedged confidence (the negated negativity of the echoic "no shadow"). The point isn't that Pip finally sees the light. Rather the opposite. Flooded by a suddenly uncurtained field of brightness, bedazzled once more by the figure of expectancy (in Dickens sustained irony), the long-enthralled subject of desire sees for a moment, at least, no darkening nonlight. All we can locate for sure in this closing moment is respite rather than repair. Transfiguring his own original intent for the passage with such "pretty" revision, Dickens develops its true beauty in the unravelling tug of elegy at the thinly stitched hem of restitution. Language for Dickens is once more the very medium of nontranslucence, elastic, volatile, and elusive, a language whose writing—delegated to his invested narrator as Pip's own "tracing out"—frays the very assurances it seems to bind. Dickens and language: the deepest pact of his genius sealed yet again in one of its most exacting and exquisite tests.

NOTES

1. The capped word is actually botched by a typo, normalized to "ARE," in the otherwise scrupulous new Norton Critical edition of the novel, ed. Edgar Rosenberg (Norton, 1999), p. 169. As a check on this misprint, see for example (following all other previous editions) *Great Expectations*, ed. Angus Calder (Harmondsworth: Penguin, 1980), p. 241.

2. George Eliot, *Middlemarch*, ed. Bert G. Hornback (Norton, 1977), p. 134.

3. *Great Expectations*, ed. Rosenberg, p. 536, quoting Dickens's letter to John Forster, 1 July 1861. This is an emendation in the novel's conclusion that has brought forth, according to Rosenberg, some "hundred-odd commentators (hyphen optional)," through whose claims and counterclaims he wittily sorts in his giant afterpiece, "Putting an End to *Great Expectations*," pp. 491–527.

Further Reading

Alter, Robert. "Reading Style in Dickens." *Philosophy and Literature* 20:2 (April 1996), 130–37.

Brook, G. L. *The Language of Dickens*. Andre Deutsch, 1970.

Newsom, Robert. "Style of Dickens." In *Oxford Reader's Companion to Dickens*, edited by Paul Schlicke. Oxford University Press, 1999, pp. 541–45.

Sorensen, Knud. "Charles Dickens: Linguistic Innovator." *English Studies* 65 (June 1984) 237–47.

Stewart, Garrett. *Dickens and the Trials of Imagination*. Harvard University Press, 1974.

JOHN COSNETT

Charles Dickens—Syndrome-Spotter:
A Review of Some Morbid Observations

A feature of Charles Dickens's novels which fascinates physicians is his ability to provide realistic accounts of illnesses and disabilities which affect his characters, with their predominant signs, and sometimes symptoms, accurately portrayed. So vivid and true are these descriptions that it is possible to make retrospective diagnoses in many cases. This facility is all the more remarkable when one considers two attributes of the author. Firstly, he had no formal medical training or experience though some such knowledge might have rubbed off from his acquaintance with doctor friends or medical students. Secondly, many of the clinical pictures and syndromes which he described had not, at the time of his authorship, been formally reported in the medical literature. Indeed, many of his more esoteric descriptions antedated formal medical description by one hundred years or more.

Medical diagnosis consists largely of Pattern Recognition. A large proportion of medical training consists of learning patterns of disease and their basis in physiology and pathology. The diagnostic process consists mostly of forming a 'differential diagnosis' which includes cataloguing those conditions which might be suspected of being present. Proceeding further, one tries to confirm the diagnosis by searching for more clinical signs, and employing laboratory tests and imaging techniques which will

From *The Dickensian* 99, 459 (Spring 2003). © 2003 the Dickens Fellowship.

exclude some conditions listed in the differential diagnosis, and, hopefully, leave one final diagnosis confirmed. In the absence of medical training, the observer, however keen, can only describe what he sees and hears. He does not know what further signs or symptoms to search for. Diagnosis is somewhat akin to shopping: the process is much easier and effective if one knows what is available, and where items can be found. Without such knowledge it is remarkable how often Dickens contrived to produce pictures of clinical situations and syndromes which are recognisable and accurate today.

The question arises: To what can this exceptional ability be attributed? That Dickens had unique powers of observation and description is obvious. Dickens applied these powers to many facets of the human condition, and to their environment. Through his narrative he conveyed, meticulously and precisely, the clinical picture that he perceived, without the embroidery which is often used by authors to dramatise (and perhaps blur) medical situations. While he sometimes portrayed common clinical conditions, he had a knack of selecting those which, though genuine and perhaps rare, tended to be bizarre, and thus able to attract the attention of readers, both lay and medical. Other authors whose fictional characters have morbid disorders often describe these in a 'woolly' fashion, or they construct miscellanies of signs and symptoms which lack veracity in the perception of the medical reader. This ability to recognise and accurately describe those real, though bizarre, conditions which he encountered may have been engendered by his experience as a newspaper and court reporter. This employment taught Dickens to focus on the newsworthy, though not usually at the expense of veracity. While his powers of observation are now axiomatic, what is not widely known is that these extended to recognised syndromes, and that analysis of many of his descriptions has earned publicity in formal medical literature.

ILL-DEFINED MALADIES

A number of Dickens's prominent characters suffered from severe, ill-defined, often febrile, illnesses from which most recovered. These include Rose Maylie, Oliver Twist, young Martin Chuzzlewit, Mark Tapley, Richard Carstone and Smike. In that era such conditions were common and often fatal. The list of causes includes Tuberculosis, Typhoid and Typhus fevers, malaria and pneumonia. To the lay observer who was not equipped to distinguish these by physical examination or diagnostic laboratory tests these diseases must have appeared rather similar.

Some characters had such relatively ill-defined illnesses, without specific features, but sometimes a single facet in Dickens's narrative offers a clue to the likely diagnosis in a relatively indistinct malady. For example, Little Nell's fatal condition had no distinguishing features but there is a single indication, in her history, regarding the nature of her illness. That is the episode, in the latter part of their long journey, when she walked 'with difficulty' on account of 'the pains that racked her joints... of no common severity, and every exertion increased them'.[1] Shortly afterwards she collapsed and suffered intermittent setbacks until her death. The severe joint pains in a young person would stigmatise this as rheumatic fever, subsequently complicated by rheumatic carditis, which caused her premature death. It is thus also possible that a similar explanation would pertain to the sudden death of Mary Hogarth, on whom the character of Little Nell is said to be based. Cardiac complications of rheumatic fever were among the more common causes of death among adolescents in the days before penicillin. The case of Maggy is another example of past medical history providing a crucial clue to diagnosis. 'When Maggy was 10 years old she had a bad fever... and she had never grown any older ever since'.[2] The fact of cognitive defect, eyes that were 'very little affected by light', and 'having one tolerably serviceable eye'[2] would indicate neurological disorder, and the likely cause would be a post-encephalitic syndrome. Complications of encephalitis at the age of 10 years would explain her chronic adult condition.

In the case of Rose Maylie the clue to the nature of her 'high and dangerous fever' and delirium came from the detail in Dr Losberne's prognostications. The 'deep sleep, from which she would waken, either to recovery and life, or to bid them farewell, and die'[3] was characteristic of the crisis in lobar (pneumococcal) pneumonia. This is rarely witnessed today with the successful and early resolution of the condition by antibiotics. The Chancery prisoner in *Pickwick Papers* was said to have been 'consumptive' in addition to his cognitive and sensory deficits.[4] This term was, however, applied to many chronic wasting diseases as well as tuberculosis. It is very likely that the chronic 'dread disease' which Dickens describes as affecting Smike, causing his 'mortal part to waste and wither away'[5], was tuberculosis, possibly in a disseminated form. Dickens's account is well-nigh pathognomonic for tuberculosis in that era. Some diseases warrant no debate: Martin Chuzzlewit and Mark Tapley suffered from malaria, contracted in America 'where fatal maladies... came forth at night, in misty shapes... creeping out upon the water'.[6] Dickens wrote this some 50 years before Sir Patrick Manson and Sir Ronald Ross demonstrated the role of swamp-living mosquitoes in the transmission of malaria.

MODIFICATION OF SYNDROMES

A syndrome is defined as 'a group of signs and symptoms that collectively indicate or characterise a disease, psychological disorder, or other abnormal condition'.[7] It happens occasionally that a clinical syndrome which Dickens attaches to a character is accurate in most respects but includes some features which tend to contradict or exclude the obvious diagnosis. For example, in the case of Jenny Wren, the dolls' dressmaker, the clinical features are manifestly those of the foetal-alcohol syndrome. Strong circumstantial support for this diagnosis comes from the history of her family. It was reported of Jenny that 'This poor ailing creature has come to be what she is, surrounded by drunken people from her cradle...'.[8] Her father and her grandfather were alcoholics. Her mother had died, presumably from a cause related to alcohol. It is thus likely that her late mother had been intemperate during her pregnancy with Jenny. But the medical reader who considers this diagnosis will immediately have reservations when he reads of Jenny's bright intellect, and of the 'remarkable dexterity of her nimble fingers'.[8] These features would tend to exclude the diagnosis of the foetal-alcohol syndrome. There are several possible explanations for this diagnostic paradox. One is that the subject of Dickens's description had acquired the syndrome in an incomplete form—a somewhat unlikely occurrence in one whose other features are those of a relatively advanced form of the syndrome. The more likely explanation is that Dickens tailored the syndrome to suit his story. It is likely that he combined the features of two children of his acquaintance. One was a bright, nimble-fingered girl who did dolls' dressmaking. The other was a child afflicted with the foetal-alcohol syndrome, together with impaired intellect, unusual face, deformed hands, and 'queer legs'.[8] But it would not have suited the narrative to have all these features in his dolls' dressmaker. So the features were, perhaps, moulded to suit the needs of the story. Even outside the clinical setting the creation of composite portraits in behaviour and mannerisms of various models was not uncommon among Dickens's characters.

In some cases Dickens uses the passage of time to allow manipulation of an otherwise chronic and incurable disability. Both Mrs Clennam and Mrs Crewler were manifestly paraplegic, having lost the use of their legs. Mrs Clennam had been paralysed for 'a dozen years'.[9] Yet at the end of the story she was able to rise from her sofa and hurry to the Marshalsea prison. Such dramatic recovery from paraplegia might be construed to indicate original hysterical paralysis, but even an hysteric would, after twelve years of assumed disability and immobilisation, have disuse atrophy and joint limitation. The conclusion must be that this was manipulation of disease to satisfy the requirements of the story. The method of publication, as a serial story in monthly parts, over 18 months, would probably contribute to this manipulation. When the bedridden Mrs Clennam was first introduced the author had probably not yet conceived the precise end of the story which required her to walk through the streets of London.

A further factor which might handicap an author in producing entirely true pictures of a subject is the need for 'political correctness' and for concealment of the model's true identity. Dickens encountered such problems when he introduced the characters of Harold Skimpole, and Miss Mowcher, who was manifestly an achondroplastic dwarf. In the latter example he was obliged to make modifications in his text to defuse an embarrassing and possibly litigious situation. Dickens was constrained to change his portrayal of Miss Mowcher's temperament, though her achondroplasia was immutable. He was not, however, swayed to polish the character of Harold Skimpole even though Leigh Hunt and his family recognised the image, and complained of the resemblance.

Doctors who describe new syndromes, or add examples to previously known syndromes, have the advantage of medical training which prompts them to search for more features in a subject along lines dictated by the disciplines of anatomy, physiology and pathology. Such a search often yields confirmation of a suspected diagnosis. In the absence of such training, the author who is creating a character can only describe what he observes in some subject in his circle, and then, perhaps, add features drawn from his own imagination. Otherwise he might graft on features of another subject's abnormality or character. In both these instances the imaginary, or grafted features, may destroy the veracity of the syndrome described. Among Dickens's characters such manipulation occurred but rarely.

ABSTRUSE SYNDROMES

Surveying Dickens's pathological characters, one feels that he was fascinated by the more bizarre and unusual presentations, just as present-day students tend to remember the odd rarities rather than the commonplace in Medicine. His penchant for noticing neurological and motor abnormalities indicates a particular interest in this facet of medicine. Pancks had Tourette's syndrome, Flintwinch had focal dystonia, Jenny Wren's father had alcoholic cerebellar degeneration, and Feenix had cerebellar ataxia. Sloppy, the 'very long boy' of which there was 'too much longwise and too little broadwise',[10] was probably a case of Marfan's syndrome. Uriah Heep was a case of palmar hyperhidrosis. The old tailor in *Martin Chuzzlewit* who had progressively bandy legs 'between which you might wheel a large barrow' must have had Paget's disease of bone.[11] This condition was first described by Sir James Paget in 1877, thirty-three years after Dickens wrote this vignette.

Several characters had strokes, which were as common then as they are now. Even in his description of strokes Dickens draws attention to some of the more unusual features such as Mrs Skewton's dysphasia and dysgraphia, and the jargon aphasia of Sir Leicester Dedlock and Anthony Chuzzlewit. Similarly pertinent observations were recorded in the case of old Chuffey. This was an old man who, following an acute episode twenty years previously, spoke little, showed perseveration when 'he never left off casting up' with his figures, had difficulty swallowing ('always chokes himself when it ain't broth;... verified the statement relative to his choking propensities... the mutton being tough') and had a 'wall-eyed expression'.[12] This combination of signs and symptoms would offer sufficient basis for a tentative diagnosis of pseudo-bulbar paralysis due to strokes. It is in his descriptions of these cases of stroke that Dickens best shows his unique powers of observation which would do credit to present-day students of medicine.

Morphological abnormalities are also prominent. The best known of these is Joe, the fat boy. Although he has earned a syndrome of his own, inappropriately called the Pickwickian syndrome, the precise pathological nature of Joe's disorder is still debatable. A diagnosis of a diencephalic syndrome is, perhaps, more appropriate than the 'cardiorespiratory syndrome of extreme obesity'. Modern imaging techniques would be necessary to settle the issue! Miss Mowcher was a classical example of an achondroplastic dwarf, though the initial impression of her indelicacy in behaviour is not a feature of this condition. While most of these descriptions have features which give some clue to the nature of the disease there are some in which the diagnosis remains uncertain, though one might offer a differential diagnosis. Paul Dombey is such an example. He was a case of failure to thrive with ultimate progressive weakness. In the differential diagnosis one must consider congenital heart disease, coeliac disease, cystic fibrosis, or some form of muscular dystrophy. The latter is probably the most likely.

This penchant for describing what is clinically abstruse, even bizarre, raises certain questions. In several cases the characters concerned seem to have no solid contribution to the plot of the story. One wonders whether some characters, with their morbidity, were introduced merely to add interest, or to illustrate that such strange abnormalities had been observed. As doctors sometimes aim to be first to describe a syndrome so Dickens might have felt some pride in his clinical observations, some of which were, indeed, unique. Among Dickens's characters, it is noteworthy that those who had bizarre or abstruse syndromes (Pancks, Flintwinch, Feenix, Joe, Cleaver) were usually not major characters. This tends to indicate that such bizarre disorders were introduced in order to demonstrate their recognition rather than for the characters to play major parts in the plots.

DICKENSIAN SYNDROMES AND THE SPECIALIST MEDICAL LITERATURE

Dickens was not, of course, writing with a medical readership in mind. That doctors have analysed and debated his clinical reports is a tribute to his descriptions, in that his characters have been able to attract medical attention, and to provoke analysis. Lay reviewers have usually concluded that some of his characters have illnesses which, they presume, remain undiagnosed. But literary reviewers are probably not aware of the numerous articles which have appeared in specialised medical journals, analysing the clinical features of certain characters, and debating their diagnoses. Table 1 lists some of these publications which have appeared in medical journals in recent years. Besides the published articles, there are some conditions which Dickens described which still await analysis in the medical literature. In addition to the bizarre syndromes, Dickens also portrayed commonplace conditions which, though the descriptions are precise and accurate, do not provoke much discussion and debate, because they are medically straightforward. A good example of such a situation is the case of Major Bagstock. In his case Dickens described many classical features of chronic obstructive airways disease with emphysema.

But let it not be thought that doctors have always agreed in their interpretation of Dickens's accounts of medical abnormalities. Even when they have a living, breathing, patient before them in a clinical situation, doctors frequently disagree about diagnosis. Modern technology often helps to settle diagnostic arguments but when doctors have disagreed about the diagnoses of Dickens's characters there is no such resolution of debates. Examples of such continued disagreement occur in the cases of Tiny Tim Cratchit and the fat boy, Joe.

EPIDEMIOLOGY

In some respects, Dickens's accounts of medical conditions have scientific value. This stems from the possibility of deducing some epidemiological conclusions from them. For example, his writings give support to the observation that alcoholism, and its complications, were rife at the time of his writing. Infant mortality was high. Strokes and 'consumption' were common. Observations, or the lack of them, might also have negative epidemiological value. For example, Dickens's works seem to contain no accurate description of a case of Parkinson's disease, a condition which is now very common, and which has signs so characteristic that they could hardly be missed. They are also of a nature that would have attracted Dickens's attention, because of his apparent fascination with disorders of motion. The obvious conclusion is that Parkinson's disease was much less prevalent at the time of Dickens's writing than it is today. This might be due to the fact that, it is essentially a disease of the aged. The average age of death in 1850 was only 45 years. James Parkinson published his *Essay on the Shaking Palsy* in 1817. So this condition was not unknown in Dickens's time, though it was less commonly seen because people rarely lived long enough to develop the disease.

The observer who attempts description and interpretation of clinical conditions without medical training brings to mind the parable of the three blind men who stumble across an elephant. One blind man feels a leg, another feels the trunk, and the third feels an ear. Each reaches a completely different conclusion in attempting identification of his discovery. This illustrates the fallacies in perception which might be associated with ignorance and lack of opportunity for full examination. Some knowledge of what is to be expected is, however, not always advantageous. A feeling of what should be seen might generate illusions, rather than perception of the true picture. The interpretation of one's sensations, and the recognition of objects depend on what the mind is prepared for. Medical training therefore prepares the mind to recognise clinical syndromes. Dickens had neither the training in observation, nor the knowledge that such syndromes existed, at the time he was writing. His contribution is that of pure observation, uncomplicated by perceptive aberrations. Indeed, had he studied the medical literature of the time he would not have found reference to many of the syndromes which he described. Formal description of some only appeared in print a century or more later.

In his oration on *Dickensian Diagnoses*, published in the British Medical Journal, Sir Russell Brain said that Dickens '... recorded what he saw, and what the patient told him, so that he often gives us accounts which would do credit to a trained physician'.[13] Had Dickens chosen a medical career he may have achieved eminence in a different arena, probably in the field of neurology.

NOTES

1. *The Old Curiosity Shop*, Penguin Classics (London 1985) Ch. 45, p. 423.
2. *Little Dorrit*, Penguin English Library (Harmondsworth 1967) Book the First, Ch. 9, p. 142–143.

3. *Oliver Twist*, Penguin Classics (London 1985) Ch. 33, pp. 294–300.

4. *The Pickwick Papers*, Collins' Clear Type Press (London & Glasgow) Ch. XLIV, p. 637.

5. *Nicholas Nickleby*, Everyman's Library No. 238; J. M. Dent & Sons (London 1907) Ch. XLIX, pp. 647–648.

6. *Martin Chuzzlewit*, Collins (London & Glasgow 1953) Ch. 23, p. 369.

7. *Reader's Digest Universal Dictionary*, (London 1987) p. 1535.

8. *Our Mutual Friend*, Penguin English Library (Harmondsworth 1971) Book the Second, Ch. 1, pp. 271–277.

9. *Little Dorrit*, Penguin English Library (Harmondsworth 1967) Ch. 3, p. 73.

10. *Our Mutual Friend*, Penguin English Library (Harmondsworth 1971) Book the First, Ch. 16, pp. 245–249.

11. *Martin Chuzzlewit*, Collins (London & Glasgow 1953) Ch. 43, p. 627.

12. Ibid. Ch. 11, pp. 185–187.

13. Brain, R.: *Dickensian Diagnoses*: Brit. Med. J. 1955; 2; pp. 1553–1556.

TABLE 1
CONDITIONS NOTED AND ANALYSED
IN THE MEDICAL LITERATURE

MEDICAL CONDITION	CHARACTER	NOVEL &c	LITERATURE REFERENCE
Post-concussional state	Wrayburn	OMF	Brain, R.: *Brit. Med. J.* 1955; 2; 1553–1556
Post-traumatic aphasia	Mrs Gargery	GE	Ibid.
Stroke, Hemiplegia, Agraphia	Mrs Skewton	D&S	Ibid.
Stroke	Sir L. Dedlock	BH	Ibid.
?Cerebral arteriosclerosis ?Uraemia, stroke	Mr Dorrit	LD	Ibid.
Serial strokes	John Willet	BR	Ibid.
Epilepsy ?secondary	A. Chuzzlewit	MC	Ibid.
Paraplegia ?hysterical	Mrs Crewler	DC	Ibid.
Hysterical paraplegia	Mrs Clennam	LD	Ibid.
Cerebellar ataxia	Cousin Feenix	D&S	Ibid.
Senile dementia ?strokes	Chuffey	MC	Ibid.

Senile dementia	Mrs Smallweed	BH	Ibid.
Chronic hypomania	Man over fence	NN	Ibid.
?Multiple personality	Dr Manette	TIC	Ibid.
Learning difficulty	Barnaby	BR	Ibid.
Post-encephalitic syndrome ?Argyll-Robertson pupil	Maggy	LD	Ibid.
Emphysema, airways obstrn.	Bagstock	D&S	Ibid.
?Schizophrenia	Mr F's aunt	LD	Ibid.
Paraplegia: ?motor neurone disease	G'pa Smallweed	BH	Ibid.
Dyslexia, Spontaneous combustion	Krook	BH	Jacoby; *Lancet*; 1992; 340; 1521–1522
Renal tubular acidosis, type 1 (diagnosis debated)	Tiny Tim	CC	Lewis, D. W.; *Am J Dis Ch*; 1992; 146; 1403–1407
Tuberculosis of spine	Tiny Tim	CC	Callahan C.; *Dickensian*, Winter 1993
Pickwickian syndrome: Cardiorespiratory syndrome of extreme obesity. ?Diencephalic syndrome (diagnosis debated)	Joe	PP	Burwell et al: *Amer. J. Med* 1956; 21: 811–818
Miss Havisham syndrome	Miss Havisham	GE	Critchley M., *The Divine Banquet of the Brain*, 1979; Raven Press p. 136–140
Tourette syndrome	Pancks	LD	Cosnett: *J. Neurol. N Neurosurg. Psy.* 1991; 54; 184
Torticollis: focal dystonia	Flintwinch	LD	Ibid.

SLEEP AND ITS DISORDERS:

Insomnia	Pickwick	PP	Cosnett, *Sleep*, 1992;
	Edith Granger	D&S	15(3) 264–267
	Florence D.	D&S	Ibid.
	Carker	D&S	Ibid.
	Pecksniff	MC	Ibid.
	Dickens	UT	Ibid.
Parasomnias	Dickens	UT	Ibid.
	Miggs	BR	Ibid.
	Copperfield	DC	Ibid.
	Barnaby	BR	Ibid.
Restless legs	Waiter	DC	Ibid.
Sleep paralysis	Oliver	OT	Ibid.
Nightmares	Walter Gay	D&S	Ibid.
	Copperfield	DC	Ibid.
	Florence D.	D&S	Ibid.
	Chester	BR	Ibid.
Automatisms	Capt. Cuttle	D&S	Ibid.
	Perch	D&S	Ibid.
Hypersomnia	Joe	PP	Ibid.
	W. Dorrit	LD	Ibid.
	Hugh, ostler	BR	Ibid.
Sleep apnoea	John Willet	BR	Ibid.
	Coffee-stall holder	UT	Ibid.

EPILEPSY: VARIOUS TYPES

	Guster	BH	Cosnett, *Epilepsia*, 1994 35(4); 903–905
	Monks	OT	Ibid.
	Headstone	OMF	Ibid.
	Spenlow	DC	Ibid.
	A. Chuzzlewit	MC	Ibid.

CONSEQUENCES OF ALCOHOLISM

Binge drinking	Sydney Carton	TTC	Cosnett, *Addiction*, 1999; 94(12), 1891–1892

Alcoholism	Wickfield	DC	Ibid.
Alcoholic cerebellar degeneration	Cleaver	OMF	Ibid.
Delirium tremens	Dying clown	PP	Ibid.
	Arthur Havisham	GE	Ibid.
Foetal alcohol syndrome	Jenny Wren	OMF	Ibid.

KEY

PP = *Pickwick Papers*

OCS = *Old Curiosity Shop*

CC = *Christmas Carol*

BH = *Bleak House*

UT = *Uncommercial Traveller*

OT = *Oliver Twist*

BR = *Barnaby Rudge*

D&S = *Dombey and Son*

LD = *Little Dorrit*

GE = *Great Expectations*

NN = *Nicholas Nickleby*

MC = *Martin Chuzzlewit*

DC = *David Copperfield*

TTC = *Tale of Two Cities*

OMF = *Our Mutual Friend*

HAROLD BLOOM

Afterthought

Charles Dickens began with *The Pickwick Papers* and ended his progression of novels with the unfinished *Mystery of Edwin Drood*, published posthumously in 1870, after the novelist's death at fifty-eight. His best novels certainly include *Oliver Twist*, *Nicholas Nickleby*, *Martin Chuzzlewitt*, *Dombey and Son*, *David Copperfield*, and *Bleak House*, generally judged his masterpiece. *Hard Times*, though critically esteemed, has not enjoyed a wide public, unlike *A Tale of Two Cities*, an immense success with ordinary readers rather than with critics. *Great Expectations* pleases all however, while *Our Mutual Friend*, despite its comic splendor, has been less famous. I have omitted *Little Dorrit*, which would be another novelist's masterwork.

So large is Dickens, who created a world, that one has to be very selective in brooding upon him. He possessed, in the highest degree, what John Ruskin credited in him: "stage fire." Though not a dramatist (his play *The Frozen Deep*, with Wilkie Collins, is still-born) Dickens was a remarkable public performer. His commercial readings from his own fiction, with the novelist acting all the roles, were highly successful but dangerously exhausting, and helped to kill him at fifty-eight.

One should not underestimate Dickens's theatrical gifts and interests. He thought nothing of directing, acting in, and touring with a play by Ben Jonson while continuing his intense novelistic career. Yet his extraordinary readings from his own work, which overwhelmed audiences, drained him, and cost us the books he might have written, after he turned fifty-eight.

Dickens was at his most passionate and personal in *David Copperfield* and *Great Expectations*, where David and Pip are all but self-portraits of the young Dickens. Together the two novels are Dickens's most personal novels. He reread *Copperfield* "to be quite sure I had fallen into no unconscious repetitions" in composing *Great Expectations*, and his wariness helped make Pip his most complex protagonist. We hear Dickens's early traumas again in Pip's voice, and yet the author maintains considerable distance from Pip, as he scarcely does from David Copperfield, whose destiny is to become a Dickensian novelist.

Pip, like Copperfield, is a superb narrator, but he is frequently unkind to himself, and the reader is not expected to share in the severity of Pip's excessive self-condemnations, which partly ensue from his imaginative strength. Pip's imagination always mixes love and guilt, which is very much the mode of Charles Dickens.

George Bernard Shaw, introducing a reprint of *Great Expectations*, remarked that "Pip, like his creator, has no culture and no religion." We need to recall that Shaw told us also that he felt only pity for an even greater writer, whenever he compared the mind of Shakespeare with his own! Shaw's religion was a peculiar kind of Creative Evolution, and his culture compares poorly with his contemporary, Oscar Wilde's. Dickens indeed was a Dickensian in religion, and was deeply grounded in popular culture, as well as in literary culture.

Whether Pip's obsessive and unmerited guilt owes more to popular traditions of shame-culture, or emanates from literary guilt-culture, is very difficult to determine. One critic, Shuli Barzilai, wisely conjectures that Pip's guilt has a deep source in what Freud called "family romances," so that his relationship with Estella is quasi-incestuous, she being (unknowingly) Magwitch's daughter, while Pip becomes the escaped convict's adopted son. What is clear enough is that both Pip and Estella seem doomed to expiate a guilt not at all their own, the guilt of the fathers and the mothers.

Dickens notoriously weakened *Great Expectations* by revising its ending, so that Pip and Estella might be viewed as living together happily ever after. This revision is manifestly at variance with the imaginative spirit of the novel, and is best ignored. Pip, properly read, remains a permanent emblem of something that Dickens could not forgive in himself.

It is impossible not to find Dickens's life in his work, but I will focus my emphasis here on the work in the writer. The effect of Dickens-the-novelist on portraits of the novelist as a young man is profound, but the autobiographical element is so strong as to indicate primarily the traditional mode of the life transmuted into literature. My quarry is subtler: the influence of Dickens's creative mind upon itself. I turn therefore to what is unsurpassable in him: *Bleak House*.

As a representation of Dickens's visionary cosmos, *Bleak House* is a vast romance-structure, free of any overt Dickens-surrogates. Esther Summerson is wonderfully sympathetic, and in a complex way she is a portrait of Dickens's Muse, his sister-in-law, Georgina Hogarth, who pragmatically presided over the Dickens household. If Dickens's imagination is directly represented in *Bleak House*, it can only be by Esther Summerson.

Esther stands apart from the other central characters, who emerge from what critics have learned to call: "The Dickens world." Great grotesques throng the chapters: the benignly idealized paternal figure, John Jarndyce; the wicked, madly attractive, and murderous Hortense the sublime bloodhound, Inspector Bucket; the Leigh Hunt parody of Skimpole; the parody of Savage Landor in Boythorn. If one adds the fantastics—Mrs. Jellyby, Miss Flute, Mr. Krook (who goes up in spontaneous combustion), and best of all Lady Dedlock, you find yourself surrounded by creatures of an invented world that both entertains and disturbs. The Dickens cosmos precedes *Bleak House*, yet its entrance into this book is marked by a difference. Composing *Bleak House*, Dickens experiences the dramatic urgency of his earlier adventures into the self and into otherness.

Chronology

1812	On February 7, Charles John Huffman Dickens is born in Portsmouth, the second child of Elizabeth and John Dickens.
1817–1822	The Dickens family moves to Chatham, where the young Charles Dickens, who is a sickly child, is educated by his mother and the books in his father's library. Later, Dickens will characterize these years as the happiest in his young life.
1822	The Dickens family moves to London.
1824	In February, John Dickens, an impractical man, is arrested for debts, and a mere two days after his twelfth birthday, Dickens is sent to work at the Warrens bottle blacking factory. At the end of the month, John Dickens is incarcerated in Marshalsea, a debtor's prison, where he is joined by all of the family except for Charles. John Dickens remains imprisoned for three months, while Charles continues to work at the factory, living on his own. His memories from this time are traumatic, and will haunt much of his future work, most notably *David Copperfield*.
1825	Dickens enters school at the Wellington House Academy.
1827–1828	Dickens takes his first adult job as a junior clerk at the legal firm of Ellis and Blackmore. By the end of 1828, he perfects

his shorthand skills, and leaves Ellis and Blackmore to become a shorthand chronicler of the affairs of Parliament.

1830   Dickens is hired as a newspaper reporter by the *Mirror of Parliament*, a publication run by his uncle John Henry Burror and whose staff includes Dickens's father, John Dickens. Charles Dickens also reports for the *True Sun*. The same year, he meets and becomes smitten with Maria Beadnell, who will remain immortalized in his imagination as his first love. Their flirtation will be terminated after three years, when Maria's family deems him unsuitable.

1832   In March, Dickens attempts to embark on a stage career by writing a letter to the manager of Covent Garden. His letter is rejected.

1833   Spurred on, perhaps, by his romantic failure with Maria Beadnell, Dickens's ambitions grow. That year, he publishes his first story, "Dinner at Poplar Walk," in the *Monthly Magazine*. He joins *The Morning Chronicle*, a considerably more prestigious paper than the *Mirror*. It is at the *Chronicle* that Dickens writes his first social sketches under the pseudonym Boz.

1834   George Hogarth, editor of the *Evening Chronicle*, persuades Dickens to do a series of sketches based on London for his own paper. Dickens befriends Hogarth in the process, and becomes a regular guest at his house, where he makes the acquaintance of Hogarth's three daughters, Mary, Georgina, and Catherine.

1835   Dickens becomes engaged to Catherine, the eldest of the Hogarth daughters.

1836   On February 8, Dickens's newspaper sketches are collected and published in one book, *Sketches by Boz*, which is met with much acclaim. Just ten days later, Dickens conceives and begins work on the *Pickwick Papers*, his first serial novel. On April 2, Dickens marries Catherine Hogarth, and the young couple moves to Furnival Inn. In November he becomes the editor of *Bentley's Miscellany*. And at the end of 1836, Dickens meets John Forster, who will prove to be his lifetime friend and also his first biographer. *The Pickwick Papers* (1836–1837) is published in monthly installments and catapults Charles Dickens to immediate fame.

1837	Queen Victoria ascends the throne at the age of 18. Catherine Dickens gives birth to a son, the first child of ten—on January 6, after which she begins to exhibit the first signs of a lifelong neurosis. In April, Dickens moves the family to 47 Doughty Street, and early that next month, his sister-in-law Mary, of whom he was inordinately fond, collapses and dies at the age of seventeen. *Bentley's Miscellany* prints *Oliver Twist* in monthly installments (1837–1838). *Oliver Twist* proves so popular that at the end of 1838, there are at least six adaptations.
1838	In January, Dickens travels to Yorkshire to examine the Yorkshire schools. The academy run by Mr. William Shaw provides a model for *Nicholas Nickleby*'s Dotheboys Hall. *Nicholas Nickleby* (1838–1839) begins appearing later that year.
1839	Dickens moves his expanding family to 1 Devonshire Terrace on December 1.
1840	Dickens begins the journal *Master Humphrey's Clock*, an ambitious project, as he alone is responsible for its content. *The Old Curiosity Shop* (1840–1841) appears in *Master Humphrey's* in monthly installations. The central, doomed character of Little Nell is generally agreed to be inspired by Dickens's beloved sister-in-law Mary, whose life was also cut short. He also attends his first public hanging. It is a shattering experience and bolsters him in his tirades against capital punishment.
1841	*Barnaby Rudge*, a socially conscious novel that Dickens had been pondering for the past couple of years, is published in monthly installments. Dickens is asked to run for MP, but declines. Nevertheless he continues his public tirades against the Tory party, the child-labor laws, and the factory conditions of the period.
1842	On January 2, Dickens, accompanied by his family, embarks on a six-month tour of America, which greets him with fanfare. He returns in June. The country's ardor towards the author cools after the disparaging comments he makes in *American Notes* (October 19, 1842). *Martin Chuzzlewit* (1842–1843), a novel which also draws from his American experiences, is Dickens's first commercial letdown.
1843	Within a few weeks, Dickens writes and publishes *A Christmas Carol*, the first and most enduring of his

Christmas books—short works that blend holiday sentiment with the supernatural.

1844   In June, Dickens and his wife Catherine travel to Italy, where they remain for eleven months. Dickens publishes *The Chimes*, the second of the Christmas books, that December.

1845   Charles and Catherine return from Italy in July. In September he directs and stars in Ben Jonson's *Every Man in His Humour*, his first appearance with the troupe The Amateurs. The Christmas story of that year is the *Cricket in the Hearth*.

1846   Dickens's foray into newspaper journalism, a paper called the *Daily News*, begins early January, and is a fast failure, folding within a month. *Pictures from Italy* comes out in May. Dickens's family spends the majority of this year in Europe, the first half in Switzerland, and the next in Paris. *Dombey and Son* (1846–1848) begins appearing in monthly installments. The end of the year, Dickens's final Christmas book, the *Battle of Life*, is published.

1847   Miss Coutte's Home for Hopeless Women, a charity with which Dickens becomes deeply involved, opens in Shepherds Bush. Dickens and his band of performers, The Amateurs, put on *The Merry Wives of Windsor* for its benefit.

1848   Dickens eldest sister Fanny dies. The year after, her son, Henry Burnett, upon whom Dickens based the character of Paul Dombey, dies as well.

1849   Monthly serialization of *David Copperfield* (1849-1850), the novel that Dickens called his favorite child, begins.

1850   *Household Words* is established with Dickens as editor and contributor.

1851   *Household Words* publishes the first installment of *A Child's History of England* (1850–1853). In March, Dickens's father passes away. The next month, Dickens's youngest daughter, Dora, dies at the age of eight months. Dickens directs and stars in The Amateurs production of Bulwer Lytton's *Not As Bad As We Seem*, which they perform in front of Queen Victoria on April 14. Dickens moves his family into Tavistock House, which will also function as the headquarters for the charity productions of The Amateurs. At the end of the year, The Amateurs go on tour throughout the country. During the tour, Dickens strikes up a friendship with Wilkie Collins, one of the theatre troupe actors. Collins is a young writer, artist, and theatre enthusiast, who will prove to be a loyal friend and collaborator.

1852   *Bleak House* (1852–1853) begins appearing in monthly installments. The Amateurs continue to play major cities around the country.

1853   Dickens finishes *Bleak House* in Bologne, spends the last quarter of the year in Switzerland and Italy, and then returns to read *A Christmas Carol* and *A Cricket in the Hearth* in Birmingham. These are Dickens's first public readings. The third and last reading is a particular triumph—Dickens designated this reading for the working people and priced the tickets accordingly at sixpence.

1854   *Hard Times* appears in weekly installments. Dickens reads *A Christmas Carol* in Reading, Sherbourne, and Bradford.

1855   Dickens directs and acts in Wilkie Collins's *The Lighthouse*, which premieres at Tavistock House. Maria Beadnell reenters Dickens life and Dickens starts to correspond with her. When they meet, he is shocked to find her fat, toothless, and silly. Maria is immortalized by the fat, alcoholic Flora Finching in Dickens's next novel, *Little Dorrit* (1855–1857). Dickens reads *A Christmas Carol* in Folkestone, Peterborough, and Sheffield.

1856   Dickens purchases Gads Hill Place.

1857   Dickens directs and stars in an Amateurs production, the *Frozen Deep*, which costars and is coauthored by Wilkie Collins. It premieres in January, and it meets with such success (Queen Victoria was purportedly very moved) that they move it from Tavistock House to larger venues, and replace the cast, who has been made up mainly of Dickens's children, with professional actors. Among the professionals they hire is the young actress Ellen Ternan, with whom Dickens falls in love. Ignoring the increasing strains on his marriage, Dickens departs to Switzerland with Wilkie Collins and Augustus Egg for the rest of the year.

1858   Catherine Dickens confronts her husband about a bracelet that he bought for Ellen Ternan, and in May, the couple separates, and in order to parry the scandal, Dickens publishes a statement justifying his actions in the *Times* and *Household Words*. Dickens's children follow their father, as does Catherine's own sister Georgina, who takes up residence as his housekeeper. Also, this year, Dickens embarks on his first set of major reading tours. In April, he has seventeen engagements, and then later that year he has 84 more throughout the country, only to return to London for a series of Christmas readings. These readings will be fundamental to Dickens's personality and his career; they draw together his love of the people, and his talents as an actor, as a speaker, and also as a writer. The response to these tours is tremendous, the results are lucrative, but for the author, they are physically and mentally taxing, and ultimately may have contributed to his final collapse.

1859   *A Tale of Two Cities* appears (April-November) in weekly installments in *All Year Round*, a new journal with Dickens as its editor. Dickens undertakes another national reading tour.

1860   Dickens settles his family into Gads Hill Place. That December, *All Year Round* begins publishing *Great Expectations* (1860–1861) in weekly installments. Dickens agrees to another 46 readings, to be spaced over the next two years.

1863   Death of Dickens's mother, Elizabeth. Death of Dickens's son Walter in India. Death of William Makepeace Thackeray. Thackeray and Dickens have quarreled several years previous, and the two authors reconcile shortly before Thackeray's demise.

1865   Charles Dickens is returning from France with Ellen Ternan, who may now be his mistress, and her mother. The train derails, and all the first-class carriages, save Dickens's, topple off the steep bridge into the river below. The fatalities are immense. The unharmed Dickens rushes to help the scattered dead and dying, an event well documented by the press. It is only until he returns to London that he goes into complete shock. Dickens completes *Our Mutual Friend*, his last finished novel (1864–1865).

1866   Dickens moves Ternan and her mother to Slough.

1867   Dickens settles Ternan permanently in Peckham. That
            November, Dickens returns to America to give a reading
            tour that covers Boston, Washington, and New York. His
            enthusiastic audience seems to be more than willing to
            forgive him for the negative things published in *American
            Notes* twenty years ago, and Dickens meets with President
            Johnson and finds himself affected by Lincoln's recent
            assassination. Ill health, however, forces him to cut his tour
            short and return to England the following April.

1869   Dickens gives his last, provincial reading tour. In these
            seventy-four engagements, he presents and perfects what is
            now an immortal excerpt from *Oliver Twist*, which he dubs
            Sikes and Nancy. The readings prove to be irrevocably
            damaging, both physically and psychologically. Again, he
            cuts the tour short for health reasons.

1870   From January to March, Dickens delivers his farewell
            readings to a London audience. He begins *Edwin Drood*, but
            only six installments of the novel appear, because Dickens
            collapses and dies on June 9, in Gads Hill, in the company
            of his sister-in-law Georgina and Ellen Ternan. His last
            words are, "Yes, on the ground."

Contributors

HAROLD BLOOM is Sterling Professor of the Humanities at Yale University. He is the author of 30 books, including *Shelley's Mythmaking* (1959), *The Visionary Company* (1961), *Blake's Apocalypse* (1963), *Yeats* (1970), *A Map of Misreading* (1975), *Kabbalah and Criticism* (1975), *Agon: Toward a Theory of Revisionism* (1982), *The American Religion* (1992), *The Western Canon* (1994), and *Omens of Millennium: The Gnosis of Angels, Dreams, and Resurrection* (1996). *The Anxiety of Influence* (1973) sets forth Professor Bloom's provocative theory of the literary relationships between the great writers and their predecessors. His most recent books include *Shakespeare: The Invention of the Human* (1998), a 1998 National Book Award finalist, *How to Read and Why* (2000), *Genius: A Mosaic of One Hundred Exemplary Creative Minds* (2002), *Hamlet: Poem Unlimited* (2003), *Where Shall Wisdom Be Found?* (2004), and *Jesus and Yahweh: The Names Divine* (2005). In 1999, Professor Bloom received the prestigious American Academy of Arts and Letters Gold Medal for Criticism. He has also received the International Prize of Catalonia, the Alfonso Reyes Prize of Mexico, and the Hans Christian Andersen Bicentennial Prize of Denmark.

G.K. CHESTERTON was a critic, poet, and novelist most well known for his Father Brown mysteries, but also appreciated for his short literary studies, especially those on Chaucer, Dickens, and Robert Browning.

GEORGE ORWELL is the pen name for Eric Blair, who was a critic, essayist, and author of two major anti-totalitarian satires, *1984* and *Animal Farm*.

GEORGE BERNARD SHAW was a famous Irish playwright, critic, essayist, feminist, health fanatic, and radical socialist. In 1925, Shaw accepted the Nobel Prize but refused the money.

LIONEL TRILLING was an American critic, writer, and Professor of Literature at Columbia University. He was the author of several collections of essays, including the *Opposing Self* and *Beyond Culture*, and the biographer of, among others, Matthew Arnold and Sigmund Freud. His novel *The Middle of the Journey* was published in 1947.

SIR ANGUS WILSON was a British writer, lecturer, and critic most famous for his fictional snapshots of English life. He was the author of, among other titles, *The Wrong Set*; *Anglo-Saxon Attitudes*; *The Old Men at the Zoo*; and the epic family novel *No Laughing Matter*. His biographies include ones of Rudyard Kipling and Charles Dickens. Wilson was lecturer of English literature at the University of East Anglia and was knighted in 1980.

WILLIAM ODDIE is the editor of London's *Catholic Herald*. He is the author of several books on literature and religion, including *Dickens and Carlyle* and *Let My People Go*.

JOHN CAREY is a critic, reviewer, and emeritus Merton Professor of English Literature at the University of Oxford. His most recent book is *What Good Are the Arts?*.

D.A. MILLER is John F. Hotchkis Professor of English at the University of California, Berkeley. Among his publications are *Jane Austen, or The Secret of Style*; *Place for Us: Essay on the Broadway Musical*; *Bringing Out Roland Barthes*; *The Novel and the Police*; and *Narrative and Its Discontents: Problems of Closure in the Traditional Novel*.

GEORGE LEVINE is Professor of English at Rutgers University and serves as Director of the Center for the Critical Analysis of Contemporary Culture. His publications include *Dying to Know*; *The Cambridge Companion to George Eliot*; *Darwin and the Novelists*; *The Realistic Imagination*; and *Lifebirds*.

PAM MORRIS is Reader in Literature at Liverpool John Moores University. Her books include *Dickens Class Consciousness: A Marginal View*, *Literature and Feminism: An Introduction* and *The Bakhtin Reader*.

GARRETT STEWART is James O. Freedman Professor of Letters at the University of Iowa. He has written extensively on Victorian fiction, and his most recent book is *Between Film and Screen: Modernisms Photo Synthesis*.

JOHN COSNETT is a Fellow of the Royal College of Physicians of London. He retired as an Associate Professor of neurology at the University of Natal.

Bibliography

Ackroyd, Peter. *Dickens*. New York: HarperCollins, 1990.

Barnard, Robert. *Imagery and Theme in the Novels of Dickens*. Oslo: Universitetforlaget, 1974.

Basta, Martha, "Charles Dickens's Warning to England." *The Dickensian*, No. 352, pp. 166–175. London, 1967.

Bloom, Harold, ed. *A Tale of Two Cities*, Modern Critical Interpretations. Philadelphia: Chelsea House Publishers, 1987.

———. *Charles Dickens*, Bloom's Major Novelists. Philadelphia: Chelsea House Publishers, 2000.

———. *Great Expectations*, Modern Critical Interpretations. Philadelphia: Chelsea House Publishers, 2000.

Bowen, John. *Other Dickens: Pickwick to Chuzzlewit*. Oxford: Oxford University Press, 2000.

Brook, George L. *The Language of Dickens*. London: Andre Deutsch, 1970.

Butt, John, and Kathleen Tillotson. *Dickens at Work*. London: Chatto & Windus, 1958.

Carey, John. *The Violent Effigy: A Study of Dickens's Imagination*. London: Faber & Faber, 1973.

Carlisle, Janice. *The Sense of an Audience: Dickens, Thackeray, and George Eliot at Mid-Century*. Athens: University of Georgia Press, 1981.

Chesterton, G.K. *Appreciations and Criticisms of the Works of Charles Dickens*. London: J.M. Dent & Sons, 1911.

Chesterton, G.K. *Charles Dickens*. London: House of Stratus, 2001. (Copyright by the Royal Literary Fund.)

Cockshut, A.O.J. *The Imagination of Charles Dickens*. New York: New York University Press, 1962.

Collins, Phillip, ed. *Dickens: The Critical Heritage*. London: Routledge & Kegan Paul, 1971.

Collins, Phillip. *Dickens and Crime* (3rd edition). London: Macmillian and St. Martin's Press, 1994.

Collins, Phillip. *Dickens and Education*. London: Macmillian, 1965.

Crawford, Iain. "Pip and Monster: The Joys of Bondage." *Studies in English Literature*, vol. 25, issue 4, pp. 625–648. Rice University, 1988.

Crotch, W. Walter. *Charles Dickens, Social Reformer*. London: Chapman and Hall, 1913.

Daldry, Graham. *Charles Dickens and the Form of the Novel*. Totowa, NJ: Barnes & Noble, 1987.

Dyson, A.E. *The Inimitable Dickens: A Reading of the Novels*. London: Macmillian, 1970.

Engel, Monroe. *The Maturity of Dickens*. Cambridge, MA: Harvard University Press, 1959.

Fein, Mara H. "The Politics of Family in the Pickwick Papers." *English Literary History* (ELH) 61.2, pp. 363–379. Baltimore: Johns Hopkins University Press, 1994.

Fielding, K.J. *Charles Dickens: A Critical Introduction*. London: Longmans Green, 1958.

Follini, Tamara. "James, Dickens, and the Indirections of Influence." *The Henry James Review* 25, pp. 228–238. Johns Hopkins University Press, 2004.

Ford, George and Lauriat Lane Jr. eds., *The Dickens Critics*. Cornell University Press. 1961.

Ford, George H. *Dickens and His Readers*. Princeton: Princeton University Press, 1955.

Forster, John. *The Life of Charles Dickens*. London: Whitefriars Press, 1928. Reprint.

Frank, Lawrence. *Charles Dickens and the Romantic Self*. Lincoln: University of Nebraska Press, 1984.

Gilbert, Elliot L. "'To Awake From History': Carlyle, Thackeray, and A Tale of Two Cities." *Dickens Studies Annual* 12 (1983): 247–265.

Gissing, George. *Charles Dickens*. New York: Dodd, Mead, and Co., 1924.

Gissing, George. *The Immortal Dickens*. London: Cecil Palmer, 1925.

Gold, Joseph. *Charles Dickens: Radical Moralist*. Minneapolis: University of Minnesota Press, 1972.

Goldberg, Michael. *Carlyle and Dickens*. Athens: University of Georgia Press, 1972.

Gross, John, and Gabrielle Pearson ed. *Dickens and the Twentieth Century*. Toronto: University of Toronto Press. 1962.

Guerard, Albert J. *The Triumph of the Novel: Dickens, Dostoevsky, Faulkner*. New York: Oxford University Press, 1976.

Hager, Kelly. "Estranging David Copperfield: Reading the Novel of Divorce." *English Literary History* (ELH) 63.4, pp. 989–1019. Baltimore: Johns Hopkins University Press, 1996.

Hannon, Patrice. "The Aesthetics of Humour in *Great Expectations*." *The Dickensian*, No. 439, vol. 92, part 2, pp. 91–105. London, 1996.

Hardy, Barbara. *The Moral Art of Dickens*. New York: Oxford University Press, 1970.

Hawes, Donald, *Who's Who in Dickens*. New York: Routledge, 2002.

Hecimovich, Gregg A. "The Cup and the Lip and the Riddle of Our Mutual Friend." *English Literary History* (ELH) 62.4, pp. 955–977. Baltimore: Johns Hopkins University Press, 1995.

Herst, Beth R. *The Dickens Hero: Selfhood and Alienation in the Dickens World*. New York: AMS Press, 1990.

Holbrook, David. *Charles Dickens and the Image of Woman*. New York: New York University Press, 1993.

Hollington, Michael. *Dickens and the Grotesque*. Beckenham, Croom Helm, 1984.

Hornback, Bert G. *"Noah's Arkitecture": A Study of Dickens Mythology*. Athens: Ohio University Press, 1972.

House, Madeline, ed. *The Letters of Charles Dickens* (vols. 1–8). Reprinted by Oxford University Press, 1963.

Houston, Gail Turley. *Consuming Fictions: Gender, Class, and Hunger in Dickens's Novels*. Carbondale: Southern Illinois University Press, 1994.

Ingham, Patricia. *Dickens, Women, and Language*. Toronto: University of Toronto Press, 1992.

James, Louis. "The beginnings of a new type of popular fiction: plagiarisms of Dickens." In *Fiction for the Working Man*. London: Oxford University Press, 1963.

John, Juliet. *Dickens's Villains: Melodrama, Character, Popular Culture*. Oxford: Oxford University Press, 2001.

Johnson, Edgar H. *Charles Dickens: His Tragedy and Triumph*. Rev. ed. London: Allen Lane, 1977.

Jordan, John O. *The Cambridge Companion to Charles Dickens*. Cambridge: Cambridge University Press, 2001.

Kaplan, Fred. *Dickens: A Biography*. New York: William Morrow & Company, 1988.

Kincaid, James R. *Dickens and the Rhetoric of Laughter*. Oxford: Clarendon Press, 1971.

Kotzin, Michael. *Dickens and the Fairy Tale*. Ohio: Bowling Green University Popular Press, 1972.

Kucich, John. *Excess and Restraint in the Novels of Charles Dickens*. Athens: University of Georgia Press, 1981.

Leavis, F.R., and Q.D. Leavis. *Dickens the Novelist*. London: Chatto & Windus, 1970.

Lettis, Richard. *The Dickens Aesthetic*. New York: AMS Press, 1989.

Lucas, John. *The Melancholy Man: A Study of Dickens Novels*. Totowa, NJ: Barnes & Noble, 1980.

Magnet, Myron. *Dickens and the Social Order*. Philadelphia: University of Pennsylvania Press, 1985.

Manning, Sylvia Bank. *Dickens as Satirist*. New Haven: Yale University Press, 1971.

Miller, J. Hillis. *Charles Dickens: The World of His Novels*. Cambridge, MA: Harvard University Press, 1958.

Miyoshi, Masao. *The Divided Self: A Perspective on the Literature of the Victorians*. New York: New York University Press, 1969.

Monod, Sylvere. *Dickens the Novelist*. Norman: University of Oklahoma Press, 1968.

Morgan, Nicholas H. *Secret Journeys: Theory and Practice in Reading Dickens*. Rutherford, NJ: Fairleigh Dickinson University Press, 1992.

Morgentaler, Goldie. *Dickens and Heredity: When Like Begets Like*. London: Macmillan Press, 2000.

Morris, Pam. *Dickens's Class Consciousness: A Marginal View*. London: Macmillian, 1991.

Nayder, Lillian. *Unequal Partners: Charles Dickens, Wilkie Collins, and Victorian Authorship*. Ithaca: Cornell University Press, 2002.

Neely, Robert D. *The Lawyers of Dickens and Their Clerks*. Union: Lawbook Exchange, 2001.

Nelson, Harland S. *Charles Dickens*. Boston: Twayne, 1981.

Newcomb, Mildred. *The Imagined World of Charles Dickens*. Columbus: Ohio State University Press, 1989.

Nisher, Ada, and Blake Nevius, eds. *Dickens Centennial Essays*. Berkeley: University of California Press, 1971.

Oddie, William. *Dickens and Carlyle: The Question of Influence*. London: Centenary, 1972.

Orwell, George, "Charles Dickens." In *George Orwell: Essays*. London: Penguin Classics, 2000.

Ostry, Elaine. *Social Dreaming: Dickens and the Fairy Tale*. London: Routledge, 2002.

Page, Norman. *A Dickens Companion*. London: Macmillan, 1984.

Praz, Mario. "Charles Dickens." In *The Hero in Eclipse in Victorian Fiction*, Angus Davidson trans., London: Oxford University Press, 1956, pp. 127–88.

Raina, Badri. *Dickens and the Dialectic of Growth*. Madison: University of Wisconsin Press, 1986.

Sanders, Andrew. *Dickens and the Spirit of the Age*. Oxford: Oxford University Press, 1999.

Schad, John. *The Reader in the Dickensian Mirror: Some New Language*. New York: St. Martin's Press, 1992.

Schilling, Bernard N. *Rain of Years: Great Expectations and the World of Dickens*. Rochester: University of Rochester Press, 2001.

Schor, Hilary. *Dickens and the Daughter of the House*. Cambridge: Cambridge University Press, 1999.

Schwartzman, F.W. *Dickens and the City*. London: Athione Press, 1979.

Slater, Michael, ed. *Dickens 1970: Centenary Essays*. London: Chapman & Hall, 1970.

Slater, Michael. *Dickens and Women*. London: J.M. Dent & Sons, 1983.

Solomon, Pearl Chester. *Dickens and Melville in Their Time*. New York: Columbia University Press, 1975.

Spence, Gordon. "Dickens as a Historical Novelist." *The Dickensian* 72, pp. 21–30. London, 1976.

Stewart, Garrett. *Dickens and the Trials of Imagination*. Cambridge: Harvard University Press, 1974.

Stoehr, Taylor. *Dickens: The Dreamer's Stance*. Ithaca, NY: Cornell University Press, 1965.

Stone, Harry. *Dickens and the Invisible World: Fairy Tales, Fantasy, and Novel Making*. Bloomington: Indiana University Press, 1979.

Stone, Harry. *The Night Side of Dickens: Cannibalism, Passion, Necessity*. Columbus: Ohio State University Press, 1994.

Sucksmith, Harvey Peter. *The Narrative Art of Charles Dickens*. Oxford: Clarendon Press, 1970.

Thurley, Geoffrey. *The Dickens Myth: Its Genesis and Structure*. London: Routledge & Kegan Paul, 1976.

Tomalin, Claire. *The Invisible Woman: The Story of Nelly Ternan and Charles Dickens*. Viking, 1990.

Trilling, Lionel, "Dickens of Our Day." In *A Gathering of Fugitives*. American Academy of Arts and Letters, 1955.

Vlock, Deborah. *Dickens, Novel Reading, and the Victorian Popular Theatre*. Cambridge: Cambridge University Press, 1988.

Vogel, Jane. *Allegory in Dickens*. Mobile: University of Alabama Press, 1977.

Wall, Stephen, ed. *Charles Dickens: A Critical Anthology*. Penguin, 1970.

Welsh, Alexander. *The City of Dickens*. Oxford: Clarendon Press, 1971.

Welsh, Alexander. *From Copyright to Copperfield: The Identity of Dickens*. Cambridge, MA: Harvard University Press, 1987.

Williams, Raymond. *The English Novel: From Dickens to Lawrence*. London: Chatto & Windus, 1970.

Wilson, Angus. *The World of Charles Dickens*. New York: Viking, 1970.

Wilson, Edmund. "Two Scrooges." *The Wound and the Bow*. New York: Oxford University Press, 1947.

Acknowledgments

"The Great Popularity" by G. K. Chesterton. From *Charles Dickens, the Last of the Great Men*, pp. 73–91. © 1942 by The Readers Club. Originally published by Dodd Mead & Company in 1906. Reprinted by permission.

"Dickens's Radicalism, Plausibility, and His Image of the Working Man" by George Orwell. From *George Orwell: Essays* (Penguin Modern Classics, U.K.), pp. 60–78. © 1940 A.M. Heath & Co. Ltd. Reprinted by permission.

"Introduction to *Great Expectations*" by George Bernard Shaw. From *Great Expectations*, pp v–xx. © 1947 The Novel Library. Reprinted by permission.

"*Little Dorrit*" by Lionel Trilling. From *The Dickens Critics*, George II. Ford and Lauriat Lane, Jr., ed., pp. 279–293. Originally published as the introduction to *Little Dorrit* (1953) and in *The Opposing Self* (1955). © 1955 Lionel Trilling. Reprinted by permission.

"The Heroes and Heroines of Dickens" by Angus Wilson. From *Dickens and the Twentieth Century*, John Gross and Gabriel Pearson, ed., pp. 3–11. © 1962 by Routledge & Kegan. Reprinted by permission.

"Mr. Micawber and the Redefinition of Experience" by William Oddie. From *The Dickensian* 63, 352 (May, 1967), pp. 100–110. © 1967 by William Oddie. Reprinted by permission of the author.

"Dickens and Violence" by John Carey. From *The Violent Effigy: A Study of Dickens' Imagination*, pp. 11–29. © John Carey, 1991. Reprinted by permission.

"Discipline in Different Voices: Bureaucracy, Police, Family, and *Bleak House*" by D.A. Miller. From *Representations* 1, 1 (February 1983). © 1983 by the Regents of the University of California. Reprinted by permission.

"Dickens and Darwin" by George Levine. From *Darwin and the Novelist: Patterns of Science in Victorian Fiction*, pp. 119–152. © 1988 by the President and Fellows of Harvard College. Reprinted by permission.

"*Our Mutual Friend*: The Taught Self" by Pam Morris. From *Dickens's Class Consciousness: A Marginal View*, pp. 120–140. © 1991 by Pam Morris. Reprinted by permission.

"Dickens and Language" by Garrett Stewart. From *The Cambridge Companion to Charles Dickens*, John O. Jordan, ed., pp. 136–151. © 2001 by Cambridge University Press. Reprinted with the permission of Cambridge University Press.

"Charles Dickens—Syndrome Spotter: A Review of Some Morbid Observations" by John Cosnett. From *The Dickensian* 99, 459 (Spring 2003), pp. 22–31. © 2003 by John Cosnett. Reprinted by permission of the author.

Every effort has been made to contact the owners of copyrighted material and secure copyright permission. Articles appearing in this volume generally appear much as they did in their original publication with few or no editorial changes. Those interested in locating the original source will find bibliographic information in the bibliography and acknowledgments sections of this volume.

Index

Characters in literary works are indexed by first name (if any), followed by the name of the work in parentheses